Reading Modern Law

Reading Modern Law identifies and elaborates upon key critical methodologies for reading and writing about law in modernity. The force of law rests on determinate and localizable authorizations, as well as an expansive capacity to encompass what has not been prefigured by an order of rules. The key question this dynamic of law raises is how legal forms might be deployed to confront and disrupt injustice. The urgency of this question must not eclipse the care its complexity demands. This book offers a critical methodology for addressing the many challenges thrown up by that question, while testifying to its complexity. The chapters in this volume – engagements, direct or oblique, with the work of Peter Fitzpatrick – chart a mode of resisting the proliferation of social scientific methods, as much as geopolitical empire. The authors elaborate a critical and interdisciplinary treatment of law and modernity, and outline the pivotal role of sovereignty in contemporary formations of power, both national and international. From various overlapping vantage points, therefore, *Reading Modern Law* interrogates law's relationship to power, as well as its relationship to the critical work of reading and writing about law in modernity.

Ruth Buchanan is Associate Professor at Osgoode Hall Law School, York University. She teaches and researches in the areas of globalization, international economic law, law and development, and political and social theory. She has published widely in international journals.

Stewart Motha is Reader in Law at Birkbeck, University of London, and Fellow of the Stellenbosch Institute of Advanced Study, South Africa. He has published widely on questions of post-colonial sovereignty, indigenous land rights, and political theology and democracy.

Sundhya Pahuja is Professor of Law at the Melbourne Law School and Director of the Law and Development research programme at the Institute for International Law and the Humanities, University of Melbourne. Sundhya's research is widely published, and focuses on the political economy of international law and institutions, jurisprudence, and post-colonial theory.

For
Peter Fitzpatrick

Reading Modern Law

Critical methodologies and sovereign formations

Edited by
Ruth Buchanan, Stewart Motha, and Sundhya Pahuja

Routledge
Taylor & Francis Group
LONDON AND NEW YORK

First published 2012
by Routledge
2 Park Square, Milton Park, Abingdon, Oxon OX14 4RN

Simultaneously published in the USA and Canada
by Routledge
711 Third Avenue, New York, NY 10017

A GlassHouse Book

Routledge is an imprint of the Taylor & Francis Group, an informa business

First issued in paperback 2013

British Library Cataloguing in Publication Data
A catalogue record for this book is available from the British Library

Library of Congress Cataloging in Publication Data
Reading modern law : critical methodologies and sovereign formations / Edited by Ruth Buchanan, Stewart Motha and Sundhya Pahuja.
p. cm.
1. Law–Methodology. 2. Law–Philosophy. 3. Jurisprudence.
4. Fitzpatrick, Peter, 1941– I. Buchanan, Ruth Margaret.
II. Motha, Stewart J. (Stewart John), 1970– III. Pahuja, Sundhya.
K212.R431 2012
340'.1–dc23 2011045290

ISBN: 978-0-415-56854-8 (hbk)
ISBN: 978-0-415-52641-8 (pbk)
ISBN: 978-0-203-11945-7 (ebk)

Typeset in Baskerville
by Wearset Ltd, Boldon, Tyne and Wear

Contents

Notes on the editors

Ruth Buchanan is Associate Professor at Osgoode Hall Law School, York University, and has been a Visiting Research Fellow at Birkbeck, University of London, and the University of Victoria, British Columbia. She teaches and researches in the areas of globalization, international economic law, law and development, and political and social theory. She has published widely in international journals, including the *Leiden Journal of International Law*, the *International Community Law Review*, *Law, Text, Culture*, the *Indiana Journal of Global Legal Studies*, and the *Nordic Journal of International Law*. She is co-editor (with Peer Zumbansen) of *Law in Transition: Rights, Development and Restorative Justice* (Hart, forthcoming).

Stewart Motha is Reader in Law, School of Law, Birkbeck, University of London, and Fellow of the Stellenbosch Institute of Advanced Study, South Africa. He has published widely on questions of post-colonial sovereignty, indigenous land rights, and political theology and democracy. His research draws on visual art and literature in examining questions of memory, home, exile, and political violence. His articles have been published in a variety of international journals including the *Journal of Law, Culture, and Humanities*, *Theory, Culture and Society*, *Law and Critique*, the *Journal of Law and Society*, and the *Australian Feminist Law Journal*. In 2007 he edited a book titled *Democracy's Empire: Sovereignty, Law, Violence* (Blackwell). A book co-edited with Karin van Marle, *Genres of Critique: Aesthetics and Liminality in Post-apartheid Jurisprudence*, is forthcoming (Stellenbosch University Press, 2012).

Sundhya Pahuja is Professor of Law at the Melbourne Law School, Director of the Law and Development Research programme at the Institute for International Law and the Humanities at the University of Melbourne, and concurrently, Visiting Research Fellow at Birkbeck, University of London. She is the author of *Decolonising International Law: Development, Economic Growth and the Politics of Universality* (Cambridge University Press, 2011), and co-editor (with Fleur Johns and Richard

Joyce) of *Events: The Force of International Law* (Routledge, 2010). Sundhya's research is widely published and focuses on the political economy of international law and institutions, jurisprudence, and post-colonial theory.

Notes on contributors

Carrol Clarkson is Associate Professor and Head of the Department of English Language and Literature at the University of Cape Town. Her research interests are in literary theory, philosophy of language, and South African literature and art within a context of transitional justice. Recent publications include *J. M. Coetzee: Countervoices* (Palgrave, 2009) and *Drawing the Line: Toward an Aesthetics of Transitional Justice* (Fordham University Press, forthcoming).

William E. Conklin is Professor of Law at the Faculty of Law and Department of Philosophy at the University of Windsor, Ontario. He teaches in the areas of jurisprudence, international human rights law and constitutionalism. He is the author of *Hegel's Laws: The Legitimacy of a Modern Legal Order* (Stanford University Press, 2008), *The Invisible Origins of Legal Positivism: A Re-reading of a Tradition* (Kluwer/Springer, 2001), and *The Phenomenology of Modern Legal Discourse* (Ashgate, 1998).

Marianne Constable is Professor of Rhetoric and holds the Zaffaroni Family Chair in Undergraduate Education at the University of California, Berkeley. She is the author of *Just Silences: The Limits and Possibilities of Modern Law* (Princeton University Press, 2004) and *The Law of the Other: The Mixed Jury and Changing Conceptions of Citizenship, Law, and Knowledge* (University of Chicago Press, 1993).

Peter Fitzpatrick is currently Anniversary Professor of Law at the School of Law, Birkbeck, University of London. He has taught at universities in Europe, North America, and Papua New Guinea, and published books on legal philosophy, law and social theory, law and racism, and imperialism, including *Modernism and the Grounds of Law* (Cambridge University Press, 2001) and more recently, with Ben Golder, *Foucault's Law* (Routledge, 2009).

Judith Grbich is Adjunct Associate Professor, Socio-Legal Research Centre, Griffith Law School, and Research Associate of the Institute of Postcolonial Studies, University of Melbourne. She is General Editor of the

Australian Feminist Law Journal, a member of the Editorial Board of the *International Journal for the Semiotics of Law*, and a past President of the Law and Literature Association of Australia. Her research interests include jurisprudential, post-colonial, and psychoanalytic approaches to juridical and cultural forms of life. She is currently working on political theologies in the cultural life of early modern and Reformation Europe.

Fleur Johns is Associate Professor in the Faculty of Law, University of Sydney and Co-director of the Sydney Centre for International Law. Fleur is author of *The Non-Legal in International Law: Limits of the Legal Imagination* (Cambridge University Press, forthcoming), editor of *International Legal Personality* (Ashgate, 2010) and co-editor of *Events: The Force of International Law* (Routledge-Cavendish, 2011).

Fiona Macmillan is Corporation of London Professor of Law at Birkbeck, University of London. Her areas of research interest are intellectual property, cultural property and heritage, and international economic law.

James Martel teaches in the political science department at San Francisco State University. Recent books include *Textual Conspiracies: Walter Benjamin, Idolatry and Political Theory* (University of Michigan, 2011), *Divine Violence: Walter Benjamin and the Eschatology of Sovereignty* (Routledge, 2011), and *Subverting the Leviathan: Reading Thomas Hobbes as a Radical Democrat* (Columbia, 2007).

Abdul Paliwala is Professor of Law at the University of Warwick and worked previously at the Universities of Papua New Guinea, Dar es Salaam and Queen's Belfast. He is involved with the International Development Law and Human Rights Research Group at Warwick and has been Director of the Programme.

Paul A. Passavant is the author of *No Escape: Freedom of Speech and the Paradox of Rights* (New York University Press, 2002) and editor (with Jodi Dean) of *Empire's New Clothes: Reading Hardt and Negri* (Routledge, 2004). He is also the author of numerous articles in law and political theory. Some of the journals in which his essays have appeared include *Political Theory, Constellations, Theory amd Event, Amsterdam Law Forum,* and *Law, Culture, and the Humanities,* among others. Passavant teaches at Hobart and William Smith Colleges.

George Pavlich is a Professor of Law and Sociology at the University of Alberta. He is the author of numerous journal articles and books, including *Justice Fragmented: Mediating Community Disputes under Postmodern Conditions* (Routledge, 1996), *Critique and Radical Discourses on Crime* (Ashgate, 2000), *Governing Paradoxes of Restorative Justice* (GlassHouse Press, 2005), and *Law and Society Redefined* (Oxford University Press, 2011).

Johan van der Walt is Professor, Faculté de Droit, d'Economie et de Finance, University of Luxembourg. He has published several articles exploring the relation between law and the sacrificial social dynamics through which communities generally maintain normative, symbolic, and semantic frameworks and identities. He is also author of *Law and Sacrifice* (Birkbeck Law Press, 2005).

Introduction

Ruth Buchanan, Stewart Motha, and Sundhya Pahuja

> A book like this, a problem like this, is in no hurry; we both, I just as much as my book, are friends of *lento*. It is not for nothing that I have been a philologist, perhaps I am a philologist still, that is to say, a teacher of slow reading: – in the end I also write slowly. Nowadays it is not only my habit, it is also to my taste – a malicious taste, perhaps? – no longer to write anything which does not reduce to despair every sort of man who is 'in a hurry'. For philology is that venerable art which demands of its votaries one thing above all: to go aside, to take time, to become still, to become slow – it is a goldsmith's art and connoisseurship of the *word* which has nothing but delicate, cautious work to do and achieves nothing if it does not achieve it *lento*. But for precisely this reason it is more necessary than ever today, by precisely this means does it entice and enchant us the most, in the midst of an age of 'work', that is to say, of hurry, of indecent and perspiring haste, which wants to 'get everything done' at once, including every old or new book: – this art does not so easily get anything done, it teaches to read *well*, that is to say, to read slowly, deeply, looking cautiously before and aft, with reservations, with doors left open, with delicate eyes and fingers ... My patient friends, this book desires for itself only perfect readers and philologists: *learn* to read me well!
>
> (Nietzsche 1881/1982: 5)

Modern western formulations of legal scholarship have been formed – and continue to circulate – around the question of the authority of the law of the sovereign state and the practices of government. Such concerns are central to the formation and maintenance of the European state in its national, imperial, and international guises. This book takes up these concerns, but 'slantwise',[1] addressing itself to the question of how to live with the law of modernity through the question of reading and, specifically, how to read the modernity of law. The essays in this volume arise out of a symposium focussed on the work of Professor Peter Fitzpatrick.

As late moderns, we inhabit a world that has been shaped by the demand for the security of both the sovereign territorial state and the power and wealth of empire. Questions of sovereignty and domination and of subordination and freedom have driven these claims of security and protection, but have driven, too, the claims of right and of justice. In turn, such questions and claims have engendered the critical scrutiny of the practices of politics, law, and morality. And even as we live in an age of neo-colonialism, the over-consumption of resources and the destruction of the environment, our responses remain shaped by the forms of law by which we live. The various chapters of this book attend to the ways that critics from within and across the common law tradition have approached what we might think of as 'sovereign formations' and the origins or grounds of law – and through this our 'situation' as subjects of law.

The origins of law have long been a central concern of the 'theoretical' branch of the discipline. This book considers *reading* as central to developing a critical methodology capable of addressing that concern, and the persistence of, and limits to, a variety of sovereign formations. *Reading modern law* as we envisage it here is an attitude, posture, and style. In this book we advocate reading slowly, attentively, again and again,[2] in order to attend to the vanishing point (or limits) of what appears substantial in law's extravagant claims. Such claims include the notions that law is autonomous, that it grounds itself, that it is ever responsive to the new, and that it carries universal values and aspirations. Here, we remind ourselves that the work of reading, like that of listening, is as much the work of the critic as is responding to injustice. Such reading, slow reading, also serves to join and re-join with the possibilities and potential law.

The strategies of reading and the styles of writing and argumentation explored in these essays draw inspiration from the work of Peter Fitzpatrick. Fitzpatrick's work spans 30 years of patient reading of the origins and (authoritative) grounds of modern law. It is a body of work that might retroactively pass under the heading of the decolonization of law, and offers a style or ethos of slow reading which tries to do justice to law, and to a life lived with law. Fitzpatrick's readings of law's grounds are thus both a challenge to law and a form of care or love for law.

In this book we take Fitzpatrick's complex formulation of the dynamic conduct of law in terms of 'determination and responsiveness' as a device for reading slowly – for undoing, resisting, and reformulating a variety of sovereign formations. In Fitzpatrick's hands the endless relation between determinacy and responsiveness gives us a point of ordering of the relations of law. His work offers us at least two ways of reading (modern law) slowly. First is the patient work of the redescription of western legal relations as a tradition forever engaged in the task of shoring up and breaching its own boundaries. In its psychic and material states, the determination of law creates grounds, establishes territory, governs populations, and seeks security. At the same time, law must also be open to change and be able to respond to the realities of the world it engages. So, second, Fitzpatrick's work calls on us, as critics, to read slowly to *recast* this dynamic, both to make visible its injustices and also to find new forms of responsiveness. The slow readings in this book also elaborate the patterns and styles created by such readings – their rhythm or tempo; the practices of re-inscription within and around the traditions of legal thought; the tracing of law as it moves; and an ethic of care that would ensure that law is not without response, or the possibility of justice.

The chapters thus open appropriately enough with the question of justice, and specifically reading justice and the archive. Marianne Constable in Chapter 1 observes that Fitzpatrick's 'insistent and persistent' citations of the writings of others 'incite us to (consider) what might otherwise remain outside of writings of and about law: possibilities of justice'. Constable is concerned with the question of authorship, and specifically Fitzpatrick's authorial style, as a key dimension of his practice of reading. The tension between an avowed willingness to be attentive to (or determined by) the specificity of the text, and the willingness to be open to that which those texts cannot contain, is an integral aspect of Fitzpatrick's work. His layered, difficult philological writing invites us to engage in the project of reading modern law differently. Fitzpatrick's work 'challenges not only the imperialism of the state and its law, but also the imperialism of a particular sort of scholarship about law – in particular, that of the empirical social sciences', as Constable puts it. Constable's chapter elucidates both challenges.

Linking Fitzpatrick's mode of reading to his approach to the question of sovereign formations, Constable begins by tracing the arc of Fitzpatrick's arguments about the United States' sovereign assertion and its arrogation to itself a style of settled determinacy that transforms the nation from one which was once (reflexively) identified with the 'revolutionary dimension of the rule of law' to a 'carrier of imperialism'. In contrast with the usual (critical) formulation, international law becomes the locus of a potential challenge to imperialism through an 'imperative and counter-imperial ethics' which is encompassed (though not contained) within it. Constable notes that, for Fitzpatrick, international law is 'both dissipated *and* state-centred'. The second, methodologically oriented challenge is developed by setting Fitzpatrick's view of the role of custom in international law alongside Sally Merry's account of the role of culture in the translation of international human rights norms to local contexts. For Merry and Fitzpatrick, culture and custom respectively are both 'fluid' and 'promiscuous', and in this respect are transgressive of legal norms. Yet for Fitzpatrick these transgressions have a constitutive dimension; indeed, it is precisely 'the effects of active opposition, disregard and violations' that 'merge to challenge law to become just'.

For Constable, Fitzpatrick's profound attention to texts is unapologetically symptomatic of 'archive fever'. This attentiveness is held in constant tension with his equally unapologetic responsiveness to that which always exceeds the capacity of those texts, and that archive. Made visible in this tension are 'unsettled silences and possibilities of response' within which Constable locates the impossible fecundity of Fitzpatrick's work. We are cautioned to be 'wary of global visions and sovereign systems, both as claims and as facts', yet the very failures of those visions and systems in relation to the 'insatiable' demands of justice are revealed as leaving spaces open for something else.

Worrying and revisiting what is 'settled', whether territorially or in text, is the subject of Chapter 2, by James Martel. Martel offers us a double account of reading, presenting some uncanny parallels between the reading styles of Peter Fitzpatrick and Thomas Hobbes. Both Fitzpatrick and Hobbes (and, by implication, Martel) offer us ways of thinking about power and authority anew through reading. Both Fitzpatrick and Hobbes are concerned with the theological remnants in putatively secular formations. In Fitzpatrick's case these remnants are made visible through practices of attentive reading. In Hobbes' case the revelation is connected to his rhetorical sensibility, which manifests a certain 'urge to truth'. As Martel points out, this urge becomes clear in Hobbes' own comments on reading texts:

> [I]t is not the bare Words, but the Scope of the writer that giveth the true light, by which any writing is to bee interpreted; and they that insist upon single Texts, without considering the main Designe, can derive no thing from them cleerly; but rather by casting atomes of Scripture, as dust before mens eyes, make every thing more obscure than it is; an ordinary artifice of those that seek not the truth, but their own advantage.
>
> (Hobbes 1651/1996: 415)

Martel shows that Hobbes wants us to be attentive to the scope and design of a text, and 'how we are to interpret and interact with (or read) the text overall'. The point is quilted when Martel guides us to read Fitzpatrick as a reader of Hobbes. Through his careful re-reading of Hobbes, and his refusal of received wisdom, Fitzpatrick seeks – and finds – a certain kind of lawfulness where others find only savagery and darkness. This reading, and rereading, enables Fitzpatrick, Martel argues, to find a 'tender' side to *Leviathan*, one that displaces the usual characterization of Hobbes as an authoritarian positivist, enabling the emergence of a different genealogy of liberal law and politics and engendering a call to a different kind of responsibility.

From author and authority we turn our gaze to sovereignty, yet still 'slantwise', not directly. The chapters by George Pavlich (Chapter 3) and Paul Passavant (Chapter 4) both share the sense that neither law nor its subjects can live without the 'enchantment' of the stories that sustain law as sovereignty and self-knowledge, judgement, and understanding. And each of them takes up the problem of how we are to read the variety of sovereign determinations through which power and authority are constituted and sustained, through which biopolitical life is administered and how critical beings resist, refuse, and rebel.

A sovereign determination, Pavlich argues with Fitzpatrick, is at once decisive and responsive to that which is beyond the determination. This is as consistent with the ungrounded ground of medieval sovereignty as it is with a biopolitical power that posits itself through law. Drawing on Fitzpatrick's account of 'the law of the law', Pavlich offers a way to read both law and sovereignty which reveals their mutuality: the law in a given instance posits itself, and in that process an associated sovereignty emerges. But the law of sovereignty is then forever caught, produced, and read between determination and responsiveness.

Like Martel, Pavlich insists on the radical potential of reading carefully, using Fitzpatrick as an exemplar of such practices of 'radical reading'. Hobbes, for example, is sometimes thought to offer a form of law and politics delimited by territory, and a form of sovereign power that is illimitable and ungovernable. For Pavlich, though, a different register of questioning sovereign power is in order: 'Can the political logic (theology?) of an ungovernable sovereign be understood as an historical event? And have new "governmentalized" forms of sovereignty transformed this logic? If so, what might the laws of such governmental sovereignty be?' Drawing on Foucault, Butler, and Fitzpatrick, Pavlich argues that sovereignty produces ungovernability as a mode of governance, and point of reading. We have seen the emergence of a 'governmentalized sovereign', a sovereign who 'becomes' through governing. These questions, which emerge through a careful re-reading of sovereign formations, enable us to 'refus[e] the ungovernable sovereign as definitive of all sovereignties'. Such refusal opens up the 'unconditional' aspect of sovereignty, drawing on Fitzpatrick again, to signal the unknown senses of a 'governable', or at least 'governed', sovereign, and open them to the possibility of other promises, including democracy.

Paul Passavant's chapter too picks up on these themes, avowedly locating his consideration of the relation between sovereignty and democracy from within 'democracy's ruins' – the United States after the torture memos. Passavant too counterposes Fitzpatrick to Agamben's work on sovereign power. In contrast with Agamben's anti-juridical, messianic view of the transition from an 'absolute sovereignty' to the 'coming community', Fitzpatrick, in Passavant's reading, mediates the relation between sovereignty and democracy within his conception of sovereignty itself. Modern sovereignty must ' "marvellously combine" being enclosed, one, corporate, and determining with also ... being illimitable, plural, responsive, determinate, and dissipating'. And it must 'combine these contradictory dimensions without recourse to a transcendental reference'. For Fitzpatrick, and for Passavant, this impossibly paradoxical combining is accomplished by the peculiar alchemy of modern law. Law, for Passavant, 'is where we take a position on democracy'. Returning us to the ethical possibilities of (re-)reading the archive, Passavant's chapter compellingly argues for the reclamation of law as 'democracy's archive' – the site within which we may 'recall principles of democracy and justice to ourselves, and send, again, this legacy to the future'.

Taken as a practice of reading and writing which both challenges law and evinces a form of care or love for law – a fecund law, pregnant with possibility – Fitzpatrick's work reminds us again and again that 'the medium is the message', or that the medium is there to be read. Yet as we see in Chapter 5, by Fleur Johns, and Chapter 10, by Carrol Clarkson, the message resonates differently within different disciplinary idioms. In her poetic chapter, Johns identifies the 'possibility' that Fitzpatrick locates within international law with the distinctive 'rhythm' of his scholarly engagements with it, and yet concludes that it is a possibility that will provide little reassurance to international lawyers.

Johns approaches Fitzpatrick's rhythm or method of reading and writing in terms of a critical practice, a way of living *in* or *with* international law, rather than the production of knowledge about it. Yet she locates her reading of Fitzpatrick both within and outside of the discipline of international law. While his 'insistence upon what he calls a "socio-logic"' in international law can be related to 'recurring attempts to restore to international law an imperative if paradoxical sociality', Johns notes that Fitzpatrick's call to imbue international law with 'positive content' may strike 'the international lawyer on the street' as risky, even retrogressive. More importantly, the critique may miss its mark, either because it is too easily accommodated within international law's 'comfortable, elastic cosmopolitanism' or because it underestimates the utility of the pragmatic anti-formalism that is the critical international lawyer's stock in trade. For an international lawyer, while the distinctive tempo of Fitzpatrick's work can be understood in terms of a refreshing, if resolutely discordant, critical ethos in respect of much that is taken for granted within the field, it also defies the pragmatic impulse so deeply embedded in the psyche of the discipline: 'nothing emerges that may be applied readily elsewhere'.

Staying with international law, and bringing together the themes of reading slowly, creatively, and collaboratively is the similarly poetic account offered by Fiona Macmillan in Chapter 6 of the 'tapestry' of the intellectual endeavour in which she understands herself to be engaged. This effort, of weaving together (in both senses), understands scholarship as a (communal) process rather than an (individualized) product. Macmillan is concerned with the 'new constitutionalisms' of both the national and the international, and the attempts to integrate and 'harmonize', at both levels, the economic and the political. Macmillan's chapter draws on the first of Fitzpatrick's lessons about reading modern law, and specifically the possibilities of critical redescription. Here that redescription is Fitzpatrick's reversal of the typical depiction of the international as being constituted by the national, and his account of the mutually constitutive relationship between the national and the international which offers us new ways of reading domestic political processes as being shaped by the international. As Macmillan compellingly shows us, the effect of this in general, and of the international trading regime in particular, is that the political has become subordinated to the economic.

Moving from the international to the universal, William Conklin in Chapter 7 engages with the question of law's forms, and in particular the understanding of those forms as universals. Conklin's chapter is a lovely illustration of what may be gained by a practice of reading slowly in contrast to more forensic styles of critique. Reading slowly has the potential to draw open a text, revealing the unexplored and unexamined possibilities that lie within it. Taking Fitzpatrick's critique of analytical jurisprudence as his starting point, Conklin reminds us that another corollary of reading slowly is *teaching* slowly, and implied in slowness in that context is an approach to the question of knowledge that resonates with the decolonization of law. Placing Fitzpatrick's constant concern with the irresolution of law's origins against the analytic tradition's equally obsessive concern to pin it down, Conklin reminds us that

> [a]n explanation of the origins of the legal order 'a priori puts us outside'. The myth and mysticism of the origins remain a secret so long as contemporary legal theorists, law teachers, and other officials colour their analyses as the rule of law and objectivity. The secrecy is reinforced by disparaging rhetoric directed towards anyone, whether inside or outside the chains of analysed forms, who attempts to pierce the veil of the invisible foundation. Social bonding among the non-expert knowers of legal forms [therefore] remains an outside possibility.

Through Fitzpatrick and Derrida, Conklin reminds us that the 'painful consequence' of this secrecy, and the asserted universality of forms, is violence and exclusion. Fitzpatrick has been especially concerned with this 'painful consequence of law with reference to the civilizing mission of the colonialist on the one hand and the indigenous experiences of the aboriginal peoples in North America and Australia on the other'. Following Fitzpatrick into a concern with foundations, we understand that as 'long as we remain in the illusion that the system (*droit*) of laws (*lois*) has a foundation, we will pursue the colonizing project'. And yet Conklin shows us that a slow reading of Fitzpatrick and, with Fitzpatrick, of Derrida may also reveal a continuation of what Conklin calls a 'territorial' knowledge which presupposes that concepts are valid if they can be situated within familiar territorial and metaphysical boundaries. Territorial knowledge raises the prospect of power and violence as an inevitable feature of a modern state-centric legal order and of the imperial and colonial condition of modern European and common law. And yet reading slowly shows us that Fitzpatrick himself is haunted by the intuition that there might be another sense of knowledge. Conklin, like Macmillan, is concerned to 'weave together', treating scholarship as a communal practice rather than individualized product. And he pushes Fitzpatrick's own concern along, to outline a different sense: of 'experiential' knowledge. For Conklin, this radically different sense of knowledge is also nested in European legal thought, and opens a question as to whether even Fitzpatrick's sophisticated account of territorial knowledge tells the whole story about contemporary legal thought. Teasing these threads out from within Fitzpatrick's texts enacts the lessons of slow reading Fitzpatrick's own writing has taught us.

The thought of the territorial and of the occupation of territory is taken up from within the tradition in another way. Like Conklin, Judith Grbich in Chapter 8 questions the inheritance of the form of law. She takes up the experience of the form of modern law and links it to Peter Fitzpatrick's work of 'internal decolonization'. Drawing on the work of Ian Duncanson in delineating relations between law, modernity, gender, and race, Grbich draws out the sense in which Fitzpatrick's project joins a long engagement with the experience and affective form of law: with Christian spirit and with the gendered and sexed understanding of the story of debt, economy, and authority. For Grbich this is a story read best in terms of Lutheran theology and Lacanian psychoanalysis. Grbich asks, what is the character of the God which dwells as a colonizer within, and who or what aspect of ourselves has this God colonized? How else should this story be told except as biography, tradition, and law? How else can this be told except as the story of the Christianization, or at least the Lutheran Christianization, of the Law of Moses?

In a sharp delineation of the Christian structure of modernity, Grbich links Martin Luther's anti-Semitic characterization of the expropriation of labour and life by gluttony and drunkenness, the cost of clothing, and usurious buying of rent charges with Freud's story of the killing of God in *Moses and Monotheism*. Economy, and the exchange of economy, is structured around the desire of brothers for access to women. Authority, life, and exchange point both to the ways in which we kill God and to the ways in which we enter into cultural life and language. For Freud this was a story to be told in terms of a family romance. For Lacan it is one told in Aristotelian terms of the making of knowledge like 'a procreation in which the masculine is the activating of a life'. Both accounts point to the ways in which 'the sexed and theologically loaded fantasies embedded in the jurisprudential archive have a central place in the ways the subject in modernity is conceived'.

Grbich draws Lacan's accounts of authority and language into law by pointing to the ways in which Lacan reveals the continuities between Martin Luther's onto-theological concerns with the discourses of trade, economy, and exchange, and contemporary forms of thinking. The New Testament and Lutheran teaching of 'love thy neighbour as thyself' transform the meaning of the Eucharist from Catholic sacrifice to the sealing of a gift from God. However, as Grbich and Lacan note, in Luther's telling of the New Testament this is a gift that turns out to be a debt – the gift of a financier and the sign of financial property. This gives us the dialectic of the Master and the Slave. It is these fantasies that put women into circulation as the creation and property of men. While Luther's interpretation of the Mass as a gift that overcomes the Mosaic law of prohibition gives us the entitlement of freedom (this is the gift of Christ), it also gives us the injunction to follow the life of Christ and give up life for the neighbour.

Johan van der Walt in Chapter 9 too is concerned with reading the modern imaginary, returning us to the question of origins or grounds in his exploration of Fitzpatrick's reading of Freud in *Modernism and the Grounds of Law* (2001). As is well known, Fitzpatrick turns to Freud in exploring the origins of human society, and the question of the grounds of law. In the quasi-ethnographic account of the primal horde in Freud's *Totem and Taboo*, we find the origin myth that serves as an allegory of the origin of law. In what seems like a completely determined fixity, the father imposes order on the primal horde and has monopoly over the women. In the face of this order and fixity another sociality emerges: that of the sons who band together to kill and consume the father. The rupture ushers in a sense that possibility and newness can enter the world. But 'taking leave' of this order, as van der Walt puts it, does not offer 'a stable abode'. The brothers find themselves

> split by two seemingly irreconcilable concerns, the concern with a stability reminiscent to some degree of the fixity formerly imposed by the father, on the one hand, and a freedom to take leave of this order when the exigencies of desire and circumstance require this leave-taking.

Driven by the need to reconcile this tension, the 'totem' is instituted. The killing of the totem is generally prohibited but occasionally allowed. This combines both order and the possibility of an occasional ecstatic overcoming of that order. As Fitzpatrick (2001: 2–3) puts it, the 'two extremities' of determinate order and what is unknowably beyond are combined in the killing of the totem. The two extremities – determination and responsiveness – characterize totemic law. Van der Walt describes these dimensions or extremities of law 'in terms of two homonyms that allow us to contemplate and trace further their *wondrous* and *unmediated* concentration and *combination*. The homonyms at issue here are *immanence* and *imminence* – where determination corresponds to immanence, and responsiveness to imminence. Following a discussion that distinguishes 'immanence' in the work of Deleuze and Guattari on the one hand, and Jean-Luc Nancy on the other, van der Walt suggests that the determinative aspect of law involves a claim that law is 'immanent to itself'. An imminent or responsive law, on the other hand, 'is never fixed but always to come'.

For van der Walt, a law that is immanent to itself fails to be hospitable or open to a law that is never fixed and always to come. In terms of the orientation to slow reading which positions this volume, van der Walt's chapter reminds us of another dimension of attentiveness – that of listening – that corresponds to the slowness in reading:

> the misleading homonymic play between immanence and imminence can in fact lead us to hear imminence when we hear immanence and vice versa, or lead us to hear both simultaneously and leave us to first think and *listen to* what is to be heard before we can respond aptly.

Modern law advances the dominance of the determinate (immanent). Or, as Fitzpatrick puts it, '[t]he modern rule of law, with its avowal of assured stability and ultimacy of determination, seems closer to the condition of the primal horde' (2001: 2). This is not to suggest that 'utter responsiveness' would be an alternative posture, as that would also return us to another totalized world. Immanence and imminence becomes dangerously fused – a condition that we experience in our mishearing and confusing of the two terms. For van der Walt,

> Between immanence and imminence is an infinitesimally small but always hugely impossible step, namely the step between the now and not-now, the step between time that is still for a moment and time that is always gone. The totem was devised to traverse this impossible step and embody this impossible threshold. And it is the consistent focus on this impossible step or threshold between the here and there and the now and then of law that renders Fitzpatrick's work so relentlessly liminal.

This liminality of law takes the place of what would otherwise be an alchemy or reliance on a transcendental reference.

But if Fitzpatrick's work of reading – and the work of reading Fitzpatrick – reminds us of the intimacy between medium and message – and between the medium and its reading – the chapter by Carrol Clarkson (Chapter 10) finds in Fitzpatrick a model of how responsiveness to law might be enacted. Writing from within the discipline of literary and aesthetic theory, Clarkson is oriented by an attention to the expressive and aesthetic forms taken up in response to the limits of law. In this, Clarkson (like Constable) attends to Fitzpatrick's own citational practices. For Clarkson, this practice itself enacts, perhaps even constitutes, a relation between what is beyond law and what is interior to law. One task undertaken in Fitzpatrick's *Modernism and the Grounds of Law* (2001), for example, is a form of responsiveness to the too literal grounding of law. For Clarkson, Fitzpatrick's work is exemplary in the way it holds on to and elaborates the gesture of responding to the limits of law. Fitzpatrick writes in response to and against the enclosed space of Carl Schmitt's European *nomos*, 'whilst determination can never be completely spatially formed, responsiveness cannot be ever completely unformed' (Fitzpatrick 2001: 91). Clarkson herself responds, with Heidegger, that what is important is not so much earth or world but the relation that is called forth or disclosed by art, or by law. The world of art is 'responsive to the earthly forms in nature ... it neither excludes them, nor does it abstract or reduce them to the supposedly determinate limits of its own world'. Rephrased in the language of limit, art and law do not simply exclude, they make possible. Fitzpatrick, argues Clarkson, identifies such a relation in terms of a response – a creative reaching out to a possibility beyond determinate existence – where law finds itself bound to its exterior. The limit or *aporia* that keeps law and justice apart also allows for the possibility of a relation – of a justice, law, or ground yet to come.

Reading, relationality, and limit are themes that take us full circle, (back) to Abdul Paliwala's evocative chapter (Chapter 11), which provides us with a fireside resting place before Fitzpatrick's own contribution to this volume. In what is the most avowedly biographical chapter in the book, Paliwala takes us back to Fitzpatrick's early engagements with law and politics in Papua New Guinea, hinting at the ways in which Fitzpatrick's 'reflexive transgressive form of participatory engagement with people who were being subordinated' has shaped his practices of reading and writing, and living with, law ever since. Paliwala uses the metaphor of reading and writing by firelight to consider the particular demands and possibilities – and limitations – of decolonizing law. 'Firelight', he observes, 'is both warmly seductive and in its flickering quality not a great medium for readers or writers', and yet the particular ethical commitments it evinces are well captured by the implicit contrast to the electric glare of modern law. This contrast becomes contradiction in the form of Fitzpatrick as a 'carrier' of modern law in Papua New Guinea, but a carrier as jurist, as reader, who speaks not as a jurist 'of the South'[3] but as a critical reader of his own traditions. Thus emplaced, Fitzpatrick, according to Paliwala, tried always to enact the resistant and transgressive possibilities of the law in a society putatively 'in rapid transition' from tradition to modernity, from colony to post-colony, while always also aware of the inescapable tension between the imperial and counter-imperial dimensions of law. In his subsequent practice, Fitzpatrick has held on to something of that emplacement, reading and writing against the grain, and teaching us to read and write in a similar vein, of critique and care, for both law and its 'critical beings' (Fitzpatrick and Tuitt 2004).

Fitzpatrick's own contribution concludes this volume, bringing together modern law's mythopoetic quality with its characteristic duality of determinacy and responsiveness, combined and made visible through the practice of reading – and writing – slowly. Here Fitzpatrick suggests that law and literature share a creative and fictive quality. But saying what this fictive quality may be is no easy matter. Almost all the contributors to this volume have pointed to Fitzpatrick's characterization of law as combining a determinate and responsive quality. In Chapter 12 he extends this to the 'receptive creativity' that both law and literature share. But he also insists on the persistence and insistence of the negative – the sense that 'poetry makes nothing happen' (Auden 1979). But as Fitzpatrick makes clear, with a citational practice we have drawn attention to, what happens is far from 'nothing':

> What Auden means with 'poetry makes nothing happen' is that it brings nothingness into happening. In the same poem he describes poetry as '[a] way of happening, a mouth' (1979: 82). Or as Blanchot puts it even more expansively: 'Nothingness is the creator of the world in man' (1999: 398–9). Or we have nothing as our 'flowering' in Celan's 'Psalm' (2002: 153). (The evocation of nothing can make the academic feel the need of copious reference.)

An attentiveness to the event of newness or happening is a consistent theme in Fitzpatrick's work. After Nietzsche, he urges us to read and write slowly – partly as a way of countering this 'age of work', but also in order to leave some doors open. This is the injunction with which we began, 'to read slowly, deeply, looking cautiously before and aft, with reservations, with doors left open, with delicate eyes and fingers' (Nietzsche 1982: 5; and see Goodrich 2005: 189–97).

As a volume, *Reading Modern Law* gathers together a collection of essays that pay close attention to a critical approach to sovereign formations and the grounds of law. The character of modern law is approached through an emphasis on the rhetorical and discursive practices which we regard as constitutive of what law is. As we have suggested, we approach the task of studying law by privileging an attitude to reading texts. This is not especially new. There are several excellent studies that have examined the nature and character of law from a critical and interdisciplinary perspective which emphasizes the ethical importance of reading (slowly), and we take our bearings from Goodrich (1986), Fitzpatrick (1992, 2001), Constable (2005), Douzinas and Geary (2008), and Pavlich (2010).

But if an attention to reading – and slow reading in particular – is not new, the study of the 'grounds' of law – understood broadly as authorization, foundation, arche, and memory of legal decisions and institutions – owes much to Peter Fitzpatrick, the leading theorist of modern law's grounding and groundlessness. From his early, path-breaking work on myth and modernity which characterized the irresolution of modern law's expulsion of mythic structures and narratives (Fitzpatrick 1992) to his later work directly on the grounds of law, what emerges crucially is the ambivalence at the core of what characterizes law and the legal decision – an irresolute combination of law's determinate and responsive qualities (Fitzpatrick 2001).

Following Fitzpatrick, we learn that treating a combination of the determinant and responsive qualities – of law, and of sovereignty – as the object of study can serve to reveal the dynamism and potential in a law that is too often regarded as radically over-determined, whether by something called the 'social', or by the sovereign exception. And so the fact that scholars and critics disagree about how to define sovereignty is less our concern here than the idea that different ways of reading sovereign formations suggest different engagements between writer, reader, and sovereign, as well as with justice and law.

Accordingly, many of the chapters of this volume can also be seen as taking a sideways glance at sovereignty, thinking about sovereignty 'slantwise' through cognate concepts such as democracy, governance, international law, constitutionalism, theology, imperialism, the force of literature, psyche, and sacrifice, each addressed here to a greater or lesser extent as sovereign formations. And although we are far from suggesting that the multiple, situated, and persistent sovereign disasters can be reduced to a text, or resisted by strategies of reading alone, we take inspiration from Fitzpatrick to think about what practices of re-reading both legal texts and sovereign events with slowness, or a kind of 'radical care', might offer.

But if the irresolution between determinacy and responsiveness, and the practices of reading that it engenders, demands, and sustains, can help us to live with modern law, the legality to be encountered through Fitzpatrick's work is a 'terminal' one (Fitzpatrick 2001: 100, 148, 175, 184). It is terminal not only because modern law has been a reliable companion of imperial death-dealing and colonial appropriations of various kinds; it is terminal, too, not in the sense of finality, but in the sense that it makes something possible – beyond. Terminus is the Roman god of boundaries; his temple is open to the sky. Holding open a place between forms of dissolution – the work of irresolution – is one of the tasks of the reader of law.

Notes

1 See Emily Dickinson, 'Tell all the Truth but tell it slant' (1960: 506 [1128]).
2 On slowness and law's time, see the lovely essay by Karin van Marle (2003).
3 See generally Black *et al.* (2007).

References

Auden, W. H. (1979) 'In memory of W. B. Yeats', in W. H. Auden, *Selected Poems*, London: Faber & Faber.

Black, C., McVeigh, S., and Johnstone, R. (2007) 'Of the South', *Griffith Law Review* 16: 299–309.

Blanchot, M. (1999) 'Literature and the right to death', trans. L. Davis, in M. Blanchot, *The Station Hill Blanchot Reader: Fiction and Literary Essays*, Barrytown, NY: Station Hill Press.

Celan, P. (2002) *Poems of Paul Celan*, trans. M. Hamburger, New York: Persea Books.

Constable, M. (2005) *Just Silences: The Limits and Possibilities of Modern Law*, Princeton, NJ: Princeton University Press.

Dickinson, E. (1960) *The Complete Poems of Emily Dickinson*, ed. T. H. Johnson, Boston: Little, Brown.

Douzinas, C. and Geary, A. (2005) *Critical Jurisprudence: The Political Philosophy of Justice*, Oxford: Hart Publishing.

Fitzpatrick, P. (1992) *The Mythology of Modern Law*, London: Routledge.

Fitzpatrick, P. (2001) *Modernism and the Grounds of Law*, Cambridge: Cambridge University Press.

Fitzpatrick, P. and Tuitt, P. (2004) *Critical Beings: Law, Nation and the Global Subject*, Farnham, UK: Ashgate.

Goodrich, P. (1986) *Reading the Law: Critical Introduction to Legal Method and Techniques*, Oxford: Basil Blackwell.

Goodrich, P. (2005) 'Slow reading', in P. Goodrich and M. Valverde (eds) *Nietzsche and Legal Theory: Half-Written Laws*, New York: Routledge.

Hobbes, T. (1651/1996) *Leviathan*, ed. R. Tuck, New York: Cambridge University Press.

Nietzsche, F. (1982) *Daybreak*, trans. R. J. Hollingdale, Cambridge: Cambridge University Press.

Pavlich, G. (2010) *Law and Society Redefined*, Toronto: Oxford University Press.

van Marle, K. (2003) 'Law's time, particularity and slowness', *South African Journal on Human Rights* 19: 239–55.

Chapter 1

Incitement to justice

Fitzpatrick's citations as counter-imperialism

Marianne Constable

Introduction

In reading Peter Fitzpatrick's work on law, one is immediately struck by the richness and breadth of his citations. Fitzpatrick paraphrases and quotes directly with great fluency from not only Foucault, Derrida, and Blanchot, but also Hobbes, Rousseau, and the Bible. He shows himself to be up to date with law and secondary literature in any number of fields: international law, jurisprudence, legal history. A UK law professor, he appears as comfortable with US national security documents as with Canadian case law concerning indigenous peoples, as comfortable with contemporary novels as with classic poetry. He analyses bestsellers in political science and refers to the most recent essays of contemporaries with whom he is both more and less attuned. Drawing insistently and persistently on the thoughts and writings of a range of others, Fitzpatrick's work nevertheless manifests an originality that challenges not only the imperialism of the state and its law, but also the imperialism of a particular sort of scholarship about law – in particular, that of the empirical social sciences.

One might simply attribute Fitzpatrick's challenge to conventional sociolegal studies to the 'post-structuralist' or 'postmodern' tenor of his work; to do so would be to apply labels without considering what they name, however. Both Fitzpatrick's substantive arguments and his writing style – if one will allow that distinction – counter what is taken for granted in law and legal scholarship. In his 2003 essay '"Gods would be needed…": American empire and the rule of (international) law', for instance, Fitzpatrick finds that international law, with its aporias and layers and contradictions, may counter the hegemony or imperialism of an American law that is linear, exhaustive, and powerful. Such law has correlates, as we shall see, in a particular sort of scholarship. And just as Fitzpatrick's account of international law, drawing on Derrida among others, counters American state law, so too Fitzpatrick's inimitable writing style – with its own citational layers and silences and conflicts – counters the hegemony or imperialism of the global sociolegal enterprise's mainstream scholarship. In the face of a perhaps now not-so-new sociolegal imperialism in the writings and circulations of law, Fitzpatrick's celebration and recollection of a multiplicity of humanistic texts and approaches incite us to what might otherwise remain outside writings of and about law: possibilities of justice.

I should mention at the outset that my comments here are offered neither as conspectus (to use a word Fitzpatrick likes) nor comprehensive analysis of Fitzpatrick's work. This essay of appreciation aims simply to say something of what I like about a recent set of pieces in which Fitzpatrick writes of the responsiveness (or not) of law to claims of justice, if I have translated properly into my own idiom. In reading for the occasion of this Festschrift, I was chagrined to find how much of Fitzpatrick's work I had not previously encountered. I have no opportunity to engage here with Fitzpatrick's anthropological and Marxian work, nor with his critiques of H. L. A. Hart, for instance. To gauge from our essays on Robert Cover's 'Violence and the word' (Sarat 2001), though, Fitzpatrick and I share the view, I think, that if state law no longer speaks of justice, then that is not a reason to ignore or neglect justice. It is, rather, a reason to reconsider the claims of state law to exhaust the category of law.

Fitzpatrick develops this argument in 'Gods would be needed…'. He turns there to international law to find possibilities – however inherently contradictory – of a law that can counter what he calls the imperialism of American state law, a state law exemplified in his essay by the 2002 US National Security Strategy. Its power is positivistic, sociologic-al in Fitzpatrick's terms, socio-logical in mine, and instrumental. Not only does Fitzpatrick suggest (and 'suggest' is more apt than 'propose' in Fitzpatrick's writing) an alternative law, but his writing itself opens one up to possibilities of law – and of justice and of ways of knowing – that counter, again, not only American imperialism and its claims, but also the imperialism of the sciences of society (sociologies) that would – that is, seek to – determine reality while themselves constituting law.

After briefly summarizing Fitzpatrick's account of the relation of 'American empire' to 'the rule of international law', my argument proceeds in two parts. I suggest, first, that international law has also become the site of a new imperialism: that of the social sciences. The best-intentioned sociolegal scholars see universal human rights as the 'best global vision' that we have. They turn international law into precisely the kind of nation-state-oriented or imperialist law that, Fitzpatrick recognizes, is but one aspect of a lovingly incomplete international law. Second, I show that, like the controverted international law that Fitzpatrick argues is both in and beyond itself, Fitzpatrick's work manifests without apology and with apt reflection the somewhat schizophrenic symptoms of what Derrida identified as 'archive fever'. Both state law and sociolegal products and productions seek to stabilize and deny these symptoms. In explicitly acknowledging them, Fitzpatrick's own legal writing emplaces (to use another of Fitzpatrick's own terms) an alternative to the current imperialism of the empirical in the writing and circulation of law, which alternative keeps open the responsiveness of law to *claims* of justice.

The new imperialism

Fitzpatrick sees the history of law as a trajectory from a 'theologic' to a 'sociologic' in which the modern 'Eternal Object' humanity is, 'borrowing Derrida's term, a "secularised sacred concept", uniting as it does an impelling force of transcendent right with a profane location in the factual' (2003: 443). Such a trajectory accords, of course, with the genealogies of reason and of law offered by Nietzsche and those who have followed. As Fitzpatrick puts it elsewhere, modern law 'can no longer resolve the divide between its determinate existence and its responsiveness by way of a transcendent reference, by way of divine right' (2010: 449); in effect, 'Gods, or a god, would still be needed' (2003: 436). For Fitzpatrick, then,

> law 'is' the settlement in terms of a normative continuity of the existential divide between a determinate positioning and a responding to what is beyond position, and it is in the necessity yet impossibility of such settlement that law is iteratively impelled into existence.
>
> (2004: 223)

In 'Gods would be needed…', Fitzpatrick shows, against this background and against the many usual critics of international law, how international law is law. He argues that although the nation-state is often viewed in opposition to both international law and imperialism, the United States, as the most powerful nation of modern nationalism and with its claims as to the sovereignty of its municipal law, is a carrier of imperialism. He turns to international law as a site of, among other things including power, an 'imperative and counter-imperial ethics' that may counter US claims to sovereignty.

The idea of the sovereignty of US law, Fitzpatrick (2003: 430) argues, relies on a completeness of power or an illimitable authority that is nevertheless determinately emplaced. Through the United States' claims to sovereignty, the once-revolutionary dimension of the rule of law, Fitzpatrick writes, its being ever-responsive to change and conducive to the unsettling of any fixed rule, becomes oriented towards determinate settlement. So – to oversimplify – in state law, according to Fitzpatrick, the rule of law, even in its aspiration, becomes fixed and static, in a manner that parallels the way that sovereignty claims to be exhaustive.

International law, by contrast – as Fleur Johns' contribution to this collection explains – potentially opposes the imperial claims of the United States to a quasi-sovereign completeness. Dependent but never completely determined by outside 'power', the 'reality' of international law is constructed in part through fictions, Fitzpatrick (2003: 452) points out – the fiction of custom, for instance. In the context of the 'savage', custom corresponds to the 'iron invariance [that reflects] unchanging practices' (ibid.: 453). In the context of '"the gentle civilizer of nations" that is international law' (ibid.: 453, citing Koskenniemi's title and epigraph), however, a 'promiscuous custom [is] freed of any enduring attachment and [becomes] ever responsive to what is ever changing' (ibid.: 454). The failure of attempts to ground international law in a more determinate custom enables international law to constitute the nation-state that ostensibly constitutes it (ibid.: 455). In other words, international law may be viewed either as a creation of custom or as what custom and transgression replace or displace (ibid.: 452). Whichever the relation of international law to custom, the fact of international law's recognition of subject states – whether creating the nation-state through such recognition or acknowledging the state's existence prior to recognition – passes through 'a constituent process' marked by 'the sociologic' (ibid.: 455). International law, that is, is both dissipated *and* state-centred. It participates in 'sociologic' in so far as society, like humanity, gives content to law, even as law affirms 'society', by adding continuity to what is otherwise the paradoxical impossibility of a totality of discrete parts belonging to a whole in the same ways (ibid.: 438–46).

A sociologic also characterizes the ways of knowing law of today's social sciences (see, for example, Constable 1994; 2004: 9–11, 28–34, 43–4, 78–92). Sociolegal studies, from legal realism on, claim to uncover the realities that underlie and exceed ostensibly fixed legal rules. The 'realities' that their empirical accounts offer, however, correspond to and rely on 'social' facts and constructions that themselves appear to circumscribe or exhaust the possibilities of modern law and policy. Anthropologist Sally Merry's recent *Human Rights and Gender Violence: Translating International Law into Local Justice* exemplifies just such logic (see Constable 2008a: 514–17, and Merry's reply, 520–2).[1] In its concern for battling static conceptions of culture, it highlights the contribution – and challenge – that Fitzpatrick's work poses not only to anthropology but to contemporary sociolegal thinking about law. ('Culture' is of course not the same as 'custom', but Merry's argument about culture in international law is comparable to Fitzpatrick's argument about custom.)

Merry argues that there exist two predominant conceptions of culture in international law. Both posit culture as static and unchanging. Both the national culture and the traditional culture to which Merry refers resemble the one-sided determinate custom of the 'savage' to which Fitzpatrick refers. According to Merry, they get in the way of the effective use of human rights and international law to secure women's rights, the topic of Merry's book. These two static and unchanging conceptions of culture prevent well-intentioned international actors from understanding local struggles and differences, Merry writes. Culture should instead be considered, she argues, as 'a consensual, interconnected system of beliefs and values' (2006: 6), as a fluid 'repertoire ... of ideas and practices that are not homogeneous but continually changing because of contradictions among them or because new ideas and institutions are adopted by members' (ibid.: 11).

Rather than using her claims about fluid culture to destabilize claims as to the sovereignty of law or to expose the character of humanity as 'ur-instance' of juridical modernity, as does Fitzpatrick (2003: 442), however, Merry ultimately reinforces such claims. She expressly concludes:

> Despite drawbacks in the way the concept of human rights has been developed and used, it is still the only global vision of social justice currently available. With all its flaws, it is the best we have. It provides at least some constraint on the operation of markets and offers a potentially powerful tool to those who learn to use it. Like the language of law itself, it serves those in power but is always in danger of escaping its bounds and working in a genuinely emancipatory way.
>
> (2006: 231)

Fitzpatrick's account of an international law 'which opposes imperial claims ... to a quasi-sovereign completeness' (2003: 431) allows one to ask – in response to Merry – how well served we are by even 'the best' of 'global visions of social justice'. Shouldn't sociolegal scholarship be wary not only of the global visions of the *imperium* of the United States that Fitzpatrick addresses, but of global visions of whatever sort (if indeed they are of different sorts)? Should we not be critical, Fitzpatrick implies, of the ways that texts like Merry's ground their claims to expertise in appeals to a transnational, English-speaking readership that constitutes both the source of the study and its audience? Sociolegal scholarship, Fitzpatrick in effect points out, must become self-conscious about the ways in which it participates, however unintentionally, in a circulation of knowledge, as Foucault might put it, that helps legitimate the particular political arrangements, institutions, and practices that would constitute and perpetuate an ostensibly global international legal system (Foucault 1984; Sarat and Silbey 1998).

In other words, both Fitzpatrick and Merry would counter static conceptions of custom and culture respectively, Fitzpatrick finding that promiscuous custom in international law allows ever-present change, and Merry battling static conceptions of culture in international law for their falsity. But there is still a big difference between them. In correcting these misconceptions and seeking to make human rights more 'effective', the language of Merry's text valorizes international law for its aspirations to what looks like sovereignty and ostensibly seeks to improve it.[2] Meanwhile, Fitzpatrick – cautiously celebrating international law's *non*-sovereignty – counters the possibility of a 'power' that could determinately fix international law and challenges the desirability of a single 'system' or sovereign vision of international order.

Fitzpatrick's work suggests that we be wary of global visions and sovereign systems, both as claims and as facts. Such a suggestion, like the international law, or rather the constituent ethics of law, that Fitzpatrick cautiously celebrates, diverges from conventional understandings of law that continually refer to law in terms of 'legal system(s)'. For Fitzpatrick, the effects of active opposition, disregard, and violation merge to challenge law to become just. As for Derrida, so too for Fitzpatrick:

> [T]ransgressive practice *both* undermines and constitutes the normative.... It is always a question, the legal question, whether, and through what remade perception of it, the norm is going to 'apply'. If the situation could always be automatically matched by an invariant norm, there would be no call for law, for the legal decision, for the 'fictional' making of law, or for custom.
>
> (2003: 453, citing in note 101 'a quite unoriginal condensation' of Derrida, 'Force of Law')

The effects of the oppositions, disregard, and violations that Fitzpatrick discerns in law reverse the character of the deficiencies that are usually attributed to public international law. They accord to public international law a potential – to counter the imperialism of the most powerful nation-state of today – that neither a more fixed system nor the defective law that international law is often taken to be could have. Likewise, in private international law or conflicts of law, which has now largely become the law of international business transactions, a recent symposium suggests a reversal similar to that which Fitzpatrick notes (Knop *et al.* 2008).[3] The symposium, as I have noted elsewhere, reveals the richness of possibilities of law introduced into private international law by the participation – even if only to find that they do not have standing – of non-state parties that deviate from the identities and rules established by state and interstate law. Acknowledging the laws of others, as conflicts law does (even when it decides in favour of the forum law or treats the foreign law selected as 'fact'), drives a wedge into the seemingly monolithic claims of domestic state and public international (or 'interstate') law to govern (Constable 2008a: 348).

Citation as deviation and repetition

The 'opposition', 'disregard', and 'violation' that Fitzpatrick uses along with their opposites to describe aspects of law can also be applied to aspects of Fitzpatrick's own citational style – to similar effect. In this context, Fitzpatrick's writing points to the limits of the ostensibly exhaustive claims to knowledge of the empirical sciences that would (claim to or seek to) exhaust what can be considered 'real' or 'actual' law.

Fitzpatrick explicitly acknowledges great debts to Derrida's 'Force of law', 'White mythologies', and 'The laws of reflection', as well as to many other thinkers and texts. He elaborates on his debts to these works – to the uninitiated reader's occasional frustration – to varying degrees. Such an approach to citation resonates with what Derrida (1996) identifies as 'archive fever'. Derrida wrote at least central parts of *Archive Fever* on the occasion of a 1994 celebration or commemoration of the opening of the Freud Museum in Freud's final (1938–9) residence in London. For Derrida, archive fever (*mal d'archive*) is a disorder we are experiencing today: a compulsive repetition and nostalgic desire to return to the origin, to a most archaic place of absolute commencement. It is a trouble – in so far as it is a need and also both impossibly preservative and destructive. And it is a trouble shared by psychoanalysis and jurisprudence, law and legal history, as Fitzpatrick would no doubt acknowledge.

Archive Fever is subtitled 'A Freudian impression'. A recent visit to the Freud Museum brings home the archaeological character of Freud's mania and of Derrida's critique and participation in it.[4] There one sees what an inveterate collector of antiquities – Egyptian, Assyrian, Greek, and Roman; busts, figures, icons – Freud was. One realizes how deep was Freud's indebtedness to a very grounded and material archaeology in his explanations of the excavation that goes on in psychoanalysis. On Freud's desk (reconstructed in the museum to resemble how it was when he worked in his study) is a set of figures, which (according to the film being shown about him) he would finger as if communicating with his elders or in a fetishistic way when meeting with others. Freud's fascination with such artefacts is legendary. On his first day in New York (according to a temporary exhibit in the museum; only on his second day and after visiting Coney Island, according to Jed Rubenfeld's (2007) mystery novel *The Interpretation of Murder*), Freud visited the Metropolitan Museum. The very morning he arrived in London from Austria, he visited the British Museum; he also returned that afternoon.

What better exemplar of an archive (after the Freud Museum), then, than the British Museum – a place where I once had lunch with Peter Fitzpatrick and which I know he loves? The upstairs rooms on Egyptian life in the British Museum – at least at the time of this Festschrift – begin with a display about Hieroglyphs and the Written Record (case 9, room 61, 'Egyptian Life'). There it is written, 'Although writing was important to Egypt, it only described certain aspects of life. Much was not written about. These silences must be filled by archaeology and comparative studies.' Or by psychoanalysis, sociology, and law, as the case may be.

The beauty I find in Fitzpatrick's work, because of and in spite of his incessant and occasionally absent references to texts that I will never master, may be that in the layers of his writing there are unsettled silences and possibilities of response that – *contra* Freud and the British Museum – are precisely *not* filled by the writings of archaeology and comparative studies – or of jurisprudence and social science. In 'Juris-fiction: Literature and the law of law' (Fitzpatrick 2004), in 'Law like poetry – Burnt Norton' (Fitzpatrick 2001), and in 'Necessary fictions: Indigenous claims and the humanity of rights' (Fitzpatrick 2010, whose citation here confirms that the 2007 Berlin Festschrift was not a wake), texts of 'fiction' that, in Fitzpatrick's hands, refuse the usual contrasts between law and literature affirm unsettled silences and possibilities of response to law.

'Law and literature', Fitzpatrick writes, citing Maria Aristodemou and Patricia Tuitt's critiques of it, is a 'settled enough field when it entails exploring literary depictions of the juridical, or when it comes to extracting literary qualities from an at-times reluctant law' (2004: 220). But Fitzpatrick pursues a more challenging enterprise, finding with Peter Goodrich that in law's separation and opposition to the poetic, law suffers (2001: 286). Drawing now on Maurice Blanchot and Jean-Luc Nancy, as well as on Derrida, Fitzpatrick argues that law and literature 'share the same ambivalence between existent instantiation and what is ever beyond yet incipient in it' (2004: 222). Legal fictions throughout Fitzpatrick's work, then, whether those of international law ('Gods would be needed...'), of the courts of the nation-state (Fitzpatrick 2010: Act III), or of the post-colonial novel (Fitzpatrick 2001, 2004), supervene on (or occur as something additional to) 'law's own positivist pretension', impelling law's '"giving" to the insatiable demand of that "justice" which is ever beyond' (Fitzpatrick 2001: 287).

Fitzpatrick's work, originally (whatever an origin could be) an anthropology rather than an archaeology and a mythology that recognizes itself as writing, necessarily has a peculiar relation to the 'archive'. In it, texts are repositories of impossible memories – both preservative and destructive – of justice. Fitzpatrick's law is/does justice neither of a determinate time nor a determinate place, but still leaves room for its emplacement in the speech or writing of law and text. Fitzpatrick's own writings of law, in his readings and quotations of grand theorists and poets as well as of lesser ones, involve a responsiveness and a non-determination that recognize the sovereignty and determinativeness of writings. At the same time, they remember the need for and the impossibility – or counter-productivity – of establishing the fixed rule that seems paradoxically necessarily supplementary to text and to law. Fitzpatrick's work reminds us that in law, as in the social science and policy that claims to exhaust it, there is always something left over.

Notes

1 My comments here follow and condense my review of this work, which appeared (with Merry's response), in *American Anthropologist* (Constable 2008b).
2 Merry (2006) uses such locutions as: 'In order for human rights ideas to be effective' (at 1); 'if they [the set of standards] are to gain legitimacy' (at 3); 'There is a critical need for conceptual clarification of culture in human rights practice. Insofar as human rights relies on an essentialized model of culture, it does not take advantage of the potential of local cultural practices for change' (at 11).
3 This began as a symposium entitled 'The Return of the Private: Private International Law Meets Global Governance'.
4 The Freud Museum is located at 20 Maresfield Gardens, London. The author visited the Freud Museum in person in June 2007. The museum can also be visited online at www.freud.org.uk.

References

Constable, M. (1994) 'Genealogy and jurisprudence: Nietzsche, nihilism and the social scientification of law', *Law and Social Inquiry* 19(3): 551–90.

Constable, M. (2004) *Just Silences*, Princeton, NJ: Princeton University Press.

Constable, M. (2008a) 'Conflicts as a law of laws? Afterword', *Law and Contemporary Problems* 71(3): 343–9.

Constable, M. (2008b) 'A global vision of social justice?', *American Anthropologist*, 110(4): 514–17.

Derrida, J. (1996) *Archive Fever: A Freudian Impression*, trans. E. Prenowitz, Chicago: University of Chicago Press.

Fitzpatrick, P. (2001) 'Law like poetry – Burnt Norton', *Liverpool Law Review* 23: 285–8.

Fitzpatrick, P. (2003) '"Gods would be needed..." American empire and the rule of (international) law', *Leiden Journal of International Law* 16: 429–66.

Fitzpatrick, P. (2004) 'Juris-fiction: Literature and the law of law', *ARIEL: A Review of International English Literature* 35: 215–29.

Fitzpatrick, P. (2010) 'Necessary fictions: Indigenous claims and the humanity of rights', *Journal of Postcolonial Writing* 46: 446–56.

Foucault, M. (1984) 'The order of discourse', trans. I. McLeod, in M. Shapiro (ed.) *Language and Politics*, New York: New York University Press.

Knop, K., Michaels, R., and Riles, A. (eds) (2008) 'Transdisciplinary conflict of laws', *Law and Contemporary Problems* 71(3): 1–18.

Merry, S. E. (2006) *Human Rights and Gender Violence: Translating International Law into Local Justice*, Chicago: University of Chicago Press.

Rubenfeld, J. (2007) *The Interpretation of Murder*, New York: Picador.

Sarat, A. (ed.) (2001) *Law, Violence and the Possibilities of Justice*, Princeton, NJ: Princeton University Press.

Sarat, A. and Silbey, S. (1988) 'The pull of the policy audience', *Law and Policy* 10: 97–166.

Chapter 2

Reading Thomas Hobbes

Peter Fitzpatrick's gentle deconstructionist style

James Martel

Introduction

This chapter will focus on Peter Fitzpatrick as a reader, and particularly as a reader of Hobbes, a canonical figure who is himself deeply concerned with language and the act of reading. In her book *Wayward Contracts*, Victoria Kahn calls Hobbes 'metalinguistic' in his approach to reading and interpretation (2004: 135). She tells us that Hobbes is deeply aware not only of how powerful language is in structuring political life but also of how language is itself the basis for politics, the building block of our collective lives. In this essay I will argue that Fitzpatrick himself shares this 'metalinguistic' dimension with Hobbes. In Fitzpatrick's own case, such a particular interest in language leads to what I call his gentle deconstructionist style of reading, entailing a deeply careful attention to the rhetorical 'bones' of texts as well as the mechanics of interpretation. His style is 'gentle' because he has an almost Talmudic reverence for texts: Fitzpatrick appreciates and follows rules of grammar and syntax; he seeks meaning and connection and even logic in the linguistic constructions he engages with. Like Hobbes himself, Fitzpatrick is above all interested in what reading does to a text, how the act of reading is not a neutral unfurling of meaning but a part of how meaning is produced. And, like Hobbes, Fitzpatrick sees reading as reflecting and responding to the rhetorical and grammatical architecture of the text itself. By reading Hobbes according to the same methodologies that Hobbes himself both calls for and demonstrates in his texts, Fitzpatrick is able to recast Hobbes as speaking against the sort of positivist orthodoxies that are usually attributed to him. By appreciating texts qua texts, Fitzpatrick manages to read a text like *Leviathan* as if anew, despite the centuries of interpretive baggage that it has accrued.

Hobbes as reader

To begin this argument, let me lay out Hobbes' own methodologies as a reader. Hobbes demonstrates his methodologies and understanding of reading throughout the pages of *Leviathan* but principally in the second half of the book, in Parts III and IV.[1] The very fact that such instruction takes place so deep into the text, long after we have begun reading the text in a more ordinary way, itself suggests how reading, for Hobbes, is not merely the neutral experience of a text but an art, a method that we can practise well or badly.

In chapter 43, right at the end of Part III, Hobbes very famously claims that when it comes to reading,

> it is not the bare Words, but the Scope of the writer that giveth the true light, by which any writing is to bee interpreted; and they that insist upon single Texts, without considering the main Designe, can derive no thing from them cleerly; but rather by casting atomes of Scripture, as dust before mens eyes, make every thing more obscure than it is; an ordinary artifice of those that seek not the truth, but their own advantage.
>
> (1651/1996: 415)

Here, Hobbes is displaying a particularly rhetorical sensibility as regards reading. To speak of 'the Scope of the writer' and 'the main Designe' suggests exactly the sorts of rhetorical constructions of texts that, as a scholar of classicism, Hobbes knew intimately. While some scholars claim that Hobbes turned his back on the traditions of classical humanism, we see the lingering effects of his classical training in the way that Hobbes approaches and produces his own text (see, for example, Strauss 1952).[2] The notion of a text having a 'Scope' and a 'Designe' that offers a key to interpretation over and above any one 'atome' (i.e. passage) of text reproduces the classical notion that we find in authors such as Aristotle, Cicero, and Quintilian whereby the rhetorical construction of a text constitutes its 'meaning'; in this view, such constructions tell us how we are to interpret and interact with (or read) the text overall.

Hobbes also tells us that 'the foundation of all true Ratiocination, is the constant Signification of words' – that is, the way we interpret or think about words – is the key to all reasoning, all knowledge (hence Hobbes' deliberate mistranslation of *nosce te ipsum* as 'read thyself' instead of 'know thyself') (1651/1996: 269, 10). Such interpretation, he goes on to tell us, 'dependeth not (as in naturall science) on the Will of the Writer nor (as in common conversation) on vulgar use, but on the sense they carry' (ibid.: 269). This idea of 'sense' seeks on the specific level what an understanding of the 'Scope' and 'Designe' of the text reveals at the more general level. Interpretation for Hobbes seems to be an adjudication between the particular sense of a term or phrase in the context of the larger structuring of a text (and to an extent that, as we have seen, can be independent of the 'Will of the Writer'). In their act of interpretation, readers should seek to discern how one part of the text fits in with that overall pattern, what these words can be said to 'mean' in the context of the book's scope and design (revealing the 'constant Signification of words').

In describing his method of reading, Hobbes has a very complicated relationship to metaphor and other tropes, once again displaying an ambivalence towards (but, crucially, not a rejection of) his own training as a classicist. In much of the reading that he engages with throughout *Leviathan* (principally reading of Scripture), Hobbes attacks poor readings of metaphors. Thus, for example, when he discusses the term 'Spirit of God' in chapter 34 he tells us that it is a mistake to take such metaphors too literally – that is to say, to forget that these are only metaphors. He battles against reading the term 'Spirit of God' as it appears in Scripture as actual examples of divine presence or possession. He tells us:

> In the Book of *Judges*, an extraordinary Zeal, and Courage in the defence of Gods people, is called the *Spirit* of God ... And of *Saul*, upon the newes of the insolence of the Ammonites towards the men of Jabeth Gilead, it is said ... that *The Spirit of God came upon Saul, and his Anger ... was kindled greatly*.
>
> (1651/1996: 272)

Here, Hobbes seems to denude the metaphor of all of its poetry and, indeed, its metaphorical nature in so far as it exposes many biblical passages as meaning only very ordinary things (such as 'getting angry' or 'being zealous').

Yet Hobbes demonstrates a real appreciation for metaphors in so far as they are, at least potentially, more legible as tools of representation than other words might be. In one well-known passage, Hobbes tells us that

> one man calleth *Wisdome*, what another calleth *feare*; and one *cruelty*, what another *justice*.... And therefore such names can never be true grounds of any ratiocination. No more can Metaphors, and Tropes of speech [serve as the grounds of any ratiocination]: but these are less dangerous, because they profess their inconstancy; which the other [names] do not.
>
> (1651/1996: 31)

In speaking of the way that metaphors 'profess their inconstancy', Hobbes is alluding to the way that this trope potentially exposes itself as being merely a sign, a representation (hence his ability to 'read' Scripture by denuding metaphor of any but the most minimal of meanings). In so far as signification is itself the grounding of ratiocination for Hobbes, an explicit awareness of the metaphorical nature of language in general is critical to avoid misattributing meanings to words. By 'profess[ing] their inconstancy', metaphors are (however paradoxically) helping to express the 'constant Signification of words'; by pointing to their own representational status (and hence 'inconstancy' as a source of truth), metaphors point us back to the 'constant' fact of signification itself, the process of producing meaning via the interpretation of signs.

In this way, we see that Hobbes' method of reading involves an explicit awareness of signification itself, over and above any one term or passage (or 'atome' of text). We get our sense both of a particular passage and of the scope of a text when we understand that text as being explicitly rhetorical in its construction, that is to say when we avoid various forms of linguistic 'idolatry' – as Hobbes considers it – wherein the fact of figurality is obscured or overwritten by some (necessarily false) claim to truth or perfect, clear meaning.[3]

Fitzpatrick as reader (of Hobbes)

In his own reading, Fitzpatrick demonstrates many of these same conceptions as Hobbes does. We can see this in much of Fitzpatrick's writings, but perhaps most clearly (as may be appropriate) in his treatment, and reading, of Hobbes himself. In his treatment of Hobbes we find a microcosm of what Peter Fitzpatrick does more generally: here, as elsewhere, Fitzpatrick brings his interest in Nietzschean philosophy, and key Nietzschean figures sich as Derrida and Foucault, to bear upon very canonical issues of law and politics. In the case of Hobbes in particular, Fitzpatrick gets some important help from Hobbes himself. Let me spend the rest of this chapter elucidating both how Fitzpatrick reads Hobbes and also how that reading is itself an example of a reading method that in many ways is remarkably similar to Hobbes' own.

Fitzpatrick engages with Hobbes' standing at the heart of canonical conceptions of liberalism and law to show that this so-called 'proto-liberal' offers a far more complex legacy for notions of law, sovereignty, and politics itself than is usually understood. For Fitzpatrick, to read Hobbes is to encounter the foundational text for – but also the exposure of – the peculiar formulations of law as they are practised in the modern West. In *Modernism and the Ground of Law* – the main, although not sole, text that I will be considering here – Fitzpatrick notes the peculiar emptiness of the understanding of law that is often attributed (at least in part) to *Leviathan*. Fitzpatrick describes the law's questionable 'autopositioning' as he puts it, following Derrida, whereby the law has no concrete ground but instead is constantly asserting its own reality by distinguishing itself from some other, pre-legal savage realm (the classic interpretation of the social contract). This distinction renders law both incoherent and greatly effective.

Among the many myths and legends of legal origin that Fitzpatrick explores to highlight this dynamic is what he describes as the 'fusing [of] common law and the national soil of England' as a way to assert the 'nomos of the earth' (a term of art he takes from Carl Schmitt's book of the same title), the ipseity of law's authority as such in connection with the very materiality of the land it reigns over (Fitzpatrick 2001: 92). The law stakes its claim even as it excludes other territories and sites as a way to assert and produce that *nomos* in the first place.

To help in his examination of the genesis of such conceptions of law, Fitzpatrick looks at Hobbes' *Leviathan* as a work that purportedly accomplishes the production of our contemporary *nomos.* As Fitzpatrick tells us, in the classic understanding of *Leviathan* the absolute power of the Leviathan is predicated on avoiding 'the savage state which made [it] necessary ... a state which Hobbes instances spatially' (2001: 93). Here, the organization of space involves two competing orientations, with the existence of the lawful order depending upon the conception (and exclusion) of the unlawful. This is where Fitzpatrick's close reading of Hobbes comes into play; he reads the text of *Leviathan* itself according to its 'Scope' and not according to the meaning that Hobbes insists on at any given point in the text. This is not so much reading against the grain of the text but rather truly 'with' it in a way that may perhaps be autonomous even from the 'Will of the writer' (i.e. Hobbes himself).

In looking at the 'Scope' and the 'Designe' of *Leviathan* overall, Fitzpatrick notes how in Hobbes' depictions of the state of nature there is in fact a kind of 'lawfulness' after all; in so far as the occupants of the state of nature are able to covenant among themselves, we see a kind of ordering that the orthodox readings of Hobbes have rendered invisible. Instead of perfect savagery serving as the ground (via its eradication) for a form of perfect order, we get instead two semi-lawful states, each in a sense contaminating – even as it renders possible – the other. This state of affairs is reinforced by Hobbes' assertion that even in the 'state of nature' we have 'natural law' producing what Fitzpatrick calls an 'anterior demotic legality', a basis for authority that resides with people as a whole rather than issuing from the sovereign (and which pre-dates both the sovereign and the social contract which produces it) (Fitzpatrick 2001: 94).

For Fitzpatrick, this alternative source of authority explains the lingering devotion we find in *Leviathan* to a demos which otherwise seems completely secondary to the rule of law itself. We find here what Fitzpatrick calls the 'tender' side of the Leviathan, the liberties of the subject (2007: 173).

In more orthodox readings of *Leviathan,* such tenderness may be hard to explain. Even liberal readers of Hobbes tend to find in him an absolutism that must be reconciled with his seeming leniency towards subjects, displayed principally in chapter 21. Such readers tend to argue that although the sovereign is absolute, it is in its interest to allow the subjects certain liberties in order to preclude social unrest. There is thus (such readers argue) a kind of happy coincidence between the sovereign's absolute power and the people's need to exercise certain forms of 'freedom' (see, for example, Skinner 2008). In so far as it gives the people no separate source of authority, such an argument reasserts the black and white, pure versus impure, reading of the sovereign's assertion of *nomos* that Fitzpatrick does so much damage to in his own reading. In this view, all decision and authority are seen as issuing solely from and on behalf of the sovereign as a kind of purely self-grounding figure. Yet Hobbes himself suggests that the people have their own, separate sources of authority in chapter 16 when he tells us, for example, that the people are the 'AUTHOR' of the sovereign's power to act on their behalf (1651/1996: 112). In Fitzpatrick's view, given the separate (and not always harmonious) strands of authority between sovereign and subject, it is not simply up to the sovereign per se to determine what rights can and cannot pertain to the citizenry.[4]

More to the point, the sovereign itself reflects the kinds of complicated authority structures that emerge from the mix of modern and 'savage' genealogies Hobbes supplies us with. As Fitzpatrick puts it 'for Hobbes, Leviathan has, in the very power of 'positive' determination, to have responsive regard to where that power came from' (2001: 94). Here the sovereign is not exactly made of different stuff as compared with the people that it rules. There are ties and connections between it and them that go both ways. As Fitzpatrick puts it further (in his essay ' "What are the Gods to us now?" '),

> Of course, it could be objected that the sovereign gives itself . . . rights, but that would be to return us to the autopositioning and the complete ipseity of the sovereign that my argument has for too long now been at pains to undermine. More explicitly, the contrary is the case: the sovereign depends on right not just to institute action but to endow and to continue its very being.
>
> (2007: 187)

In a similar vein, Fitzpatrick shows how the attempts by positivists to read Hobbes as producing an entirely secular apparatus for law disguises (in a way Hobbes himself never does) the degree to which sovereignty remains a theological construct.[5] Taking a page from Derrida, who notes that the secularization of sovereignty 'means the inheritance of a theological memory', Fitzpatrick shows how the 'sovereign Leviathan is both the worldly creation of freely covenanting "men" and a manifestation of God's tremendous power' (2007: 168). Here, theology itself becomes a means to mutually contaminate the so-called purity or ipseity of the law with the savage 'before' that it is distinguished from. Fitzpatrick shows how the theology of *Leviathan* hides in plain sight, including through the metaphorical references to Job. Fitzpatrick notes how the social contract itself is 'found to resemble "that *fiat*, or *Let us make man*, pronounced by God in the Creation"' (2001: 106). This construction produces a sovereign who amounts to, or is at least associated with, what Fitzpatrick calls a 'savage God' – that is to say a figure who smuggles into itself the very savagery and pre-legal power that the inculcation of sovereignty was supposed to banish (ibid.: 107). Calling the sovereign a 'Mortall God', as he does, Hobbes may not so much be signalling a break with past sources of authority, or the production of a radically self-generating law, but instead revealing the ongoing contamination of law by exactly what it sets itself against (1651/1996: 120). The savage other is brought into the so-called 'modern' grounds of law, and in exchange – and by the very same process – the savage before is shown to contain within itself the means for covenanting, for authority and for law itself.

In focusing here on the metaphorical nature of Hobbes' argument, Fitzpatrick is once again following or duplicating Hobbes' own methodology of reading. Fitzpatrick illuminates the way that Hobbes metaphorically connects law, theology, and politics in *Leviathan*, especially via what is perhaps the most 'metafigurative' (to cite de Man) metaphor of all: that of representation and the relationship between ruler and subject that it suggests. As we have already begun to see, in his reading, Fitzpatrick offers how for Hobbes representation does not merely imply a one-way exchange in which the sovereign does as it pleases. Law is not merely dictated but is a kind of exchange of information. Fitzpatrick writes:

> [F]or Hobbes ... people incapable of knowing the law cannot be bound by it, and even those who are capable must be given adequate means of knowing it.... But the issue becomes more intimate than a matter of simple knowing. Command may be made one and ultimate in the person of the sovereign, but Hobbes is no banal positivist: 'all laws ... have need of interpretation'.
>
> (2001: 95)

Here Fitzpatrick begins to demonstrate the power of Hobbes' (and his own) 'metalinguistic' approach to reading. Just as Hobbes' readers are told to '*Read thy self*' in order to 'read and know, what are the thoughts, and Passions of all other men, upon the like occasions', so too must the subject 'read' the law that the sovereign has produced in order to understand it and in fact to make it 'law' in the first place (Hobbes 1996: 10). This power of reading and interpretation once again hearkens to an 'anterior demotic legality', the forms of authority that predate the formation of the social contract itself. The sovereign's authority does not and cannot displace this anterior source of authority (for it is indeed the basis of its own power).

In making us aware of how reading is not merely passive but is an active form of interpretation, Fitzpatrick helps to render the internal architecture of the text of *Leviathan* more visible. The metalinguistic focus on reading and interpretation complicates a text that seems to demand both a passive reader and a passive political subject. When we read *Leviathan* as Fitzpatrick does (that is to say, read in a way that accords with Hobbes' own interpretive methodologies), our reading produces not our subjection but our active participation in a polity, which the text formally seems to exclude us from. By engaging in his own deep and careful reading of the text, Fitzpatrick allows for the 'Scope' and 'Designe' of *Leviathan* to emerge more clearly (and hence influence or alter the way we read and interpret the text).

Reading *Leviathan*

When we read *Leviathan* the way Fitzpatrick does, many long-standing debates about the meaning or inner workings of the text vanish or are radically altered. We can spare ourselves the lengthy conversations that we find with many positivists (and even some non-positivists) about how the social contract could have happened in the first place when the ability to contract itself is purely a function of a law that only arrives at that precise moment when law comes into being. We see that the power of promising, contracts, and law all pre-exist the social contract.

We can also see how the all-important division between a 'before' and 'after', a kind of secular eschatology of sovereign power, is undermined by another eschatology that the book pays homage to, that of the Immortal God and the theological remnant that haunts even the modern iterations of authority. In this way the concept of 'modernity' itself becomes a question rather than an assertion.

This articulation of a power and authority that is both determinant and responsive, both pure and impure, is for Fitzpatrick a microcosm of law more generally. Thus, in reading Hobbes as carefully and clearly as he does, Fitzpatrick discovers even in the heart of positivism a responsiveness that is embedded in all law. Here, law is not purely of itself; it comes out of a relationship to a demos and also, more darkly, to an outside (a category that is not always perfectly separated from the demos). The brilliance of this reading lies in the way that Fitzpatrick does not undermine the force of law as it is produced from positivist readings. He does not deny the distinctions that are read into *Leviathan*, nor the functions they play in supporting law as it is practised and produced in Hobbes' and our own time. But he shows how this very same text simultaneously complicates and possibly subverts these distinctions, suggesting a law that is both more vulnerable but also in some sense more enduring than we have often been led to understand.

As already suggested, in Hobbes, a figure who could not be more canonical, more mainstream, and more redolent of liberalism (or at least 'proto-liberalism'), Fitzpatrick notes various peculiarities that speak to a different genealogy of law and political order. By a close reading of Hobbes' state of nature, the social contract, and the question of political obligation and responsiveness, Fitzpatrick discovers a more 'tender' side to this author, one that exposes as much as it enables the *aporias* of law. Typical of his gentle deconstructionist style, Fitzpatrick's reading is in a sense more powerful, more devastating even, exactly because he approaches texts with such attention to detail. He follows the rules of grammar and rhetoric without giving his reading up to those orthodoxies which usually are smuggled into such a keen respect for texts. Fitzpatrick shows how you can be both a radical and respectful reader at the same time. And, in keeping with his own philosophy, this mutual contamination of reading styles is both effective and endlessly productive.

Notes

1 He demonstrates his method of reading in other works as well, such as *De Cive*, but it is in *Leviathan* that Hobbes most clearly demonstrates his reading methodology.

2 Richard Tuck argues that Hobbes never truly abandoned his interest in classical rhetoric (1989). Other scholars, such as David Johnston, argue that Hobbes briefly abandons his classical roots but returns to them when he realizes (via the events of the English Civil War) that the people of England require rhetoric to be convinced of the basic principles of order he sought to (re)establish (Johnston 1986; see also Skinner 1996).

3 Hobbes' main example of such linguistic idolatry is what he calls the 'Error of *Separated Essences*'. Here a sign or figure takes on a life of its own, obscuring or overwriting what it purports to represent (Hobbes 1651/1996: 466).

4 In my own reading I argue that in fact the sovereign can be read as an idol (by Hobbes' own theory of religious representation): something that purports to represent the people but replaces them with its own inflated status (see Martel 2007).

5 Here once again, Fitzpatrick is on Carl Schmitt's turf, but in an entirely different way as compared with Schmitt himself (see Schmitt 1985).

References

Fitzpatrick, P. (2001) *Modernism and the Grounds of Law*, New York: Cambridge University Press.

Fitzpatrick, P. (2007) '"What are the Gods to us now?": Secular theology and the modernity of law', *Theoretical Inquiries in Law* 8(1): 161–90.

Hobbes, T. (1996) *Leviathan*, ed. R. Tuck, New York: Cambridge University Press.

Johnston, D. (1986) *The Rhetoric of Leviathan: Thomas Hobbes and the Politics of Cultural Transformation*, Princeton, NJ: Princeton University Press.

Kahn, V. (2004) *Wayward Contracts: The Crisis of Political Obligation in England, 1640–1674*, Princeton, NJ: Princeton University Press.
Martel, J. (2007) *Subverting the Leviathan: Reading Thomas Hobbes as a Radical Democrat*, New York: Columbia University Press.
Schmitt, C. (1985) *Political Theology: Four Chapters on the Concept of Sovereignty*, Cambridge, MA: MIT Press.
Skinner, Q. (1996) *Reason and Rhetoric in the Philosophy of Hobbes*, New York: Cambridge University Press.
Skinner, Q. (2008) *Hobbes and Republican Liberty*, New York: Cambridge University Press.
Strauss, L. (1952) *The Political Philosophy of Hobbes: Its Basis and Genesis*, Chicago: University of Chicago Press.
Tuck, R. (1989) *Hobbes*, Oxford: Oxford University Press.

Chapter 3

Unconditional laws and ungovernable sovereigns

George Pavlich

Introduction

The dangers associated with ungovernable sovereignty haunts much western social and political thought, grounding liberal calls for a 'separation of powers', the 'rule of law', and so on. Attached to influential, and no doubt excessively absolutist, readings of Bodin or Hobbes, a worry over wayward Leviathans who can do anything to anyone at any time remains (cf. Fitzpatrick 2009). In retrospect, Hobbes' reassurances will appear injudicious to those who have suffered the violence of an unfettered sovereign:

> And though of so unlimited a Power, men may fancy many evill consequences, yet the consequences of the want of it, which is perpetuall warre of every man against his neighbour, are much worse. The condition of man in this life shall never be without Inconveniences; but there happeneth in no Common-wealth any great Inconvenience…
>
> (Hobbes 1651/1985: 260, ch. 21)

For them, as for Agamben (1998), there is little consequential difference between Hobbes' imagined 'state of nature' and the reign of a sovereign. Indeed, far from quelling, or peaceably resolving, the 'war of all against all' – as Hobbes' commonwealth is supposed to do – Agamben will insist that the logic of sovereignty creates, realizes, and perpetuates this state of nature. The matter may be complicated further in current contexts where sovereign political logics have undergone consequential changes, the effects of which unfold as national sovereignties are exceeded by more encompassing (global, international) sovereignties and laws, and where vast agglomerations of 'life' are managed through governmental techniques – all of which magnify questions pertaining to whether sovereignty is intrinsically ungovernable.

Conventionally, debates around how to check a sovereign with illimitable power, who is radically ungovernable, are framed around 'absolutism' versus 'constitutionalism'. However, the following pursues the matter by questioning whether a sovereign is always ungovernable, beyond law, beyond a law of sovereignty. Ultimately, at stake here is whether or not modern sovereignty politics ought only to be engaged – as Agamben (1998, 2001) might allege – by overcoming its basic forms. Or are there ways to reinvigorate engagements with sovereignty politics opening continuously to horizons in excess of existing forms thereof, relentlessly pursuing ways to place any sovereign before, say, an illimitable justice, or democracy (Pavlich 2010)? If that finite calculation is to be made through deconstructible laws of sovereignty, one need not be addressing constitutional law, but a law of constitutions. To be sure, any capacity to order an unconditional, yet historically gathered, sovereign being is a momentous, if always contingent, political accomplishment. As Foucault (2007) aptly depicts, a significant achievement of modernity is to have associated an unconditional sovereign with a defined territory, and to posit a supreme authority that expresses the will of a society, the people, a commonwealth, and so on.

But what if the restless grounds that shape medieval images of an ungovernable sovereign shift? Limiting this question, the following discussion pursues an expressly theoretical inquiry: can the political logic (theology?) of an ungovernable sovereign be understood as an historical event? And have new 'governmentalized' forms of sovereignty transformed this logic? If so, what might the laws of such governmental sovereignty be?

This chapter explores such questions through three modulations. First, it outlines an enduring western logic that posits the sovereign as an unconditional, ungovernable entity. Thereafter, it turns to residues of that logic through a confrontation between Agamben and Foucault/Butler on the question of an 'ungovernable sovereign', taking account of Foucault's argument that medieval forms of sovereignty were gradually, in the fifteenth and sixteenth centuries, 'governmentalized' alongside an emerging modern 'administrative state' (2007: 109). Here, one finds two different ways to understand the 'ungovernable' sovereign: Agamben's view that a liberal sovereign is inherently ungovernable (and so should be overthrown) versus Foucault's more nuanced idea that modernity's 'ungovernable sovereign' is made possible by discipline and (biopolitical) governance. The point is sharpened by Butler's (2004) sense that new forms of sovereignty are generated by governmental political horizons. Third, I turn to Fitzpatrick's (2005: 8) formulation of 'the law of the law' to consider the logic of sovereignty not as something that is fundamentally ungovernable, but as an emerging governmental calculation of a radically ungovernable terrain. The illimitable indeterminacy of the latter is the stuff of history; the need to 'cut' determinate aspects is part of current forms of life. And the law of the sovereign's law 'ties' the two together in what Fitzpatrick would call a 'determined responsiveness', or perhaps a 'responsive determinism'. Reversing command theories of law, one might explore the law of sovereignty (in both meanings) as both 'determining' and 'responsive' to what is always ungovernable, illimitable, and incalculable. In this sense, a 'democracy to come' persistently haunts attempts to posit democratic, governed sovereigns (Derrida 2005).

Logic, sovereign commands, and the law of the excluded middle

We have already alluded to an influential interpretation of Bodin and Hobbes as protagonists of an absolute sovereignty: the unconditional sovereign who declares a law must thereby except itself from that law which gives it force (see Fitzpatrick 2007). Schmitt's overused 'sovereign is he who declares the exception' line abounds in recent analyses of contemporary states (e.g. Agamben 2005). And the exception involves a paradox whereby the sovereign emerges as one who initiates the law and is thereby excluded from it.

Bertrand Russell's references to a hypothetical Sicilian barber who shaves *only and all* the men in his village who do not shave themselves indicates the claim at hand (see Rasch 2004: 90). What of the barber – does he shave himself? If he does, then he contradicts the *only* requirement of the above statement. If he does not shave himself, then he cannot be considered to shave *all* men of the village. In other words, the ambivalent position of the barber is consequential for how we grasp the proposition. Indeed, for it to be meaningful the barber must be placed outside of the enunciation, must be exempted from its decrees. In the matter of shaving he is paradoxically both a member of the village and *simultaneously* above it; he literally 'rules' in matters of shaving.

That logic is echoed in the foundations of western philosophical logic. Logic's 'law of the excluded middle' states that 'All propositions are either true or false.' But what is the status of *this* proposition? Is it true or false? Can the laws of logic be subjected to their own laws? Does that law include itself in its own decree, or does it except itself from that law? To make any sense in this context, the laws of logic cannot apply to themselves; they are of a different dimension. The law of the excluded middle is thus neither true nor false; it incarnates a sort of excluded middle – it is the excluded spacing that opens up the possibility of a law in which statements are to be considered true or false. It *proclaims* absolutely without subjecting itself to the demands of its own laws of truth and falsity. Is there a law that governs this 'excluded middle' or is it radically ungovernable?

In still another version of the paradox, Derrida evokes La Fontaine's fable of the wolf and the lamb. It begins with the line 'The strong are always best at proving they're right' before telling the story of a lamb drinking from a serene brook who unfortunately is spotted by a hungry wolf. The wolf tells the lamb he (or she) will pay for the gall of mucking up his 'beverage'. The lamb protests by way of reason that there is no way he could have done so, since the brook is vast and he is still nursing from his dam. The wolf retorts that someone in the lamb's clan has done so and forthwith proceeds to eat his 'midday snack': 'So trial and judgment stood' (Derrida 2005: x). The sovereign wolf declares, judges, and executes his law, and in so doing carves out the space for the existence of a particular kind of law. The story indicates this paradoxical feature that is intrinsic to the logic of sovereignty: the sovereign declares that her or his law is universal (i.e. applies to all), which means that a form of sovereignty arises which cannot be subject to that law without renouncing a sovereign prerogative. That is, the logic of sovereignty excepts the sovereign from the laws that she or he declares as applicable to all. Moments of successful declaration and enforcement, decision, yield particular versions of the sovereign. And here one senses traces of an ungovernable sovereign, an unrulable ruler, the definer of law who is beyond the law, etc. La Fontaine solicits a sovereign beyond, nay above, the reach of laws that are to subject all others.

All three cases – the barber, the law of the excluded middle, and La Fontaine's wolf – intimate a political logic, which generates a sovereign out of an exception. At the heart of that logic is an impossible, if mystical, leap through which a sovereign event declares a law and excepts her- or himself from it. There is no rational justification for the violent initiation of a regime's law, or the creation of a domain that enables the enunciation of what is normal and what is not; of what is true and what is not; of who is friend and who is enemy, etc. The rationales for the regime are always *ex post facto* and occur within the laws of language, logic, politics, etc., initiated by founding events. One is here reminded of the theological auspices – God the unconditional sovereign – of sovereignty. But as we move further from modernity's founding myths, including the denial of myth (Fitzpatrick 2001b, 2007), so another question arises: is this medieval logic of sovereignty on the move? One could explore the impossibility that contours these sovereignty rationales. For instance, what if the distinction between generation and effect were blurred to the point of enabling a law of the excluded middle, a law of ungovernable sovereignty? Is there another law in play here – not one that 'includes law by excluding it', but one that relentlessly 'cuts' a finite law from what is infinitely beyond? Let us defer this question to a later discussion of Fitzpatrick's sense of 'the law of the law'. For now, we might attend to another burning question: can liberal sovereignty ever be restrained by the power relations out of which it is constituted?

Agamben, especially in works like *Homo Sacer* (1998) and *State of Exception* (2005), says no. Modern 'biopolitical sovereignty' generates a critique of the West's liberal politics centred on the idea of a radically ungovernable sovereign with the power to except itself from the laws that it generates. The ground of sovereign power is ultimately, and by logical definition, 'the sovereign's preservation of his natural right to do anything to anyone' (1998: 106). His analysis is quite different from that of Foucault, who posits that the sovereign has become 'governmentalized' and so is arguably subject to governmental powers. More precisely, the deployment of governmental techniques to vast areas of modern being has enabled diluted forms of medieval sovereignty to persist in modern political arrangements (2007: 59). For Foucault (and developed by Butler), in its modern incarnation the sovereign is more and more constituted by practices of governance (biopolitics) and discipline. In this sense the modern sovereign is enabled by governance, and is not therefore absolutely ungovernable. Without rehearsing the nuances of the debate between Agamben and Foucault, which has attracted much attention elsewhere (see French 2007; Genel 2006; Gratton 2006; Norris 2005; Fitzpatrick 2001a), I shall here focus exclusively on questions of governance and sovereignty.

Ungovernable sovereigns and the 'state of nature'

Referring to the 'exceptional' political logic of modern sovereignty, Agamben (as noted) argues that the opening moment of western political thinking is not the contract between Hobbesian subjects who – through a social pact – form a society to escape an imaginary and brutish 'state of nature'. Rather, he reinterprets Nancy's (1993) discussion of the *ban* as the founding moment of western politics: the 'originary juridico-political relation is the ban' (1998: 111). The sovereign contains a biopolitics that transforms its illimitable power 'into a power to decide the point at which life ceases to be politically relevant ... In modern biopolitics, sovereignty is he who decides on the value or non-value of life as such' (1998: 142). That 'decisive act' enables a sort of sovereignty where

> the realm of bare life – which was originally situated at the margins of the political order – gradually begins to coincide with the political realm, and exclusion and inclusion, outside and inside, *bios* and *zoe*, right and fact, enter into a zone of irreducible indistinction.
>
> (ibid.: 9)

As is now well canvassed (Mills 2008; Norris 2005), the totalitarian logic here effectively emaciates Aristotelean political distinctions between *zoe* and *bios*. It restricts sovereignty politics to 'states of exception' that simultaneously exclude and capture bare life (Agamben 2005). This excluded inclusion forms 'the hidden foundation on which the entire political system rested' (1998: 9). Recovering politics beyond such a logic is most likely only possible by interrogating the 'link between bare life and politics' that founds the modern Leviathan. This 'secret' grounding of sovereignty and bare life needs to be challenged, to 'bring the political out of its concealment and, at the same time, return thought to its practical calling' (Agamben 1998: 5). Agamben (2001) holds out the possibility of an indistinct, somewhat anarchistic, revolutionary political space that nurtures forms of life in limbo, always in excess of modern law, state, community, and bare life – a way to overcome the totalitarianism intrinsic to the politics of an 'ungovernable' sovereign.

He argues further that most political analyses ignore the 'foundational event' – 'the politicization of bare life as such' (1998: 4) – in which biopolitical sovereignty creates vacuous categories and oppositions (e.g. public/private) to fabricate the 'bare life' and 'docile bodies' of capitalist politics (ibid.: 3–4). Agamben further asserts that Foucault's untimely death prevented him from providing a sustained analysis of biopower and perhaps from engaging with Arendt, or analysing the paradigmatic case of biopolitics in totalitarian states of the twentieth century. Had he done so, Agamben believes, he would have alighted on the ways that – throughout history – various versions of biopolitical sovereignty have created 'bare life' in a 'state of nature', ensconcing homologous notions of sovereigns and subjects. Here, Agamben posits the unfettered and ungovernable sovereign ban as producing the state of nature, rather than containing or escaping it. Moreover, the contorted logic of sovereignty politics requires the ungoverned sovereign to ban unconditionally, for such decisions generate (and preserve) sovereignty. Yet they also create the brutish and violent 'state of nature' in which, as Hobbes detects, all have an equal ability to kill one another. The making of a brutal state of nature is central to sovereignty politics:

> Far from being a prejudicial condition that is indifferent to the law of the city, the Hobbesian state of nature is the exception and the threshold that constitutes and dwells within. It is not so much a war of all against all as, more precisely, a condition in which everyone is bare life and a *homo sacer* for everyone else.
>
> (Agamben 1998: 106)

The mutual constitution of sovereignty and state of nature secures their 'homologous' ungovernable conditions: the sovereign's unfettered will resembles Hobbes' egotistical subject that engages in a war against all, just as bare life excluded from politics is rendered, like a sovereign, outside of law and politics. The sovereign fashions a radically disordered bare form of life through its continuous decisions (ibid.: 109). Sovereignty politics, that is, does not bring peace to a commonwealth; instead, it realizes the horrific Hobbesian state of nature through the ungovernable, illimitable sovereign bans that abandon 'bare life' to a state of nature. The operation of the 'camp' (refugee camps, concentration camps) is paradigmatic here

(Agamben 1999). The 'bare life' generated by 'biopolitical sovereignty' involves 'an unconditional subjection to a power of death' (1998: 90) because 'not simple natural life, but life exposed to death (bare life or sacred life) is the originary political element' (1998: 88). In this sense, to repeat, for Agamben, the ungovernable sovereign is central to modern liberal politics; to govern the sovereign is to destroy the logical and practical foundations of that political being.

Governed sovereigns

I do not know of a specific text where Foucault specifically ponders whether, or how, sovereigns can be governed, but he certainly argues that governmental powers contour contemporary forms of sovereignty (see also Pavlich 2010; Butler 2004: 50–100). Indeed, for him, sovereignty has persisted in modernity only because of the creative effects of both disciplinary normalization and governmentality (Foucault 2007: 46–9). As to the latter, he tells us:

> We live in the era of a governmentality discovered in the eighteenth century. Governmentalization of the state is a particularly contorted phenomenon, since if the problems of governmentality and the techniques of government have really become the only political stake and the only real space of political struggle and contestation, the governmentalization of the state has nonetheless been what has allowed the state to survive.
>
> (ibid.: 109)

If one takes Foucault here to reference a broader model of sovereignty through its historical incarnation of the modern state, one might even say that, for him, the modern sovereign is increasingly a governed being, or rather the product of governmental political agendas and reasons

> and it is likely that if the state is what it is today, it is precisely thanks to this governmentality that is at the same time both external and internal to the state, since it is the tactics of government that allow the continual definition of what should or should not fall within the state's domain ... if you like, the survival elements of the state should be understood on the basis of the general tactics of governmentality.
>
> (ibid.: 109)

And even more explicitly, in a well-traversed passage, we are told that

> we should not see things as the replacement of a society of sovereignty by a society of discipline, and then of a society of discipline by a

> society, say, of government. In fact we have a triangle: sovereignty, discipline, and governmental management, which has population as its main target and apparatuses of security as its essential mechanism.
>
> (ibid.: 107–8)

Foucault here rejects the absolutist case for the sovereign exception, as referenced in Agamben and his reading of Hobbes, for this would misunderstand the degree to which governance and discipline help to constitute the modern sovereign in the first place. At least in its modern incarnation, the sovereign is less an ungovernable entity than one produced by complex and hybrid powers that increasingly govern through managing 'life', conceived through aggregates such as the 'population' (as opposed to correcting normal individuals, or spectacularly coercing through the threat of death). So, far from the contemporary sovereign being ungovernable, it is *produced* – at least in part – by governance. Governmentality is included as an exclusion and a tactics of governance that increasingly generate versions of the contemporary sovereign. Since these depend on governance, they are not 'ungovernable' but are, at the very least, 'governmentalized'.

Butler usefully works with this insight to develop what she takes to be a contemporary incarnation of medieval sovereignty as developed through governmental regimes. As she puts it, in such contexts 'Sovereignty's aim is to continue to exercise and augment its power to exercise itself; in the present circumstance, however, it can only achieve this aim by managing populations outside the law' (2004: 98). Echoing Foucault's images of a 'governmentalized state', Butler notes a 'resurgence' of sovereignty in governmental politics, and particularly an animation of anachronistic forms thereof. This politics is 'animated by an aggressive nostalgia that seeks to do away with the separation of powers' and is generated by a suspension of law: '[W]e have to consider the act of suspending the law as a performative one which brings a contemporary configuration of sovereignty into being or, more precisely, reanimates a spectral sovereignty within the field of governmentality' (ibid.: 61). In other words, the many 'performative acts' through which law suspends itself (declaring emergency conditions, allowing indefinite detentions, etc.) actually generate a new version of sovereignty, not vice versa. This new sovereign is no longer imagined through a central state commanding through law; nor is it completely independent of governance. Instead, it disperses itself within and across the tactics of governmental management regimes. If this sort of sovereign fashions itself across governmental horizons, it also operates by 'managing' subjects extra-legally without clear time and space constraints. Versions of such extra-legal powers previously existed in medieval contexts. Now, however, there is an indefinite quality to the sovereign as it extends without limit, and into an open, illimitable future. Through multiple and diverse suspensions of the rule of law, a new version of the 'unaccountable' sovereign power emerges, focused on managing security with or without the law. It is on such grounds that she describes a situation in which

> [t]he future becomes a lawless future, not anarchical, but given over to the discretionary decisions of a set of designated sovereigns – a perfect paradox that shows how sovereigns emerge within governmentality – who are beholden to nothing and to no one except the performative power of their own decisions.
>
> (ibid.: 65)

As intriguing as Butler's interpretation is, let us leave it here to suggest more precisely that for Foucault, if there currently is an ungovernable sovereign, that sovereign is paradoxically created out of governmental powers. And moreover, the sovereign is yielded not simply as the author of law but, increasingly, through multiple contexts where the law withdraws. One might note, in passing, an expanding notion of sovereignty of the kind that Derrida (2005) references. The withdrawal of law has, in many ways, constituted a governmental sovereign – allowing sovereigns to venture beyond medieval terrains of law, territory, and principality. In this sense we are dealing with a 'governmentalized sovereign', one that has not elided the hands of governance, one that becomes through governing, and through that governing is in an important, if not constitutive, sense governed.

Contrasting sovereigns

Agamben's image of an ungovernable sovereign contrasts with (this interpretation of) Foucault's governmentalized sovereign. It also allows us to see that Agamben's claim to correct and expand Foucault's work may be misplaced. He challenges (1998: 3–9, 142, 187) at least two ideas he attributes to Foucault: first, that sovereignty and biopower are distinctly opposite forms of power that cannot be unified; and second, that sovereignty was a dominant medieval modality of power but has been surpassed by modern discipline and biopower. The first, for Agamben, is 'incorrect' because, as noted, biopolitics is the founding moment of sovereignty politics: 'bare life' is constitutive of sovereignty from the latter's earliest expressions, and is the hidden foundation on which the entire political system rested (1998: 9). His point is that even if discipline and state power oppose one another, they 'converge insofar as both concern the bare life of the citizen, the new biopolitical body of humanity' (1998: 9). Ultimately, then, modern politics is best characterized through a logic of sovereignty that excepts itself from legal degrees and rules unconditionally over 'bare life'. Sovereignty is, in this sense, profoundly ungovernable.

Second, Agamben argues that Foucault wrongly conceives of sovereign models of power as dominant in medieval political arrangements, and declining in modern political contexts. Rather, for Agamben, sovereignty's reach is as formidable and dominant in western politics as it was in Roman conceptions of sovereignty; the paradigmatic figure of bare life in Roman law – the *homo sacer* – may have become transformed into the twentieth century's Muselmann of concentration camps and refugees camps (1999). However, the exemplary ungovernable governor remains an abiding purveyor of life that barely survives, in interstices, between life and death. In each case, Agamben challenges Foucault's sense that a medieval logic of sovereignty is in decline. For him, sovereignty pre-dates the Middle Ages; it is always concerned with biopolitics, especially in an 'age of biopolitics' where power is 'transformed into a power to decide the point at which life ceases to be politically relevant … In modern biopolitics, sovereign is he who decides on the value or non-value of life as such' (1998: 142). To resist such embedded powers, one has to escape sovereignty's reach.

This is, for me, a rather odd debate because there appears to be a misunderstanding of key terms at hand. Agamben consistently refers to biopower as a conceptual corollary of discipline and sovereignty, whereas Foucault (2001, 2007, 2008) uses governance–sovereignty–discipline as the significant conceptual 'triangle'. Agamben's emphasis on biopower thus misses the broader governmental framework within which Foucault developed his work. In Foucault's scheme, governmentality and practices of governance provide the general framework within which a more specific biopower operates. He understands the relationship between governmentality and biopolitics in this way:

> [I]t seems to me that the analysis of biopolitics can only get under way when we have understood the general regime of this governmental reason I have talked about.… Consequently, it seems to me that it is only when we understand what is at stake in this regime of liberalism opposed to *raison d'Etat* … [that we will] be able to grasp what biopolitics is.
>
> (Foucault 2008: 21–2)

For example, biopolitics 'manages' broad swaths of life, especially 'the biological existence of the population' – not an individual body, but the body of a population (ibid.: 21–2). Consequently, biopower is concerned with improving a population's health, decreasing its mortality and obesity rates, increasing its longevity, etc. Yet biopolitics is an instrument of a much wider and far more historically entrenched 'governmentality', in which modern liberal subjects are increasingly called upon to govern themselves outside of direct, formal institutions (ibid.: 21–2). And Foucault does not deny that governmentality's lines of descent include Greek, Roman, and early Christian contexts, where images of a shepherd (pastor, ablative leader) caring for a flock contoured images of appropriate governance (2007: 135ff.). Also, it is within this broader context that the more specific rise of biopower can be understood. The governed sovereign is one that develops within the logic of that framework, not the more specific biopolitical sovereign that Agamben declares ungovernable.

This difference raises the question of the relation between law and the governed sovereign. As we have seen, both Butler and Agamben appear to conceptualize contemporary circumstances in which the law suspends itself, and in the process enables either an ungoverned state of exception (Agamben) or a governmentalized sovereign that animates older versions of an extra-legal sovereign (Butler). Of course, much of this depends on what one means by 'law', a question that extends beyond the scope of this particular chapter. However, Agamben and to a lesser extent Butler appear to understand the law as a new kind of 'tactic', a contentless force at the disposal of, but yet creative of, biopolitical or governmental sovereignties. Whatever one makes of the specifics of their views on law, one could emphasize a common recognition that the sovereign – governed or not – is born out of performances that constitute law. And here, Golder and Fitzpatrick's overview of a debate around Foucault and the law (2009) allows us to focus more precisely on what Fitzpatrick calls 'the law of the law' (2005) – the law through which a given instance of law posits itself and in that process an associated sovereignty.

The sovereign's law

In referencing 'the law of the law', Fitzpatrick could be taken to address the law of the sovereign – governed or not – in two senses. First, the law associated with the contemporary sovereign harbours a very distinctive logic to decide in the here and now. It makes authoritative determinations and decisions, yet keeping open its ability to face ever-changing conditions. Second, I want to argue that Fitzpatrick's 'the law of the law' enables us to think about the law of sovereignty as one forever caught between 'determination' and 'responsiveness'. This allows one to understand the 'groundless ground' of medieval conceptions of ungoverned sovereigns that transform into the governmental sovereigns nowadays. As is by now well known, Fitzpatrick argues as follows:

> For law to rule, it has to be able to do anything, if not everything. It cannot, then, simply secure stability and predictability but also has to do the opposite: it has to ensure that law is ever responsive to change, otherwise law will eventually cease to rule the situation which has changed around it.
>
> (2001b: 71)

Therefore, law is never finally intact, for it is persistently called upon to respond to the diverse circumstances that confront it. It cannot be encircled within clear limits, because it must hold itself 'constantly responsive to all that is beyond what it may at any moment be' (ibid.). And it is not consistent, for 'how could law, in extending to what is continuously other to itself, avoid pervasive contradiction?' (ibid.). So how are we to understand the 'groundless grounds' of law (2001b)? Here Fitzpatrick refers us to the 'persistent squabbles' of jurisprudence in which law appears as a fixed, 'determinate' entity, and also as one that must be highly responsive and adaptable to change. This leads him to this intriguing notion:

> Rather than seeking law in that which simply conforms to either side or both sides of the opposition, perhaps we could seek a law which 'is' in-between the opposed dimensions, which 'is' the experienced combination of them, and which has its being because each dimension is inexorable yet to unable to be experienced by itself. And perhaps these dimensions are equivalent to the divide between law's autonomy and law's dependence.
>
> (Fitzpatrick 2001b: 72–3)

Consequently, he focuses on the law that resides 'in-between' the positing of law as something autonomous, determinate, etc., *and* law as perpetually responsive to differently conceived alterities beyond such determinate existence. That is,

> [L]aw, if it is to rule effectively and secure the requisite certainty and predictability in the world beyond, must constantly relate to the ever-changing nature of society, the economy, and so forth. There is a constituent requirement for law to respond to the infinity of relation which can impinge upon its determinate position. And yet, whilst the law cannot simply ossify in the determinacy of its position, neither can it dissipate itself in a pure, unalloyed responsiveness to the other and to the changing world 'outside' it.
>
> (Golder and Fitzpatrick 2009: 80)

Fitzpatrick's reading of Derrida (1997) allows him to explore how law 'becomes the combination of determination with what is beyond determination' (2001b: 76). However, he argues that the law cannot only and simply be a form of calculation that 'cuts into' and renders incalculable justice present, because 'justice, responsiveness, responsibility' always also enable law to become. So, law's ground rests on a moving contradiction: it enunciates a determinate existence while simultaneously responding to what is beyond that. The 'tie' between responsiveness and determination brings 'existence to normative futurity' and surpasses any 'contained condition', making law 'the most independent yet the most dependent of things' (2005: 9). And here Fitzpatrick detects law's 'incipient alterity':

> Law is continually oriented to, continually opening to, the possibility of its being otherwise. Law moves beyond the assertion of any singular, even predominant power and in some ultimate sense receives power in its, in law's, own terms, filtering an intrusive power and ultimately constituting its content.
>
> (Fitzpatrick 2005: 10)

Clearly, the law of the law rests, like Derrida's notion of justice (1997), on an ultimately incalculable, illimitable, and unconditional 'platform'. It is insufficiently 'monadic' to enable such claims as 'law creates sovereignty'; however, the law of the law brings together the selfsame determination and responsiveness that is tied to the idea of sovereignty, of sovereign declarations that calculate and are thereby always exceeded by illimitable horizons to which they respond. This law of the law is also simultaneously a law of sovereignty, of the sovereign who relentlessly seeks to govern over what for ever remains in excess of any given instances of governance. No doubt this complicates the assertion of an 'ungovernable' sovereignty, just as it exceeds the idea of a governmentally structured image of sovereignty.

Governing as the ungovernable

Where does all of this take us? The unconditional sovereign, when deemed ungovernable, is a feature of much western political thinking, evident in the muses of such early modern thinkers as Hobbes and Bodin as it is in recent writers like Agamben. What I have tried to do here, with Fitzpatrick, is to unhinge the putatively irreducible connection between the unconditional and ungovernable sovereign. Appropriating Derrida (2005), the aim is to separate these 'two exigencies' and to conceive of the ungovernable sovereign as one image of sovereignty – not *the* definitive form thereof. In that light, we might engage any logic of sovereignty as but a conditional calculation exacted from the unconditional excess that is always to arrive. This sort of analysis could be framed on the strength of

> an unconditional rationalism that never renounces – and precisely in the name of the Enlightenment to come, in the space to be opened up of a democracy to come – the possibility of suspending in an argued, deliberated, rational fashion, all conditions, hypotheses, conventions, and presuppositions, and of criticizing unconditionally all conditionalities.
>
> (Derrida 2005: 142)

Herein lies the basis for refusing the ungovernable sovereign as definitive of all sovereignties. The point is rather to address the prospects of a democracy to come that confronts all sovereigns as conditional beings founded on illimitable, unconditional promises (e.g. democracy and justice). Such promises enable conditional calculations, like ungovernable or governable sovereigns. But this orientation turns us away from mythologies that imagine a conditioned version of sovereignty, no matter how well entrenched, to be *the* necessary, or unassailable, form. Even the governed production of an ungovernable sovereign rests – as the paradoxical logic described at the outset indicates – on an impossible structuring. The unconditional resists, no matter how much we condition or calculate, and no matter how much we insist upon the necessities of a given horizon. Opening up to, say, the unconditional promise of democracy could again signal – as Fitzpatrick's law has done – unknown images of a democratically governed sovereign that never fully arrives.

References

Agamben, G. (1998) *Homo Sacer: Sovereign Power and Bare Life*, Stanford, CA: Stanford University Press.

Agamben, G. (1999) *Remnants of Auschwitz: The Witness and the Archive*, New York: Zone Books.

Agamben, G. (2001) *The Coming Community*, Minneapolis: University of Minnesota Press.

Agamben, G. (2005) *State of Exception*, Chicago: University of Chicago Press.

Butler, J. (2004) *Precarious Life: The Powers of Mourning and Violence*, London: Verso.

Derrida, J. (1997) 'Force of law: The "mystical foundations of authority"', in J. Derrida and G. Anidjar (eds) *Acts of Religion*, New York: Routledge.

Derrida, J. (2005) *Rogues: Two Essays on Reason*, Stanford, CA: Stanford University Press.

Fitzpatrick, P. (2001a) 'Bare sovereignty: *Homo sacer* and the insistence of law', *Theory and Event* 5(2): 34–67.

Fitzpatrick, P. (2001b) *Modernism and the Grounds of Law*, Cambridge: Cambridge University Press.

Fitzpatrick, P. (2005) 'Access as justice', *Windsor Yearbook on Access to Justice* 23: 3–16.

Fitzpatrick, P. (2007) '"What are the Gods to us now?": Secular theology and the modernity of law', *Theoretical Inquiries in Law* 8(1): 61–179.

Fitzpatrick, P. (2009) 'Leveraging Leviathan', in C. Barbour and G. Pavlich (eds) *After Sovereignty*, London: Routledge-Cavendish.

French, M. (2007) 'In the shadow of Canada's camps', *Social and Legal Studies* 16(1): 49–69.

Foucault, M. (2001) *Essential Works of Foucault, 1954–1984*, vol. 3: *Power*, New York: New Press.

Foucault, M. (2007) *Security, Territory, Population: Lectures at the Collège de France, 1977–1978*, Basingstoke, UK: Palgrave Macmillan.

Foucault, M. (2008) *The Birth of Biopolitics: Lectures at the Collège de France, 1978–79*, Basingstoke, UK: Palgrave Macmillan.

Genel, K. (2006) 'The question of biopower: Foucault and Agamben', *Rethinking Marxism* 18(1): 43–62.

Golder, B. and Fitzpatrick, P. (2009) *Foucault's Law*, London: Routledge.

Gratton, P. (2006) 'A "retro-version" of power: Agamben via Foucault on sovereignty', *Critical Review of International Social and Political Philosophy* 9(3): 445–9.

Hobbes, T. (1651/1985) *Leviathan*, Harmondsworth, UK: Penguin Books.

Mills, C. (2008) *The Philosophy of Agamben*, Kingston, Ontario: McGill-Queen's University Press.

Nancy, J.-L. (1993) *The Experience of Freedom*, Stanford, CA: Stanford University Press.

Norris, A. (2005) *Politics, Metaphysics, and Death: Essays on Giorgio Agamben's Homo Sacer*, Durham, NC: Duke University Press.

Pavlich, G. (2010) 'On the subject of sovereigns', in C. Barbour and G. Pavlich (eds) *After Sovereignty*, London: Routledge.

Rasch, W. (2004) *Sovereignty and Its Discontents*, London: Birkbeck Law Press.

Chapter 4

Democracy's ruins, democracy's archive

Paul A. Passavant

Introduction

Giorgio Agamben's work condemns sovereignty and aspires to found a new politics, or a 'coming community', beyond sovereignty and law. He describes sovereign power as determining, unitary, and absolute. This sovereign must be overcome by its equally absolute or all-encompassing other. This other to sovereignty has been conceptualized as pure potentiality, pure singularity, belonging itself, contingency, creativity, excess, or absolute democracy (Agamben 1993: 2, 67; Hardt and Negri 2000). I argue that Peter Fitzpatrick's work on sovereignty and law shows that absolute sovereignty is not capable of existing as such. Nor, for that matter, is absolute democracy capable of existing as such. 'Sovereignty' and 'democracy' are not absolutely opposed to each other. Instead, politics takes place in the torsion of these impossibilities.

Many postmodernists today are allergic to anything with a whiff of sovereignty (Hardt and Negri 2000). Unfortunately, this has the consequence of asking those with democratic sensibilities to give up on the project of popular sovereignty at the exact moment that the right in the United States is seeking to ruin democracy by asserting sovereign prerogatives under various theories of absolute and uncheckable presidential powers.[1] We are faced, presently, with the ruins of a law opposed to unchecked presidentialism, torture, and camps.[2] Fitzpatrick's attention to sovereignty's paradoxical requirements, and to its near-mythic reliance upon law for temporary resolution of these contradictory demands, teaches us that law, and hence democracy, is always vulnerable to ruin of this sort. Instead of sharing the hopes of messianic postmodernists for a final resolution to these challenges, Fitzpatrick indicates where we must begin our political labours: among democracy's ruins. These ruins are legal remainders of past struggles against tyrannies and, as such, material for an archive of democratic remains. I contend that our political work should be mindful of law as democracy's archive. These reminders can help us to recollect the persistence necessary to take down or overcome tyrannies, to recall the fidelity necessary to keep a commitment to popular sovereignty. If we fail to labour on behalf of the future this archive anticipates, then the scriveners of George W. Bush's administration will continue to consign us to a dwelling among democracy's ruins.

Messianic postmodernism

According to Giorgio Agamben, sovereign power is absolutely determining. In *Homo Sacer*, Agamben accepts Carl Schmitt's theory of state sovereignty, positing the sovereign as the one who decides the exception to the normal juridical order (Schmitt 1988, 1996; Agamben 1998: 15–16).[3] Against liberalism, which seeks to debilitate the state from acting through individual rights and multiplying checks on decision, Schmitt's theory of the political relies on a concept of sovereignty where sovereignty is the one place where the decision on the 'critical situation' or 'exception' resides (1996: 61, 38–9). For Schmitt, and therefore for Agamben's understanding of sovereignty, it is clear where sovereignty lies, in so far as the sovereign is not hampered by checks and balances. It is the unitary place of decision (1988: 5, 7).

For Agamben, the place of the sovereign is a place where the outside is brought inside the community (1998: 35, 38, 83). *Homo sacer*, the one who is 'captured in the sovereign's ban', the one who may be killed without committing homicide but not sacrificed, exists in a parallel relation to the sovereign in the sense that he also is outside the normal juridical order (1998: 83). Political space is thus constituted through a double exclusion. The political sphere, the place of sovereignty and the referent of the sovereign's decision, is created in its separation from the divine and the juridical. This is where political power confronts bare life without mediation.

The concentration camp, Agamben contends, the 'pure, absolute, and impassable biopolitical space', is the 'hidden paradigm of the political space of modernity', and the 'hidden matrix of the politics in which we are still living' (1998: 123, 175). The concentration camp is the creation of a declaration of a state of emergency or exception, and thus placed outside the normal legal order (Agamben 2005a: 2). The camps are the spatialization of the suspension of law that is inhabited by bare life (Agamben 1998: 175). By identifying the German body through the negation of the Jew, the Nazi camps produced the Muselmann, an 'absolute biopolitical substance' (Agamben 2002: 85). In these concentration camps that are the logical extreme of sovereign power, biopower sought to produce, through the Muselmann, a complete separation of living being from speaking being, a kind of absolute biopolitical substance forced to survive as an entirely separated stratum – an absolute separation of *zoē* from *bios* (ibid.: 156).

Because, for Agamben, politics must be immanent to being, he must find a passage from the contemporary state to the 'coming community' from within human being as it is presently manifested. This means, paradoxically, that he must look to the camps as the political matrix of the present – and the state of exception generally – in order to find this passage. Agamben must locate the seeds of change, the potentiality of the coming community, within the camps and within the state of exception. At this point, Agamben requires a theory of political action. Yet Agamben has described the camps such as Auschwitz as 'the most radical negation of contingency; it is, therefore, absolute necessity' (2002: 148). What, within the realm of human possibility, could overcome sovereign power defined as 'absolute necessity'? Faced with absolute necessity, Agamben must evacuate the terrain of the political and rely upon the messianic to overcome sovereign power.

In an extended consideration of the messianic, Agamben describes the word of faith as an 'experience of pure power (*potenza*)'. It is a 'pure potentiality of saying' (2005b: 136). Paul's faith, expressed as 'Jesus Messiah', can be understood through J. L. Austin's conception of performative speech acts (Agamben 2005: 131; Austin 1962). The apostle's joyful message might be likened to a performative speech act where language is not functioning denotatively but where language is action. A successful performative speech act, however, relies on particular conditions of possibility for its effectivity.

In Austin's initial introduction of performatives, he notes that they rely on 'appropriate circumstances' (1962: 6). What are the preconditions for a successful speech act? If we are referring to the process of becoming a citizen of the United States, we would want a ceremony, someone to administer the oath of citizenship, dress appropriate to the occasion, and so on. In other words, the success of the performance is contingent upon its staging or conventions. We also need to believe in the performance – that this is not a group of actors, say, being filmed (a simulation of the oath of citizenship) – or, as Agamben helpfully reminds us, the announcement needs the complement of faith for it to pass from potentiality to actuality (2005b: 90). Finally, we would need to be able to secure this situation and perhaps this space against other possible uses, at least for the time it takes to perform the ceremony. This means that other possible performatives – like a promise to sell the site to a developer in response to a decision to develop the site with luxury condos, a shopping mall, and a sports arena – must not have occurred. Therefore, a particular situation, the preconditions for a successful performative speech act, must be secured for the announcement's success. The faithful, that is, would have to make *political* decisions and perhaps even act with a certain measure of militancy to continue to maintain the security of the situation that enables the possibility of the truth of the announcement against other possible speech acts and their corresponding subjects and situations (Badiou 2001, 2003; Passavant 2007: 162–5). Agamben's acknowledged reliance upon the messianic functions as a displacement of attention from politics, although it must presuppose unacknowledged political commitments.

Agamben believes, along with other 'new ontologists' such as Michael Hardt and Antonio Negri, that today's political problems cannot be solved within politics or political philosophy. Instead, the problem of sovereignty must be solved at a more fundamental level by removing inquiry from the level of political philosophy to 'first philosophy' by creating a new ontology (Agamben 1998: 44; Hardt and Negri 2000). A thread ties the modern state to the ancient creation of the political sphere in the western tradition. Likewise, there is an 'inner solidarity between democracy and totalitarianism' (Agamben 1998: 10). The production of bare life – the human life exposed to an ever-present vulnerability to being killed, the exclusion that founds the city of men – is the 'originary activity of sovereignty', and this decision constitutes the 'originary "political" relation' (ibid.: 7, 83, 85). Agamben traces the production of bare life to the distinction for the ancient Greeks between *zoē* (biological life) and *bios* (a way of life), and the exclusion of *zoē* from public or political space by confining it to the *oikos* (home). The human being with *logos* dwells in the *polis* 'by letting its own bare life be excluded, as an exception, within it' (ibid.: 8). The seeds of the camps are located in the ancient Greek distinction between *zoē* and *bios* at the beginning of the western political tradition. Therefore, the problems of politics and law cannot be solved at the level of political or legal theory. We must shift our attention to the more fundamental problem of ontology and *be* otherwise (ibid.: 44).

Agamben looks favourably upon Negri's effort to rethink constituent power as potentiality, as a category of ontology, although he suggests that Negri's continued use of the terminology of constituent power means that potentiality still, unfortunately, remains tied to sovereignty (Agamben 1998: 43–4). This is significant for Agamben as he seeks to 'think the Being of abandonment beyond every idea of law', towards 'a politics freed from every ban', and cites Walter Benjamin's aspiration for a world that 'absolutely cannot be appropriated or made juridical' (1998: 59; 2005a: 64). In other words, Agamben shares Negri's anti-juridicism, even suggesting that Negri himself might still go further in this respect.

Political theory is embedded ontologically such that the outcome of camps – a spatialization of law's suspension where bare life is confined – is predetermined. To correct these injustices, then, we must found a new ontology for our politics of the future. Where would we find these new subjects or this new experience of being? To stop the present and to found a new ontology, however, presumes an Archimedean point on which to pivot from present to future, or messianic salvation inexplicable to human being, if sovereignty is as determining as Agamben suggests in his *Homo Sacer* project. Thus, the approach of this new ontologist shares a problematic weakness with deontological theories of justice and politics: the belief that we can find, invent, or *experience* totally new grounds for our politics of the future.

To accede to Agamben's coming community, we must experience messianic salvation. This act of salvation would have to occur without ruin, remainder, or excess. Otherwise, we would not experience pure belonging in the coming community. Either something would be lacking in the coming community, which would mean that it was less than belonging itself, although Agamben theorizes the coming community as 'without remainder' (1993: 28), or there would be the coming community and something more than the coming community that continued to reside within it. This would require, however, a subsequent act of representation in order to come to grips with that which exceeds the coming community, and a concomitant exclusion or limit to belonging or to pure potentiality, although Agamben considers the coming community to be 'unrepresentable' (1993: 25). It would require a consideration of that which is inessential to the coming community, a consideration, therefore, of the coming community's purpose, yet Agamben conceptualizes the coming community as 'without presupposition' (and without a state) in its being such (1993: 83). Passage from absolute sovereignty to the coming community, then, must be messianic.

Agamben's proclivity to substitute a project requiring the invention of new metaphysics for political inquiry and political struggle is messianic. Present injustices are too pressing to wait for this. Peter Fitzpatrick's work on sovereignty, I believe, presents us with a more productive post-structuralism – one with less need to resort to messianic diversions.

Sovereignty's paradoxes

Peter Fitzpatrick understands modern sovereignty as something that eludes us all. It cannot be possessed. This might seem odd in light of the standard understandings of sovereignty, where the latter would be that political and legal locus of the final decision, that place from which there can be no appeal. The standard account of modern sovereignty suggests that sovereignty is singular in its self-possession. Sovereignty is a place, as Schmitt (1996) contends, that must be unitary. Contemporary scholars like Agamben, then, borrow from Schmitt to evoke the image of an all-powerful sovereign who decides matters of life itself as the origin of contemporary law and politics today, as well as its catastrophes. The sovereign, according to this image, decides and the act the decision mandates occurs without delay, a perfect translation of the decision into the action required by the sovereign.

Fitzpatrick asks, what would be required of this sovereign, of pure sovereignty? This sovereignty would have to be *enclosed*.[4] It would have to be a distinctive and unitary space. Otherwise, it would fall prey to the confusions of pluralism to which liberal governments are vulnerable, on Schmitt's accusation. It must be enclosed, or else we would have trouble locating the exact place of sovereignty. It must be *this* place and not another. Sovereignty is in its place and not, therefore, the place of the non-sovereign. Sovereignty must be its own entity and not the entity of another or else it is not sovereign, but governed by the other that possesses it. In other words, sovereignty must be self-possessed and not possessed by another. Thus, it must be enclosed and set apart from the rest who would be non-sovereign. Sovereignty cannot be with-in the rest if it is to be sovereign.

Sovereignty also must be *one*. If sovereignty were plural, then, as Schmitt points out, confusion ensues. What if there is a difference of opinion among the many? Which would govern or decide the matter? If there were more than one, then there might be another place to lodge an appeal. If there was division among the multiple with sovereign pretences, then the multiple itself might split and divide in conflict. In this case we would have struggle, and not the simplicity and decisiveness of a unified decision made by the sovereign. With unity, there is self-possession. Without unity, there is struggle and one entity would then be determined, in part, by the course taken by its struggle with another. Thus, sovereignty must be one.

Relatedly, sovereignty must be corporate. We must know the body of sovereignty. Otherwise, if sovereignty is not enclosed within its own body, if it is not self-possessed, then its powers would be shared among many bodies. If power were shared among many bodies, then we would not be speaking of sovereignty. Rather, we would be speaking of sharing and pluralism, if not democracy. We would not be able to locate the unitary place of decision.

Sovereignty must also be *determining*. Sovereignty determines the fate of others with its decisions. If one were determined by another, then one would not be sovereign, but the entity that decided one's fate would be sovereign over one. One would be subjected to other, determinant forces. Therefore, sovereignty must be determining if it is not to be subjected to others.

Fitzpatrick shows, however, that sovereignty to be sovereign must also be the opposite of the above. That is, to be sovereign, sovereignty must not only be enclosed, one, corporate, and determining, but also illimitable, plural, responsive, and determinate yet dissipating as well. Sovereignty must be *illimitable* because if something limited sovereignty, then the limiting entity would be determining, and not sovereignty. Sovereignty must be capable of reaching all. Sovereignty, to be sovereign, must be illimitable.

Sovereignty must also, paradoxically, be *plural*. It must be capable of representing itself in multiple places for it to be relevant and indeed sovereign over all. So, the sovereign decision must be amenable to reproduction in a place other than its place of origin for the decision to have its determining effects for others. The decision's mandate must appear in the place of the other, yet it must be of the locus of sovereignty. Because sovereignty must be in the place(s) of the many to be sovereign for the many, sovereignty must of necessity be many, plural, and perhaps shared if not democratic, as it re-presents and reproduces itself along a chain of reiteration, and ultimately in the place of the other.

Sovereignty must be not only determining but also *responsive*. If sovereignty was not responsive then it could no longer be sovereign – it could not be sovereign *for us*. The sovereign, for example, might dictate a rule. Because of the flux of life, however, circumstances might arise that were not immediately contemplated when the rule was decided upon. Sovereignty, then, must respond to these new conditions and cover them as well. For sovereignty to be sovereign for us, for it to be continuing in its sovereign power, sovereignty must be responsive to us, and not stuck unresponsively in another place and time.

Paradoxically, sovereignty must be not only determining but determinate. That is, we must know where sovereignty lies so that it is not mistaken for another. Confusion if not struggle ensues if those who must act on the sovereign's decisions do not know whether the rules issue from this place or that. We must know the sovereign – it must be determinate – so that we are not fooled by imposters. Sovereignty must be distinguishable from the rest. Yet once sovereignty becomes determinate, it becomes subject to that which identifies it or gives it meaning. Sovereignty becomes determined by that which points it out, defines it, and gives reasons to justify it (see further Derrida 2005: 101). Once sovereignty is determinate for us, it has become determined by the creative forces of determination.

Finally, sovereignty must be dissipating. By being 'responsive to the illimitable plurality beyond its present existence', by being 'attuned and receptive' to plurality, sovereignty dissipates over space and time (quoting Fitzpatrick 2007: 4). The decision moves from one place to another along a chain of institutions, disappearing from one place as it reappears in another. The decision is also translated and thus becomes subtly different from what it was once as it is reformulated to fit new circumstances. The sovereign decision becomes other than what it was in order to continue to be – to be for the many and indeed in the infinite. Sovereignty must no longer be what it was in order to be for us, now. So, modern sovereignty must 'marvellously combine' being enclosed, one, corporate, and determining, with also, simultaneously, or by turns, paradoxically, being illimitable, plural, responsive, determinate, and dissipating. Modern sovereignty, unlike earlier or other forms that govern with reference to the sacred, has to combine these contradictory dimensions 'without recourse to a transcendental reference' (Fitzpatrick 2007: 3).

In order to combine these contradictory dimensions without transcendent reference, modern sovereignty 'has to be a process of continual constitution'. Borrowing from Jacques Derrida's discussion in *Rogues*, Fitzpatrick describes this process of sovereignty as 'gathering itself by tending toward simultaneity' as it responsively incorporates and assembles the 'multitude of disparate forces that continually come to (re)constitute it' (2007: 3, quoting Derrida 2005: 12). Since sovereignty cannot be confined to what it presently is for it to be in the infinite future, sovereignty must take on a position, constantly, that enables it to be 'other than what it is, a position that is an incipient vacuity – ultimately "nothing"' (Fitzpatrick 2007: 3–4). In other words, in Fitzpatrick's rigorous examination of what pure sovereignty would have to be, we wind up ultimately, paradoxically, with nothing.

Pure sovereignty is impossible. Sovereignty, or rather sovereign aspirations, always risk ruin. Sovereignty, to be truly sovereign, would have *to be* simultaneously. The decision, the announcement, the act to make the decision real would all have to occur in the same instant without ruin or remainder or else the ruin or remainder would be indicators that something eluded sovereignty. In other words, ruins and remainders indicate that which is beyond the grasp of sovereignty, that which is beyond its control – the limits of sovereignty indicating other powers.

The sovereign, to be sovereign for us, would have to relate to us somehow. For example, the decision to torture – or not to torture – must be related, through a bureaucracy, to the one who would carry out the order, and to the one vulnerable to the tyrannical abuse. At each stage in the relay the sovereign's legal ruling risks ruin through the interpretive acts of his or her officers. Yet for the sovereign to do otherwise would be to tend towards one's self in a way that would not relate to us; it would be alien from us. We could not, however, be subject to that which does not relate to us, to that which is absolutely other to us in its radical separation from human being (Gasché 1999). So, to be *our* sovereign, the sovereign cannot be *absolutely* sovereign; it is impossible.

Sovereignty cannot be a purely unitary place if it is to relate to us. Sovereignty must be plural if it is to be; sovereign decisions must be re-presented in other places if they are to reach us. The sovereign's power achieves extension precisely through chains linking multiple decision points through the modern state – a phenomenon that Michel Foucault (1982) analysed perspicaciously through his concept of government.[5] Foucault's understanding of government grasps how the state is able to govern at a distance precisely because it accounts for pluralized forms of power, and an element of freedom. The modern state seeks to conduct the conduct of institutions and peoples constituting society. The modern state brings different forms of power under its control and activates them as an ensemble towards its ends over space and time.

'Sovereignty' achieves extension through plural institutions articulated with each other in a chain. Because of this, sovereignty is not sovereign. It relies on others. Sovereignty must share power in order to be. As

Fitzpatrick puts it, when he uses the term 'sovereignty' he is cheating (2007: 5; see also Passavant 2007: 159–60). Sovereignty, as I have already said, borrowing from Fitzpatrick, would be nothing. That which we have been analysing under the name sovereignty is really the 'supposedly modern occidental notion of the state' (Fitzpatrick 2007: 5). This state is better understood as an 'assembly' or an 'assemblage'. And that which gives the assembly power is also that which can put this state in ruins. Sovereignty, the state, liberalism, democracy – none of these can be without their scriveners, but all are potentially subject to ruin at the hands of their scriveners.

'Absolute' sovereignty now looks a great deal more vulnerable than posited by Agamben. As sovereignty becomes more 'absolute', or 'encompassing', it appears more proximate to democracy, as its powers become increasingly responsive, shared, and plural. Fitzpatrick's helpful exploration of 'pure sovereignty', in fact, suggests that sovereignty and democracy are not mutually exterior to each other, despite the assertions of Hardt and Negri in *Empire* (2000).

How are the paradoxical and impossibly contradictory dimensions of sovereignty resolved, according to Fitzpatrick? Through law. Modern political theory's attempts to 'account for sovereignty in some existentially or conceptually contained way' fail, a failure symptomatic of modern society's inability to account for itself. It is law that occupies this area of a-position, in between such determinate and infinite possibilities (Fitzpatrick 2001: 54; 2007: 9). Modern society cannot cohere through reference to transcending gods or sacred myths, and it tries, with futility, to achieve fixity through particular, determinate positivities. Ultimately, modern society coheres through a 'mythology of modern law', a law that takes on the determinant yet responsive qualities of the sacred, enduring not through a relation to the transcendent but in negative relation to what modernity is not – often unfortunately racialized conceptions of the uncivilized or the savage (Fitzpatrick 1992).

Agamben's attempt to contain modern sovereignty through a totalizing theory, to borrow an example from Fitzpatrick, becomes yet another instance of mythic paradox as Agamben tries to anchor sovereignty upon the ostensibly solid ground of 'bare life itself' (Fitzpatrick 2005: 51, quoting Agamben 1998). Yet *homo sacer*, sacred man, cannot anchor sovereignty through 'reference beyond, [because] beyond life in the world there is no position surpassing that life from which it can be observed or rendered as bare'. Therefore, without this 'resolving reference, we are left with what created *homo sacer* "in the first place", with law'. Law takes the place of the sacred for allegedly disenchanted moderns, combining the determinable here and now with 'responsiveness to what is ever beyond' (ibid.: 51).[6] It is law that mythically combines sovereignty's impossibly paradoxical attributes.

To confer meaning upon sovereignty is, Derrida writes, to justify sovereignty, giving reasons for it, to subject sovereignty to rules, to law, and thus to 'divide it, to subject it to partitioning, to participation, to being shared' (2005: 101). Law, that which renders sovereignty determinate, introduces a democratic element to sovereignty. Law is expressed through language, a potentially universalizable medium. Moreover, in addressing others in this way one relies upon prior linguistic conventions, borrowing from them while sharing this linguistic commons with others and, perhaps, those whom one addresses, even as one seeks to inflect this linguistic code so that it might be adequate to present circumstances – circumstances which would be, to some degree, both unprecedented and determined (hence determinable). Through this law and language, 'sovereign' acts, or acts performed in the name of the 'people', seek justification. Law gives credit or credibility to sovereignty. Absolute sovereignty is thus impossible.

Pure potentiality and absolute democracy

The categories of ontological reason are not those of normative political theory. Even if more primary in terms of categories of reason, they do not assist us in addressing fundamentally political questions. These questions include how to organize ourselves to avoid tyranny, identifying current forms of tyranny, identifying who is not counted – but should be – for matters of distributive justice, identifying how existing distributions should be altered, and identifying the particularities of institutionalized exploitation.[7]

To be open to potentialities and singularities without condition means being open to the flux of life, good or bad.[8] To embrace pure potentiality without qualification is to be open to infinite possibility. Moreover, producing combinations of these possibilities means being open to what is formally designated as an unthinkable number of possibilities (Meillassoux 2008). Unthinkably wonderful. Unthinkably horrible. The work of avoiding the unthinkably horrible while remaining open to, if not actively pursuing, the wonderful, if not the merely good welfare of society, however, is the work of law and politics.

Although Agamben describes sovereign power manifested in the camps as 'absolute necessity', a contrary embrace of contingency or excess is neither more democratic nor more just. To be self-governing means that we are not dictated to by other forces, be it the power of a tyrant or the contingencies of other forms of necessity. For example, the retraction of certain state services from places like the Bronx in the late 1970s, in conjunction with other intentionally regressive economic policies at both the local and the national levels, led to excessive economic duress for those who lived in the Bronx, among others. Not only were these results unjust, but these contingencies had incapacitating effects.

The practices of democratic government presuppose some collective capacity to direct and achieve collective purposes. The incapacitation of the people, by chaos, violence, and other forms of socio-economic deprivation, then, is both undemocratic and unjust. The categories of normative political theory are not identical to those of ontology. While politics, indeed democratic politics, or the possibility of creating greater justice in the world, would be impossible under conditions of absolute necessity or determination, contingency is not the same thing as either justice or democracy. Indeed, the powers of self-government refer, in part, to a capacity to govern or to mitigate certain contingencies: to determine our collective destiny within the worldly flux. Any social formation, in fact, is a complex mix of contingency and determination.

Because conditions and qualifications are explicitly not placed on the potentialities embraced by the new ontologists, no possibility, no matter how awful or torturous, can be logically opposed with-in this embrace. Agamben's potentiality is similar to the moment that Derrida describes preceding the legal decision. If one aspires to do justice to a situation, according to Derrida, one must approach the task with a 'sense of a responsibility without limits' that is necessarily incalculable and excessive. One must not simply apply a rule mechanically 'without a spirit of justice'. To play to the letter of the law in this manner, playing with this text simply as a manipulation of simulacra without a consideration of ends, might shelter one from criticism since one ruled according to the letter of the law, but one 'would not be just' in so doing. One considers law, concepts of justice, values and norms long sedimented within the law – in short, one takes on the task of 'historical and interpretive memory' when one approaches a legal decision with a spirit of justice. One also suspends, for a moment, the credit or credibility of a rule or rules of law apparently applicable to the case. This is done before deciding, where the legal decision – which would not be justice, as a legal decision is a finite calculation enabled and constrained by a logic of iterability, while justice would be infinite – may very well 'conform to a pre-existing law'. This legal decision, though, would have reinstituted or reinvented the law in a conservative and reproductive act of 'fresh' judgement in this case, reinventing the legal principle in this case that differs from the situation of the legal principle's earlier appearance, its instituting or founding. For Derrida, then, there is a moment of 'suspense' prior to the legal decision that is a 'structurally necessary' moment in so far as one approaches the legal decision with a sense of responsibility and not in a 'dogmatic slumber'. This moment is described as 'anguishing'. This moment of suspension might *seem* to be a move towards irresponsibility, but it is a necessary act of responsibility. It is a moment where transformations, even revolutions, can occur (Derrida 2002a: 244–55). Here one confronts the limits of knowledge, of time and space. But justice cannot wait, and so one must render a decision – make a finite determination – if one aspires to be responsible to the call of justice. And this decision will have been too late, too incomplete, produced with insufficient knowledge, and so forth, to have done justice, since it will have been constrained by the limits of calculability.

Agamben embraces an 'ontology of potentiality' (1998: 44). This is a 'supreme power' both to be and to not-be, a capacity for one's own impotentiality, a welcoming of non-being that he describes as a 'fundamental passivity' (1999: 182–3). Agamben exemplifies this pure potentiality with the figure of Bartelby, a scribe who can write but prefers not to write, exhibiting the potential to not-write even as he possesses the capacity to write. Poised between writing and not writing, 'resisting every possibility of deciding', to conserve all possibilities, is like a moment of suspense Derrida describes before a decision (Agamben 1993: 37; 1998: 48).

Here is where we can dramatically contrast Derrida's and Fitzpatrick's attention to law with Agamben's aversion to the concept of responsibility because of its relation to the juridical (Agamben 2002: 20ff.; Mills 2008: 102–4). If one is motivated by justice, if one wants to give force to the requirements of justice or make the powerful more just, then one must calculate, with a spirit of justice, what decision to make.[9] One cannot simply maintain the point of suspense. Not if one wants to prevent the awful possibility of camps. Therefore, the experience of passivity, this openness to innumerable possibilities described by Agamben, is like the infinite responsiveness required by considerations of justice in the suspended moment prior to a legal decision. To leave matters at this suspended point is consistent with Agamben's anti-juridicism, since responsiveness is only one dimension of the law; pure receptivity would be vacuous and ultimately nothing. The demands of justice, however, mean that we must make a determination – one that admittedly will come too late. Consequently, to leave matters at a moment of passivity or receptivity, as Agamben does with his embrace of pure potentiality, is to do neither law nor the work of justice.

The categories of ontology in themselves do not enable us to address the most pressing injustices in contemporary law and politics today, such as the revival of camps. To translate our terms of political theory into the terminology of ontology, as the new ontologists do, leads to significant confusions. To embrace pure, infinite, or unthinkable possibilities for their own sake gives us no normative grounds on which to resist camps. To contend that the opposite of sovereignty is contingency or potentiality does not suggest another force or capacity of greater normative value than sovereignty. Furthermore, if pure sovereignty is 'determinant', for example, then it cannot be described ontologically as 'absolute necessity'.

Absolute democracy, exterior to sovereignty, is also an impossibility.[10] In contrast to Agamben, though, let us give credit to the achievements of the people in the centuries of struggle against the tyranny of absolute monarchy, and consider the quest for *popular sovereignty*. Democracy is already an articulated concept – an articulation of *demos* or people, and *kratos* (or *kratein*), which refers to having power, the force of law, rule, or to have or to be right (Derrida 2005: 22). That is, 'democracy' itself refers to popular sovereignty, a situation where people are sovereign, or where people govern themselves. In a democracy, people give themselves laws, and share power equally. By referring to popular *sovereignty*, I emphasize the normative element of democracy: it is *right* that the people should rule, the people have a right to rule. This is the rule or law of democracy.

A new beginning is always both less and more than democratic. A new beginning must borrow its terms. Likewise for a democratic beginning: the people of popular sovereignty do not invent the language of their self-governance out of nothing. Indeed, the possibility of democracy is given by language, and the many discourses of democracy, with meanings attributed to these words, rules of grammar, and discourses that the people did not give to themselves. The beginning of democracy cannot be absolutely democratic. When we begin – even a project of democracy – we begin from a place or a position already given to, or imposed upon, us (Derrida 2000, 2002b). Our beginnings are always less than democratic as they have been legislated in advance of us.

Additionally, because we must borrow our terms, the 'people' of popular sovereignty are always more than themselves. The 'people' of popular sovereignty share their power with others who preceded them. Furthermore, democratic acts are oriented to the future, to keeping democracy – that is, they are oriented towards future incarnations of democratic subjects. Moreover, because democracy opens itself to others, the 'anyone' of democratic participation may include those who lack a commitment to democracy. Therefore, the 'people' of democracy are always more than themselves. There is never just democracy here. There is always democracy plus something else.

The 'people' of popular sovereignty are also always less than themselves. Never fully present, and defying origins, democracy reaches out to others in order to be. These others are past and future. Because we must begin somewhere, on some haunted grounds, using terms the meaning of which has, to some extent, been previously determined by others, democratic beginnings are always less than democratic. Concrete democratic acts are necessary to fulfil promises or claims for democracy. But, like considerations regarding justice, there is always a limit to our knowledge, or a finite limit to our accounting of a problem, or our memory. In these ways, democracy is always lacking. There is never just democracy here.

Because popular sovereignty is lacking at any moment, it requires a supplement. This is law. When we take a position – such as a position for democracy – we rely on law to recall the commitments necessarily implicated within this position. To bring our (democratic) selves back to ourselves. Law occupies the area of a-position, in between the determinate commitments necessary to making life more democratic or more just, and the infinitely responsive dimension of democracy, of justice; in between our democratic position and that to which we must respond if we are to maintain our democratic position. Like 'law', democracy's condition is always unresolved, calling for incessant decisions and judgements. Democracy also persists through a relation of negativity – in condemning and addressing manners of tyranny. Democracy takes a position – comes from a position – as law 'comes from and returns to a position'. Law is where we keep our commitments to democracy, reinstituting and re-sending these commitments in the moments of decision, when, as always, our commitment to democracy seems to be dissipating and we must respond to a different challenge. Democracy must be open, but in this opening it risks becoming something other than democracy. Alternatively, democracy risks being trapped by past determinations in the face of new and different challenges – an enclosure that would render democracy less than democratic in its lack of responsiveness. Law resolves, for the time being, these paradoxical dimensions of popular sovereignty.[11]

In sum, displacing inquiry from politics to the categories of ontology will not resolve pressing injustices. Moreover, both absolute sovereignty and absolute democracy are impossibilities. While sovereignty must take on certain democratic attributes to achieve extension – like sharing power through institutional assemblies and assemblages – democracy always begins in a place with terms in some way legislated for it by an other in advance. Both sovereignty and democracy must contain paradoxical, if not contradictory, attributes in order to be. And both rely on law for temporary and unstable resolution of these ambivalent tendencies. That which enables either the absolute sovereignty of a tyrant or a recording of a democratic success, however, makes these forms of power vulnerable to ruin. Tyranny requires the assistance of scriveners. Likewise, democratic struggles produce victories that can never be absolute as its plural institutional assemblages create opportunities for ruinous resistance to democracy's commitments. Democratic victories are always partial – succeeding in one place or another, while remaining vulnerable to the John Yoos of the world who remain embedded deep within the bureaucracies of the modern state or who remain in its assemblies. They will come with remainders and they will be lacking in some way.

Camps, or democracy's ruins

In his book *The Powers of War and Peace*, which finds that the president is not bound by international law, John Yoo, a member of the Office of Legal Counsel (OLC) between 2001 and 2003 in George W. Bush's administration, and the author of the infamous 'torture memo' of August 2002, justifies the internment of Japanese Americans in concentration camps during the Second World War by the US government (Yoo 2005). He does this in the context of illustrating a distinction he makes between 'total war', in which Congress augments executive war powers with a public declaration of the factual existence of hostilities, and other wars that are conducted without such a public declaration by Congress. He finds internment camps to be constitutional when they are created under the 'pressing public necessity' of a 'total' war. Nevertheless, Yoo is typically ambiguous about whether the wholesale round-up of Americans or others would still be constitutional without such a congressional declaration. He says, 'one doubts' whether 'courts' would have allowed 'wholesale internment' of 'Panamanian Americans', 'Yugoslavs', or 'Iraqis Americans [*sic*]', in reference to recent conflicts conducted without the benefit of a congressional declaration of war, although he does not clearly rule out the possibility that courts *might* have upheld such actions. Moreover, his speculations are on the subject of *court action*; he does not clearly state whether he believes such an action to be properly constitutional even if he is clear that internment should be considered permissible when there is a congressional declaration of war (ibid.: 151, 333). To support this position he cites favourably in a singular endnote the repudiated, though never overruled, Supreme Court decision *Korematsu v. United States* (1944), which sustained Fred Korematsu's conviction for refusing to abide by the military's internment order applicable to 'all persons of Japanese ancestry', and remaining in a prohibited area: his hometown (Yoo 2005; Irons 1983).

During the 1940s the United States fought a war against the Nazis' camps. Today, however, the United States maintains a camp at a military base in Guantánamo Bay, Cuba, and another at the Baghram airbase in Afghanistan.[12] In these camps, hundreds of people have been subjected to executive detention, and many have been tortured (ICRC 2007).

Every law is a sending, and this deeply worried a dissenter from the majority's opinion in *Korematsu*, Justice Jackson, who was concerned that the validation of racial discrimination would lie around like a 'loaded weapon', to be picked up by a future tyrant claiming 'urgent need'. Law, Jackson realized, has a 'generative power of its own', and every repetition of the principle of 'racial discrimination in criminal procedure' and the 'transplanting' of 'American citizens' would embed the principle more deeply in Americans' 'law and thinking', enabling its expansion to 'new purposes' (*Korematsu v. United States*, with Justice Jackson dissenting at 246). These, as Jackson recognized, would be ruinous repetitions.

Legal struggles, or democracy's archive

How are we to resist the ruinous aspects of tyranny and keep faith with democracy? Messianic postmodernism would have us abandon law to oppose absolute and total sovereignty in the name of absolute democracy, for Hardt and Negri, or to experience pure potentiality, for Agamben. I have shown, however, that neither absolute sovereignty nor absolute democracy can exist as such. The perfect absence of democracy and its pure presence are both foreclosed by the force of necessary iteration, iteration that enables both democracy and tyrannical sovereignty to be, spectrally. Moreover, pure potentiality gives us no position from which to oppose the particularities of tyranny, such as camps. Drawing from Fitzpatrick, I have also indicated that law facilitates the resolution of (popular) sovereignty's – of democracy's – paradoxical dimensions for the time being: the determinate political position of democracy with democracy's openness and responsiveness, for example. Law subjects political power to sharing. It is where democracy is claimed, permitted, and promised. Even as law is always already 'ruined, in ruins, ruinous', law also provides for democracy being posited and preserved (Derrida 2002a: 273). Law is where sovereignty is divided or shared, and it is how we (re)send democracy (Derrida 2005: 34). It is where we enact our fidelity to democracy – where we cut into history and take a *position* on democracy (Derrida 2002a: 289).

Law is where we take a position on democracy. Law must come from a position, and there must be a position, or a place, to which law can then return. Law is how we enact our commitment or responsibility to democracy and to justice, the commitments and responsibilities we have made here to those impossibly necessary tasks. In this, law assists our memory and acts as a resistance to forgetting even as law's repetitions are generated by the fact that we have always already forgotten some of these commitments. We cannot keep such infinite responsibilities in mind at once. In this resistance to a forgetting that constantly tracks us, law is like an archive (Derrida 1995: 76, fn. 14).

An archive is where archives, and archiving, *take place* (Derrida 1995: 2). *There* where a social order is exercised. Archive, deriving from the Greek *arkhe*, articulates a principle of beginning, a law according to which a practice was begun, a place of depositing, and the question of who exercises legitimate hermeneutic authority – who has the 'right to make or represent the law' (ibid.: 1–3). The notion of an archive implies a particular region of thought or place, as well as a law – no archiving without law (ibid.: 40). An archive both conserves and generates. It gathers in preparation for a future. It is a promise to others, to our legatees (ibid.: 36). On the one hand, when one interprets an object of an archive, one's interpretation becomes inscribed into the archive. The archive is a spectral corpus that never closes since the archivist produces more archive: the archive opens out to the future (ibid.: 67–8). Yet, on the other hand, an archive must also exclude: 'No archive without outside' (ibid.: 11, emphasis removed). The laws of an archive – principles of value and classification –

will regulate not only that which has been included and how it is to be included, but also that which should be excluded to conserve this trust, so we know how to go on in the future (ibid.: 40). Nevertheless, as Derrida points out, even that which we exclude shapes our laws as its phantom continues to haunt us (ibid.: 61).

By thinking of law as where we take a position, for democracy, for example, and by thinking of law as an archival practice, we cross a conceptual argument with an ontological one. The conceptual argument that we share our powers, our law-making, with others indicates the impossibility of either the pure absence of democracy or democracy's pure presence. Therefore, even if law and politics do not have in essence a tendency towards democracy (which is implicated in the conceptual argument), there remains an ineradicable democratic element.[13] Law as archive meets this conceptual argument with ontic and ontological principles. An archive takes place. It is deposited somewhere. There is no archive without substance: there is no archive without a trace (Derrida 1995: 26–7).

Could the claim of popular sovereignty, could a democratic beginning or performative speech act, could the exercise of self-government, could politics take place where the people, there, decide to give themselves laws, and could this democratic sending or legacy disappear without a trace? Could the struggles against tyranny disappear, totally, without a trace? Would it be responsive or responsible to democracy or to justice to try to make these things disappear in order to constitute an absolutely new ontology? Such a beginning, like any beginning, would have to take place somewhere and therefore it would have to account for what had given place to such a beginning. This is the paradox of a democratic beginning: it is never equal to itself, it is never just democracy. It begins in ruins. This is where and how we begin, even if we want to begin democratically. But this is not all bad. Not if there is a resistance to forgetting these struggles against tyranny as we begin again.

We are constituted by democracy's archive, by democracy's remainders. By its echoes. We are not totally foreign to democracy. Not now, and perhaps not ever. Our contemporary politics takes place within the echoes of languages (some even dead? Or would that be an impossibility?), making possible our constitution as political subjects and even as subjects capable of democracy in ways beyond or perhaps behind our ability to comprehend (Heller-Roazen 2005).

Constitutional law in the United States bears the impression of confronting fascism nowhere more disturbingly than in the internment of Japanese Americans, and the Supreme Court's infamous decision *Korematsu* v. *United States* upholding the conviction of Korematsu for violating the order, which Yoo cites favourably. How has this case been archived previously? The dissenters in *Korematsu* recognized at the time that the decision had fallen into the 'ugly abyss of racism', that the 'legalization of racism' plays no justifiable part in a 'democratic way of life' (with Justice Murphy dissenting at 233, 242). One of the dissenters expressed concern regarding the decision's dangerous repetitive potential, as I have already mentioned.

Peter Irons is the author of the definitive study of the law and politics around the internment of Japanese Americans. Discussing his sources, Irons notes that the decision faced immediate and scathing criticism in major law review articles published as early as 1945. Writing in 1983, Irons finds that in the 'years since the publication of these articles ... not a single legal scholar or writer has attempted a substantive defense of the Supreme Court opinions' (1983: 371).

Aside from the fact that this legal decision found that courts must apply 'strict scrutiny' (a legal term of art meaning that the classification in question must be subjected to the most searching inquiry and that there is the greatest presumption against the constitutionality of the governmental policy at issue) to racial classifications, legal scholars do not view this legal opinion as 'good law'. The decision was made at a time when racial segregation was still allowed in the United States, but the Supreme Court found racial segregation to be unconstitutional in *Brown* v. *Board of Education* (1954). Law students and others who study constitutional law are taught how the racial classification in *Korematsu* cannot stand up to the most basic forms of equal protection analysis (because the classification is under-inclusive by failing to include German or Italian Americans, and because it is also over-inclusive by including both loyal and disloyal Japanese Americans; all of this lets us see that the governmental policy is motivated less by security concerns and more by racism).[14] The conviction of Korematsu has been overturned because the government was found to have committed misconduct through the suppression of evidence and the inclusion of misinformation. And the United States has both apologized and paid reparations to those interned or their families (Sullivan and Gunther 2004: 668–9, fn. 3). As matters of law and policy, *everything* about *Korematsu*, except the notion that there is the strongest presumption against racial classifications, has been repudiated and apologized for.

The democratic narrative of *Korematsu*, based on this archive, is shame and a sense of responsibility for overcoming the outcome of the case, while maintaining the strongest presumption against invidious racial classifications. The ruling was represented as a failure in the struggle against tyranny when it was issued, and in the manner it has been archived since. Yoo's legal opinions attempt to eviscerate the narrative archiving the outcome of *Korematsu* as wrong, and the principle of racial discrimination as wrong for a democratic society. These, as Justice Jackson recognized, are ruinous iterations. The ideas that a president's word is law or that racial guilt is an acceptable premise for government must be excluded to keep democratic commitments or to send the possibility of a legacy hospitable for democracy.

Any archive must have an outside. But an archive also constitutes resources to be drawn upon – at present, and for the future.

Taking a position

No wonder, then, that messianic postmodernists – those who wait for being alien to law – wind up invoking law either to denounce present injustices or to seek a better, more just, or indeed a more democratic and less tyrannical future. If these are our purposes – if we are taking a position against tyranny – then being passively open to infinite possibilities or potentialities will not actively further those commitments. This is why, when we have specific purposes or commitments to which we are faithful, such as taking a position for democracy, or when we critique a process of repetition sedimenting the tyranny of camps in order to open the space for their rejection, we invoke the law and draw from democracy's archive.

Likewise, when Agamben seeks to preserve a community of the faithful who will think the 'relation of every instant to the Messiah', who will 'strain forward' towards salvation, he puts aside the antinomialism of *Homo Sacer* to embrace 'messianic law', or the law of faith (2005b: 76–8, 95). There would be an infinite number of actions (not) to do if the faithful are to make messianic potential become active or operative, if they are to live exclusively in the joyful announcement (*euaggelion*). To be sure, these infinite actions and inactions implicated in *pistis* (faith) would exceed any finite list of dos and don'ts exemplified by the Mosaic law of the Ten Commandments, and messianic law, or *nomos pisteos*, refers to this excessive aspect. How can the faithful know or remember what is required of them at each moment to dwell within messianic law if law is not textualized? Agamben explains, '[I]t is not a letter written in ink on tables of stone; rather, it is written with the breath of God on hearts of flesh'. It is 'not a *writing* but a *form of life* ... "You are our letter"' (2005b: 122, quoting 2 Cor. 3:2, emphasis in original).

This privileging of the spirit over the letter of the law attempts to make calculable, measured law identical to incalculable, immeasurable life by emphasizing the excessive aspect of law, and maintaining law's openness or responsiveness to the future. Through infinite openness, law and life are one, with no ruins or remainders. If, however, 'law' is not to be merely vacuous, infinitely open to anything and everything, hence no law at all, then we must not forget what it means to be faithful *to the messiah*. Appropriately, then, Agamben does not fully forgo textualizing law, citing St Paul's recapitulation of the entirety of God's law with the formula 'Love your neighbor as yourself.' It helps to learn, to know, to remember what is required of the faithful, to recall the messianic. To this end, Agamben refers to law as a '"*pedagogue*" leading to the messiah' (2005b: 76, 120, citing Gal. 3:24, emphasis added). Law is an archive even for those faithful to the messianic.

Similarly, in *State of Exception* Agamben critiques recent practices in the United States, such as the camps at Guantánamo Bay and the USA PATRIOT Act of 2001. He argues, 'At the very moment when it would like to give lessons in democracy to different traditions and cultures, the political culture of the West does not realize that it has entirely lost its canon' (2005a: 18). Here, Agamben denounces the United States, among others, for having lost its law. He condemns people in the United States for forgetting their law and losing their archive, their *aide-mémoire.* Indeed, Agamben rightly denounces them – us – for it. His denunciation – accusing them, us – for forgetting our law pays homage, as Jean Baudrillard would have noted, to the law (1988: 173). His denunciation relies on recalling a law, an archive, and its presently forgotten, suppressed, or repressed democratic commitments. Thus, to the extent that messianic postmodernists are actually concerned with specific principles of justice, democracy, or even the messianic, as opposed to whatever, they contradict their postmodern antinomialism and invoke law.

When we take a position against the abusive exercise of tyrannical sovereign power, as Agamben does, we invoke law. Coming from a position, law combines determinate political commitment with a responsiveness to future circumstances. This paradoxical, if not impossible, combination of determinacy with responsiveness required by popular sovereignty is 'resolved', as we can understand in light of Fitzpatrick's work, by law. The paradoxical co-implication of determination and responsiveness, necessary for popular sovereignty to be, is why democracy relies on law.

The sense of pure whatever potentiality Agamben promotes corresponds with the dimension of law as infinite openness tending to vacuity. If law is figured solely as vacuous, then it is open to anything, even to Yoo. Law, however, comes from and returns to a position, and understanding law as democracy's archive is an attunement to the determinate place and commitments from which we begin, again. Any archival practice supplementing our memory of positive commitments to democracy, of re-calling our (democratic) selves to our selves, of re-calling society's commitment to democracy or principles of justice to society, must necessarily have an outside. So, an archive of democratic commitments – a law dedicated to democracy – must also be constituted through exclusions if we seek faithfully to keep or to promise the prospect of democracy. This legal archive is animated through a negative relation to tyrannies. As we enumerate tyrannical mentalities and deeds, we will be engaged, in part, with the project of constituting an archive for democracy, a law to keep democracy for the future. When we labour, in our fidelity to resisting tyranny, among democracy's ruins, we are engaging in a practice of re-calling and re-sending democracy, faithful to its coming, labouring for its return. Perhaps.

Therefore, when we engage in critique of camps, and the way that some legal thought reintroduces this potentiality, we re-send our archived commitments against this tyranny as a faithful pledge to the future. In other words, the constituent force of law may indeed generate the 'very social bond of modernity, the means of our relation and being-with each other' (Golder and Fitzpatrick 2009: 85). But what manner of sociality, of 'being-with each other', shall we endure, share, or aspire to? What manner of being are we starting from, orienting towards, or have we vowed to keep for the time being? If our position is a democratic resistance to camps, then we will not be content to remain open to all potentialities, including camps – not when we have commitments to which we must remain faithful. Law as democracy's archive is our resistance to forgetting these commitments. An archive is a 'pledge' of the future (Derrida 1995: 18). Likewise, law as democracy's archive is a pledge of and for the future, a future we have no certain grounds for knowing will keep this pledge, much as we have no certain grounds to count on just democracy ourselves, not as we begin again among democracy's ruins. There is, however, no democracy 'without an act of faith' (Derrida 2005: 48).

Much as we must begin our labours among democracy's ruins, John Yoo has been hard at work already. Yoo's numerous legal memos written on behalf of the Bush administration, many of which remain secret as of this writing, constitute a warp. As geological layers evidence a protrusion, or another force repressed by layers of sediment, so too do these memos. Even their very numerousness serves to remind us of the doubts they are intended to cover over, the democratic doubt they are meant to contain.

Yoo is also currently at work writing books, publishing law review articles, uploading SSRN (Social Science Research Network) papers, crafting op-eds, presenting congressional testimony, giving interviews, teaching law school courses, and responding to government reports questioning his faithfulness to the law. He is an archivist as well, seeking to invent the legal archive that will have justified his earlier work. This is why we must persist in our faithful labours among democracy's ruins. Otherwise, democracy's archive will be put to a 'new use' and will be 'play[ed] with just as children play with disused objects'. It will become like the dead letter Agamben's 'new attorney' reads bemusedly, but without attachment, 'leafing through "our old books"' (2005a: 63–4).

Conclusion

In this chapter I have argued that recent postmodern aversions to law and sovereignty, such as the work of Agamben, which favours the coming of a new ontology – a messianic preoccupation with the absolute arrival of new being exterior to law or sovereignty – is not helpful in addressing present tyrannies and injustices. Fitzpatrick's work on sovereignty, emphasizing its tension between finite determination and extensive, encompassing responsiveness, indicates a more productive post-structuralism. Rather than a picture of absolute determination, Fitzpatrick shows how sovereignty must also be determinate. The impossibility of pure sovereignty elucidates the vulnerabilities popular sovereignty faces – the way that democracy is vulnerable to ruin. Any beginning, such as a democratic beginning, must commence on terms not of its own making. Therefore, there is never just democracy here. Fitzpatrick's understanding of sovereignty, and the way that a fraught combination of determinacy and responsiveness takes place through law, allows us to comprehend, then, the dual impossibilities of absolute sovereignty and absolute democracy. Contemporary law and politics take place within the torsion of these impossibilities.

Law, which is where popular sovereignty undergoes continual constitution, must come from a position, and it must also return to a position or a place. It is where we take a position on democracy, and it is where we archive democracy's ruins in resistance to the necessary finitude of our being forgetful human beings. If an archive is a pledge to the future, then considering law as democracy's archive means that it is with-in law that we recall principles of democracy and justice to ourselves, and send, again, this legacy to the future. In other words, we do not begin our struggles against the camps with a vacuous receptivity to pure potentiality that cannot take a position. We begin, again, in democracy's archive, with democratic remains. It is there that we find the legal principles that gave place to us, those of equal protection, due process, and that political leaders must take care that those laws are faithfully executed that are anathema to the camps. We can find these determinate commitments in democracy's archive, recall them, and extend these determinations faithfully as a response to the tyrannies of today, for the future. It is with-in democracy's archive where democracy undergoes a process of 'continual constitution'.

What is the fate of law and democracy after Yoo? Rather than a messianic aversion to law or politics, Fitzpatrick's work points us in the direction of recommencing our labours among democracy's ruins. It points us to the persistence of law, the possibility of democracy, and the faithful labours necessary to resist tyranny. We cannot expect a messianic blow to replace, totally, a non-existent absolute sovereignty, without ruin or remainder. Because of the impossibility of absolute democracy and absolute sovereignty, we must start where we are, in the torsion of politics, labouring among democracy's ruins, reconstructing its archive, if we want better than Yoo gives us. Democracy is never just here. It is never *just* here. This is the urgency of law and of politics.

Acknowledgement

I would like to thank Ruth Buchanan for reading an earlier version of this chapter, and Jodi Dean's sharp attention to detail in her reading of the essay's penultimate inception.

Notes

1 'Here, the application of these statutes to the conduct of interrogations of unlawful combatants would deprive the sovereign of a recognized prerogative' (Yoo 2003: 15).
2 I address the problem of camps here. For a discussion of unchecked presidentialism and its relation to torture in the United States, see Passavant (2010).
3 Here my argument tracks Passavant (2007).
4 What follows builds from Fitzpatrick (2005, 2007). Peter was kind enough to share with me his conference paper 'Surpassing sovereignty' before he delivered it. In turn, it formed the major ground of my discussion when I presented the first version of this paper at his 'fest-conference'. Thus, I was technically commenting upon a work to come, as it were.
5 Agamben, however, and to his detriment, feels compelled to try to 'correct' Foucault.
6 In the prior paragraph, Fitzpatrick notes the 'involving legalism' of one of Agamben's main sources for *homo sacer*.
7 I attempt to be fairly specific in identifying tyrannical attributes of contemporary politics in Passavant (2009); Jacques Rancière argues in relation to Agamben that politics is about disputes in counting, of drawing lines between different lives or who is concerned in a particular question, where politics brings the line drawn back into question (2004: 303). Iris Marion Young (1990) discusses a variety of forms of injustice.
8 On the coming community as singularities without qualification, see Agamben (1993: 1–2, 18–19, 67, 85–7).
9 Derrida (2002a: 238–41) discusses a fragment from Blaise Pascal to consider these dual goals of justice in order to argue that 'force is an essential predicate of justice' (at 240).
10 On the paradoxes of democracy, see Mouffe (2000), Keenan (2003), and Derrida (2002a).
11 In this paragraph I have been inspired by Fitzpatrick (2001: 52, 54, 73).
12 These particular camps do not follow precisely from Yoo's arguments since they are not located in the United States. Yoo is considering the legality of creating camps within the United States and interning American citizens.
13 Hence I disagree with Rancière (1999), to the extent that he equates politics with democracy.
14 See Tussman and tenBroek (1949: 341–81) for a discussion of the logic of equal protection analysis and critical commentary upon the Japanese internment cases. According to the authors, 'the Court can hardly be said to have made an adequate investigation of the genuineness of the emergency and of the good faith in dealing with it', and they remark upon long-standing 'anti-Oriental animus on the West Coast' (ibid.: 374). Although this classic essay on equal protection reasoning was long excerpted and archived within Gunther's *Constitutional Law* (1975, 1980) to teach students of law the basics of equal protection analysis, and more specifically the critical weaknesses of the Court's equal protection analysis in *Korematsu,* I regret to note that Kathleen Sullivan has removed it as she has taken over editorship of this classic casebook in constitutional law (Sullivan and Gunther 2010). I fear we may forget that internment camps wrongly violate the 'unfinished Constitutional struggle for democracy', marked by the '*pledge* of the protection of equal laws' (342, 381, quoting Justice Matthews, emphasis added).

References

Agamben, G. (1993) *The Coming Community*, trans. M. Hardt, Minneapolis: University of Minnesota Press.

Agamben, G. (1998) *Homo Sacer: Sovereign Power and Bare Life*, trans. D. Heller-Roazen, Stanford, CA: Stanford University Press.

Agamben, G. (1999) 'On potentiality', trans. D. Heller-Roazen, in D. Heller-Roazen (ed.) *Potentialities*, Stanford, CA: Stanford University Press.

Agamben, G. (2002) *Remnants of Auschwitz: The Witness and the Archive*, trans. D. Heller-Roazen, New York: Zone Books.

Agamben, G. (2005a) *State of Exception*, trans. K. Attell, Chicago: University of Chicago Press.

Agamben, G. (2005b) *The Time That Remains: A Commentary on the Letter to the Romans*, trans. P. Dailey, Stanford, CA: Stanford University Press.

Austin, J. L. (1962) *How to Do Things with Words*, Cambridge, MA: Harvard University Press.

Badiou, A. (2001) *Ethics: An Essay on the Understanding of Evil*, trans. P. Hallward, London: Verso.

Badiou, A. (2003) *Saint Paul: The Foundation of Universalism*, trans. R. Brassier, Stanford, CA: Stanford University Press.

Baudrillard, J. (1988) 'Simulacra and simulations', in M. Poster (ed.) *Jean Baudrillard: Selected Writings*, Stanford, CA: Stanford University Press.

Brown v. Board of Education, 347 US 483 (1954).

Derrida, J. (1995) *Archive Fever: A Freudian Impression*, trans. E. Prenowitz, Chicago: University of Chicago Press.

Derrida, J. (2000) *Of Hospitality*, trans. R. Bowlby, Stanford, CA: Stanford University Press.

Derrida, J. (2002a) 'Force of law: The "mystical foundation of authority"', trans. M. Quaintance, in *Acts of Religion*, ed. G. Anidjar, New York: Routledge.

Derrida, J. (2002b) 'Hostipitality', trans. M. Quaintance, in *Acts of Religion*, ed. G. Anidjar, New York: Routledge.

Derrida, J. (2005) *Rogues: Two Essays on Reason*, trans. P. A. Brault and M. Nass, Stanford, CA: Stanford University Press.

Fitzpatrick, P. (1992) *The Mythology of Modern Law*, London: Routledge.

Fitzpatrick, P. (2001) *Modernism and the Grounds of Law*, Cambridge: Cambridge University Press.

Fitzpatrick, P. (2005) 'Bare sovereignty: *Homo sacer* and the insistence of law', in A. Norris (ed.) *Politics, Metaphysics, and Death: Essays on Giorgio Agamben's Homo Sacer*, Durham, NC: Duke University Press.

Fitzpatrick, P. (2007) 'Surpassing sovereignty', paper presented at the Law and Society Association Annual Meeting, Berlin, 24–27 July.

Foucault, M. (1982) 'The subject and power', *Critical Inquiry* 8: 777–95.

Gasché, R. (1999) *Of Minimal Things: Studies on the Notion of Relation*, Stanford, CA: Stanford University Press.

Golder, B. and Fitzpatrick, P. (2009) *Foucault's Law*, London: Routledge.

Gunther, G. (1975; 10th edn 1980) *Cases and Materials on Constitutional Law*, 9th edn, New York: Foundation Press.

Hardt, M. and Negri, A. (2000) *Empire*, Cambridge, MA: Harvard University Press.

Heller-Roazen, H. (2005) *Echolalias: On the Forgetting of Language*, New York: Zone Books.

International Committee of the Red Cross (ICRC) (2007) 'ICRC report on the treatment of fourteen "high value detainees" in CIA custody', February. Online, available at: www.nybooks.com/icrc-report.pdf (accessed 8 April 2009).

Irons, P. (1983) *Justice at War: The Story of the Japanese Internment Cases*, New York: Oxford University Press.

Keenan, A. (2003) *Democracy in Question*, Stanford, CA: Stanford University Press.

Korematsu v. United States, 323 US 214 (1944).

Meillassoux, Q. (2008) *After Finitude: An Essay on the Necessity of Contingency*, trans. R. Brassier, London: Continuum.

Mills, C. (2008) *The Philosophy of Agamben*, Kingston, Ontario: McGill-Queen's University Press.

Mouffe, C. (2000) *The Democratic Paradox*, New York: Verso.

Passavant, P. A. (2007) 'The contradictory state of Giorgio Agamben', *Political Theory* 35: 147–74.

Passavant, P. A. (2009) 'We should be liberals (at least)', *Law, Culture and the Humanities* 5: 173–93.

Passavant, P. A. (2010) 'Yoo's law, sovereignty, and whatever', *Constellations* 17: 549–71.

Rancière, J. (1999) *Dis-agreement*, trans. J. Rose, Minneapolis: University of Minnesota Press.

Rancière, J. (2004) 'Who is the subject of the rights of man?', *South Atlantic Quarterly* 103: 297–310.

Schmitt, C. (1988) *Political Theology*, trans. G. Schwab, Cambridge, MA: MIT Press.

Schmitt, C. (1996) *Concept of the Political*, trans. G Schwab, Chicago: University of Chicago Press.

Sullivan, K. and Gunther, G. (1997; 2004 15th edn; 2010 17th edn), *Constitutional Law*, 13th edn, New York: Foundation Press.

Tussman, J. and tenBroek, J. (1949) 'The equal protection of the laws', *California Law Review* 37: 341–81.

Yoo, J. (2003) 'Memorandum for William J. Haynes II, General Counsel of the Department of Defense, Re: Military interrogation of alien unlawful combatants held outside the United States', Washington, DC: Office of Legal Counsel, US Department of Justice, 14 March.

Yoo, J. (2005) *The Powers of War and Peace*, Chicago: University of Chicago Press.

Young, I. M. (1990) *Justice and the Politics of Difference*, Princeton, NJ: Princeton University Press.

Chapter 5

Living in international law

Fleur Johns

Introduction

In international law, Peter Fitzpatrick locates a possibility. That possibility inheres in Fitzpatrick's vision of an international law in which the truncation of certain ethical claims is 'not so generalized' – in which openness to or of those claims is 'more receptively maintained' – than in (most) municipal law (Fitzpatrick 2003: 457). That there may be something 'positively and resistantly "in"' international law and that the 'something' in question may not (always or entirely) be reducible to power, *imperium*, sovereignty, nationalism, humanity, or some other 'Eternal Object' is a recurring theme of Fitzpatrick's gentle goading to the discipline (ibid.: 441, 458). In that claim, Fitzpatrick both communes with international law in its contemporary incarnations and, in a variety of ways, stands apart from it.

This chapter will trace some of the distinctive inflections of Fitzpatrick's note amid the cacophony that is international legal scholarship. It will seek to explore, in particular, that note's perplexing relation to a predominant chord within the discipline: that of pragmatism. In so doing, this chapter draws attention to one of the most vital and distinctive dimensions of Fitzpatrick's contribution to legal scholarship, international and otherwise: its rhythm. In Fitzpatrick's work one sees enacted a practice of reading and re-reading – a rhythm of pause, attention, return, unfolding – that that is as much a contribution to international legal scholarship as the words in which it is enveloped.

In examining the method and metre of Fitzpatrick's engagement with international law, this chapter looks primarily to chapter 5 of Fitzpatrick's 2001 book *Modernism and the Grounds of Law* and his 2003 article in the *Leiden Journal of International Law*. It begins by focusing on the lawfulness that Fitzpatrick would have us recognize in international law – that is, in Fitzpatrick's term, positivity (as distinct from positivism). This call to recognize the potency of positivity will be related here to modern international law's invocation of 'the social' as a strategy for renewing and reorienting the discipline. Far from conforming with the trajectories of international legal thought, however, Fitzpatrick's engagement with international law works against some of its governing tendencies. This chapter then turns to the uneasy relationship of Fitzpatrick's work to international law's (more or less) prevailing pragmatic, anti-formal disposition. Finally, the chapter concludes by focusing on the tempo of Fitzpatrick's work. In the cadence of his writing, and the gentle persistence with which he reaches from text to reader and back again – slowly folding and unfolding a set of ideas – this chapter discerns an enactment of the theorization of international law that Fitzpatrick advances. That is, it locates in Fitzpatrick's 'method' of pacing and punctuating his work a critical practice – hints of a way of living *in* and *with* – rather than a methodological key unlocking some untapped repository of knowledge (cf. Charlesworth 2004).

Law with qualities

To a discipline long wearied of defending its lawfulness, Fitzpatrick's writing has brought a characteristically generous gift: celebrate, he has said, that which is 'positively and resistantly "in"' international law (2003: 458); its failure is, he argues, its fruitfulness. There is something deliciously contrarian about such an appeal to the positive. For the post-war discipline of international law has tended to measure its 'success' in terms of its cleaving close to power, and this 'success' has, in turn, been seen to depend on its capacity to empty itself more or less of anything enduringly positive. Instead, international lawyers have sought to navigate what one international lawyer has described as a dynamic of 'ascending' and 'descending' lines of argument (Koskenniemi 2006) – to live what Robert Musil (1952–3) might have characterized as a 'hovering life'. All this has been, on occasions, with a view to speaking 'truth to power' from the margins of decision-making. Yet it has also been in the hope of remaining proximate enough to power to whisper sweet nothings or avuncular words of reproach in its proverbial ear, or so it is often seen (Koskenniemi 2004: 482–94; Berman 1999: 1525).

In place of this savvy, sometimes self-righteous and sometimes servile navigation, Fitzpatrick would have us plunge into the void between the 'inter' and the 'nation', or between, to borrow Fitzpatrick's terminology, the 'responsive' and the 'determinate' dimensions of international law (Fitzpatrick 2001: 33–4; 2003: 440) and to find that space inhabited by peoples other than statesmen, diplomats, and imperial valets (more on those inhabitants in a moment). In Fitzpatrick's account, international law possesses content – a 'life' (2003: 458) – that 'resists and counters *imperium*'; or at least it might. The positivity which Fitzpatrick would have international lawyers cherish is not, however, that of positivism (2001: 70–84; 2003: 432). The 'law' of international law in which this resistance resides is both extant and something other than a body of law to which positive reference may be made. It may be discerned in the 'efficacy' of international law whereby 'dissonance or divergence' persists in the relation between international law and empire (Fitzpatrick 2003: 465; cf. Derrida 1987). Yet its amenability to being carried into 'law made determinate' remains in question in view of the 'absence of "overarching" markers of law within international law' (Fitzpatrick 2003: 458, 466).

In this respect, Fitzpatrick's project to make international law rule anew *as law* parallels scholarly effort to rejuvenate 'the political' as against the givens of politics and prevailing political programmes. The persistent figure of 'the law' within international law to which Fitzpatrick would have international lawyers be more attentive can, like 'the political', 'only be discussed by reflecting on society's (absent) ground, not by describing society's structural or institutional differentiation'. The law in this sense stands opposed to 'the "ontic" practices of conventional [legalism]', just as 'the political' stands opposed to politics as 'the particular and, eventually, always unsuccessful attempts at grounding society' (Marchart 2007: 52, 57; cf. Mouffe 2005: 9). This rendering of 'the law' stands for an ever-present capacity to displace or oppose one or other international legalism that seems to prevail at any given moment – a capacity that is coextensive with that very prevalence and as such depends not on looking 'forward,... backward, no[r] in all eternity' (Nietzsche 2000: 714).

Sociologic

In Fitzpatrick's work, this ever-present capacity has quite a precise significance. For Fitzpatrick, paraphrasing Jean-Luc Nancy, international law is a 'place where community as such is brought into play' (Nancy 1991: xxxvii). Fitzpatrick's effort to demarcate a theoretical site at which international law's lawfulness is produced and to 'find' that site inhabited is, for this reader, to evoke the peripatetic lineage of 'the social' in international law, a lineage that is quite distinct from the pedigree of that term within political theory – the latter indicated, for example, in Arendtian thought (Pitkin 1998: 3–4). This is the first sense in which I should like to configure the relationship between Fitzpatrick's writings on international law and other incarnations of this discipline: by relating Fitzpatrick's insistence upon what he calls a 'sociologic' (or elsewhere a solidary 'ethics of the existent') to recurring attempts to restore to international law an imperative if paradoxical sociality (Fitzpatrick 2003: 438, 451, 454).

In international law, impulses towards solidary renewal of and through law have been related to, though not wholly synonymous with, broader trajectories of thinking 'the social' in law. In Duncan Kennedy's work the term is shorthand for the rise and diffusion of 'socially oriented legal thought' over the first two-thirds of the twentieth century impelled by 'the failure of coherently individualist law to respond to the ... social needs of modern conditions of interdependence' – in particular, 'the problem of war, understood as the product of failures of an international order based on the logic of sovereignty' (Kennedy 2006: 19, 38). In other words, as Austin Sarat has put it, 'the liberal rationality of government associated with laissez faire and methodological individualism was generally reordered around the social as terrain for positive knowledge' (2004: 5).

In international law this reorientation partially took the form of an 'instrumental subjection of law' to 'an idea of society as a "ruling idea"' – an idea that Fitzpatrick dubs yet another 'overweening sovereignty' (2003: 438). Yet international legal theorists have also generated a sense of sociality in law that does not depend on society (or social fact of one kind or another) simply accounting for itself, such that the possibilities of law are wholly expressed in variants of the prevailing social order. Rather, international lawyers have long sought to articulate an idea of society that, in Fitzpatrick's terms, exceeds 'what is "for the time being"' and does so, moreover, 'in law' (ibid.: 440).

Such an orientation animated, for instance, Georg Jellinek's late-nineteenth-century insistence upon the 'normative power of the factual' (1929: 338). For Jellinek, law did not arise from 'the soul of the people by which it is sanctioned, nor from the common conviction that something is law on the strength of its inner necessity, nor from a silent act of the people's will', but rather from shared perceptions of the quotidian extant – 'from the general psychological human characteristic that regards the constantly repeated fact as normative' (ibid., quoted in Weinberger 1991: 26). A 'community of individuals' exhibiting such psychological characteristics retained 'an original power to rule', by self-restraint, in the furtherance of its own interest (Jellinek 1929: 180–1, cf. 161). Yet no legal expression of that 'community' could ever exhaust its existence; any particular rule of international law was always subordinate to the law-making capacity of the 'community'.

Of course, Fitzpatrick does not share Jellinek's optimism about 'the intrinsic rationality of the European political order' such that 'the self-legislating freedom of States would not lead into anarchy or imperialism' (Koskenniemi 2004: 207). What is shared is the sense in which law's 'infinite possibility has to be drawn in repeatedly' (Fitzpatrick 2003: 444) in order to account for the concrete.

This drawing in of possibility through close examination of the ways that law sustains 'the sociologic' (Fitzpatrick 2003: 444) enlivened too the solidarism advocated by Alejandro Álvarez in the first half of the twentieth century (Obregón 2006). For Álvarez, the renewal of international law depended upon an abandonment of 'the pretensions of absolute sovereignty' as well as the belief that 'the law has an existence in and of itself, or that it is founded on human nature' in favour of an international law 'that is the product of its surroundings': the work of a 'juridical consciousness ... in perpetual evolution' (Álvarez 1918–19: 34, 37).

More recently, a concern with the 'sociologic' embedded in international law's effective dynamics has animated the reflexive sociologies of Yves Dezalay and Bryant Garth (1996, 2002a) and the studies that their work has inspired (Dezalay and Garth 2002b). In Dezalay and Garth's writings the international legal order appears as both a product of, and a stake in, competitive struggles among governing elites in many nations – struggles characterized as 'palace wars' (1996: 11; 2002a: 5). Far from being an inert instrument of power, however, international law is positioned 'at the core of the processes that structure, produce, and reproduce the field[s] of power' as 'symbolic fields with specific logics' (2002a: 5, 13). Like Fitzpatrick's (2003: 444), Dezalay and Garth's account of the imperial work of law is one of both dependence and independence.

It may seem odd to compare Fitzpatrick's approach to writing international law with sociological research so explicitly empirical as that of Dezalay and Garth (Garth 2007). Qualitative data sets, professional biographies, and institutional genealogies – these are not features of Fitzpatrick's work. Likewise, the comparison to a scholar as programmatic and modernist as Álvarez may seem inapt – concerned, as Álvarez was, with the systematization, renewal, and universalization of an international law identified explicitly with Latin American history and interests (Becker Lorca 2006; Esquirol 2006; Landauer 2006). So too the comparison with Jellinek might take readers aback: a neo-Kantian defender of the *Rechtsstaat* Fitzpatrick is most certainly not (see generally Lindenfeld 1997; Kelly 2004).

Nonetheless, the connection that may be drawn among this unlikely grouping of scholars arises from the provocative or resistant inflection of their divergent gestures to the social within international law, and their attention to the propensity for international law to overflow its 'ties to the pre-existent' (Fitzpatrick 2003: 445). In Fitzpatrick's hands, as (to varying degrees) in the hands of the scholars named, amplifying the sociality of international law has not entailed an attempt to affix that law to a 'reassuring materiality' (Fitzpatrick 2001: 157). Rather, gesturing to the social has been a way for international lawyers to enact negotiability within and through international law. Invocations of 'the social' within international legal thought have taken on a variety of political tenors (see generally Kennedy 2006). Yet throughout, the turn to 'the social' has been a marker of unease. It has coincided with an impetus towards a 'something else' latent within the here, and a persistent dissatisfaction with one or other effort of 'reform' as such. As Kennedy writes of the rise and spread of 'the social' in legal thought between 1900 and 1968 and its 'legacies', 'It was not just a matter of reconceptualizing, reformulating, and then reforming the maladaptive, ideologically individualist doctrinal substance.... The antiformalist strand in the social current emphasized gaps, conflicts, and ambiguities in the corpus of positive law' (2006: 45). That the terms of this engagement are, in Fitzpatrick's case, meta-ethical or meta-political (not, it must be said, in Rancière's sense (1999: 61–94)), rather than directed towards the purification of law per se, is made obvious, in his account, in part by the personages by whom international law's sociality is inhabited at its fraught inception. Those personages are the Catholic theologian Francisco de Vitoria and the 'Indians' of the Americas (Fitzpatrick 2003: 447–9). To read international law as structurally dependent on the irrecuperable alterity of the 'savage' in the violence of the colonial encounter, as Fitzpatrick does, is to read it away from any lulling re-inscription of its modern antinomies (cf. Fitzpatrick 2001: 11–36). In this respect one can, in passing, relate Fitzpatrick's work on international law to the work of Antony Anghie, Nathaniel Berman, and Annelise Riles, three international legal scholars long engaged in a productive rewriting of modern international law's genealogies, in part by locating its structural and stylistic genesis in the colonial encounter (Anghie 1999, 2004; Berman 1999; Riles 1995). Each has, in different ways, argued for colonial confrontations between European and non-European peoples to be seen as central to the formation of international law and to many of its doctrines, institutions, discursive tics, and characteristic preoccupations (see, for example, Fitzpatrick 2001: 146–82).

For all the humility and humour of his writing, however, accommodating or affirming international law's scholarly or disciplinary lineage has not been Fitzpatrick's goal. His engagements with international law have been characteristically thoughtful, but they have been neither timid nor acquiescent. Indeed, in some respects they are quite antithetical to the inclinations of the discipline.

Anti-anti-formalism

Despite the qualified parallels drawn above, the terms of Fitzpatrick's engagements with the 'universal content' (Fitzpatrick 2003: 460) of international law are likely to strike many in the disciple as unfamiliar – unfamiliar, that is, both in target and in tempo. Let us turn our attention first to the former: the critical objectives to which Fitzpatrick's writing seems directed.

Fitzpatrick's work seeks to provide for the 'drawing in of content to [international] law' as such, or rather, a 'generative intimation of such content', without that content demanding any 'constituent commitment' or 'primal attachment' (2003: 440, 444, 456). The content in question is to be '*some* being-in-common inhabiting and limiting [social] entities "in" their very distinctness' or some 'regardful community of law' (ibid.: 440, 466). This strategy strikes me as both defensive and offensive. In its offensive mode its target is the pretence to monadic solidity of each and every

'Eternal Object' (to adopt Fitzpatrick's preferred phrase: 1992: 49; 2003: 441). Primary among such objects for international law, in Fitzpatrick's reading, are the sovereign nation and the would-be sovereign scholar-statesman. Defensively, then, this drawing in is a drawing away from international law's instrumental subordination to exterior content, in part by showing that exterior content to be constitutively suffused by law.

This insistence upon something 'positively and resistantly "in"' international law (Fitzpatrick 2003: 458) strikes a discordant note because international law has come to understand itself, in large part, as a discipline of negation. This is something Fitzpatrick (ibid.: 443, 448, 460) acknowledges, yet it is a schema not easily dispensed with or argued away. For instance, accommodations to realist political science notwithstanding, the critique of sovereignty – or the attempt to negate the force and centrality of unfettered sovereign will – has long been, and continues to be, functionally deployed as a way for the discipline to renew and extend itself (Kennedy 1994, 2000; Marks 2006). This propensity to renew through negation is related to the chronic (albeit not terminal) anti-formalism of modern international law. In view of these disciplinary proclivities, to speak in terms of positive content or enduring ethics (even in the open and generative terms in which Fitzpatrick does) is likely to strike the international lawyer in the street, so to speak, as risky, possibly even retrogressive.

Of course, this risk may be one to be relished. The international lawyer may look in vain for affirmative evidence of this ethical content or, pragmatically speaking, its effects. No programme offers itself up in Fitzpatrick's work for those who would seek it. The ethos of which Fitzpatrick writes is a question of experience, yes, but also a question of faith, and above all a *question*.

Yet the acuity of critically engaging international law in these terms remains, itself, open to question. Modern international law's relative anti-formalism may explain, in part, its articulation with the diffuse, masterless promise with which capital comes so devastatingly loaded. For all the claims and condemnation voiced in its terms, international law often seems to speak most persistently in an enabling mode: smoothing the globe into a frictionless whole in one or other mould, welcoming the obstreperous, the insufficiently secular, and the inefficient onto its ever-lengthening to-do list. In this mode, international law is always open for business; ever willing to digest a 'new' idea, another 'perspective'; always reaching out and moving on. Against this, one wonders whether Fitzpatrick's appeals to positive content can insinuate themselves into the comfortable, elastic cosmopolitanism with which international law bewails global inequities, let alone address those inequities.

In the 'irreducible openness' of international law, in its never being tied to any 'pre-existent differentiation', Fitzpatrick locates an 'incipient ethic of equality' (2003: 444). Given modern international law's perennial launchings into openness, there is something worryingly reassuring about this promise. Holding things open seems, in many ways, international law's default posture. If mastery no longer purports to inhabit a master – and no longer affects the 'overweening' affect of autarchic force – should one associate an unsettling of the monad (sovereign or societal) with a move towards some incipient equality? Does hierarchy supervene, above all, at the moment of determination or through the assertion of dependence, or has it colonized the anterior as well? And if so, might the mode of that colonization be not an insistence upon 'conjoint insularity' but rather insistence upon an 'inextinguishable openness' (Fitzpatrick 2003: 454, 464)?

To be sure, the Bushes, Kagans, Bobbits, and Fukuyamas of this world have been ranting and raving over the past decade or two, to the tune of a rising body count (with many yet uncounted). But are *they* the high priests of inequality or its opportunistic beneficiaries? Cheney walked and talked like a Sun King, and sometimes it has *seemed* as though the World Bank were ruling the world. However, such figures and institutions have repeatedly abjected themselves before unattributed 'business interests' and narratives of freedom, and those interests and narratives seem more viral than monadically founded. The rhetoric of the Bush administration was beguiling in its directness. The 2002 US National Security Strategy (exemplary in Fitzpatrick's 2003 article) may have been a relatively easy target (cf. Byers and Nolte 2003). What, then, becomes of the 'incipient ethic of equality' in the time of Obama? Where are critical footholds to be found within the global change-a-thon in which international law is currently immersed? Does Fitzpatrick's appeal to 'inextinguishable openness' have the same potency at a time of 'transparency' and let's-make-this-work-centrism (Obama 2009a, b, c)?

All openness is evidently not made the same: this is the point that Fitzpatrick makes when he talks about the 'contained "openness"' of the United States' National Security Strategy (2003: 464). Still, I worry that modes of constraint other than containment might too readily evade a critical project so framed. Here one might recall Foucault's premonition that 'the author function will disappear, and in such a manner that … polysemous texts will once again function according to another mode, but still with a system of constraint … which will have to be … perhaps, experienced' (1977: 119). It could of course be the case that rallying what might otherwise be 'in' international law, if only evanescently, *is* an effective way of critically engaging the more or less authorless international law of today. There are certainly others who think so. Martti Koskenniemi is an important ally in Fitzpatrick's mission from within the international legal establishment: witness Koskenniemi's appeal to cultivate a 'culture of formalism' within international law, continually reaching towards a horizon of universality (2004: 494–509). Just as Fitzpatrick appeals to a positivity that does not correspond to positivism, so Koskenniemi's 'culture of formalism' is insistently not formalism as customarily known.

Nonetheless, I wonder about Fitzpatrick's inclination to dispense with the pragmatic anti-formalism by which so much international legal scholarship is inflected, reading it as yielding a 'law determined by external objectives, structures or necessities' (Koskenniemi 2004: 508), or 'mere instrumentalism' (Fitzpatrick 2003: 457). At their best moments, critiques in the anti-formal vernacular yield, rather, narratives of incompletion – accounts, that is, of the leakiness of international law as a receptacle for power, and the pervasiveness of that law within the very structures and objects on which it supposedly depends. 'Mere' instrumentalism does not rule every pragmatic page.

In this readiness to reject a dominant dialect, it is as if Fitzpatrick's contributions to international law enact yet another encounter between Europe and the Americas. Of course, to place Fitzpatrick's work 'in' Europe is to gut its unsettled core. Yet let me be reckless and reductive enough to try to chart a mutual antagonism in these terms, by reference to terrain: this more or less European terrain of resistant interiority (painfully attentive to the exteriority within) seems remote from the more or less North American field of unfolded exteriority (cut through with ambivalent interiority) that is its sometime target. What distinguishes itself as critique on one terrain presents as 'subject to the censorships of ... pure reading' on the other (Bourdieu 1984: 494). We see (without the same geographic inflection) a comparable antagonism at work in Pierre Bourdieu's rejection of Jacques Derrida's reading of Kant's *Critique of Judgement* in *Distinction* (ibid.: 494–6). Bourdieu regarded Derrida's reading as 'circumscribed by the interests linked to membership in the philosophical field', a field from which Derrida's text was, in Bourdieu's account, unable to withdraw (ibid.: 495–6). So, too, Fitzpatrick's work might strike some international legal readers as overly invested in mastery of a 'repository of consecrated texts' (ibid.: 496), while Fitzpatrick, in turn, seems to read much international legal scholarship as tethered to one or other 'ruling idea' or idea of rule (2003: 438).

Perhaps, in part, what emerges in Fitzpatrick's work on international law is a phenomenon on which Frederic Jameson remarks: the 'fundamental dissymmetry between the United States and other cultures' (1998: 63). If the encounter between Fitzpatrick's formidable critical faculties and the unwieldy (yet rather US-dominated) field of international law is marked by some degree of dissymmetry and disregard – each for another way of living critically in international law – then it serves only to recall the difficulty of maintaining the sort of 'regardful community' of which Fitzpatrick writes (2003: 445) – a difficulty continually stressed in Fitzpatrick's work.

Rhythms of regard

Recalling this difficulty brings me, finally, to the rhythm of incantation in Fitzpatrick's work. Among the qualities that have struck me in reading Fitzpatrick's work are its patient insistence; the gentle persistence of his reading and re-reading. His work betrays unwillingness to compromise alongside the most attentive regard for what has come before and what might yet come after. This rhythm of returning and unfolding lends Fitzpatrick's work a distinctive tempo: a tactus that one experiences in the company of the person – a presence at once monastic and expansive. This rhythm stands apart from the jangling beats of scholarly fad. On occasion it seems to bespeak another time altogether – a way of living in international law unfamiliar to many of its minute-managing, jet-hopping, page-flipping practitioners. This tempo is measured historically, and yet measureless in standard progressive terms. And it is this tempo, above all, that conveys to me some sense of what Fitzpatrick is evoking when he intones the ethics of the existent within international law. At this tempo, Fitzpatrick's work generates a mode of existence within international law and within the legal academy: a mode not reducible to expressive values, formal transformations, themes, or concepts (Foucault 1977: 117).

In the face of ever-burgeoning academic managerialism and associated emphasis upon inputs and outputs of a measurable kind, the tempo at which Fitzpatrick's work demands reading – and the tempo of rumination to which it testifies – might enact one version of an 'art of not being governed [like that] quite so much' (Foucault 1997a: 28–9). This suggests a way of living in the academy, but it may suggest a way of living in the international legal academy in particular. For it could be that international law has been especially afflicted by the impulse to hasten on to the next issue, text, or crisis (Charlesworth 2002), rotations and returns notwithstanding (Kennedy 2000).

In this sense, the alienation of Fitzpatrick's work from predominant tendencies in international legal thinking may be more than a matter of geography or training. It may be a matter of critical attitude, and associated withdrawal or sequestration. Far from issuing a set of ethical or political prescriptions, Fitzpatrick's work communicates, through 'the tempo of [its] signs', an 'inward state' (which is, at the same time, an outward state – a matter as much of doing as of thinking) with potential ethical and political implications (Nietzsche 2000: 721). For Fitzpatrick's work sustains this tempo at a cost – at the expense, for instance, of realistic prospects of popular or policy embrace, particularly among those for whom cost–benefit analysis of one kind or another is the reliable measure of worth. In its refusal to accommodate prevailing predilections for measurement (a refusal as much of pace as of argument), Fitzpatrick's work enacts a critique of much that is taken for granted in international legal policymaking and in the institutional settings in which it is produced. In this sense, that which may read, for some, as a 'philosophy of truth in general' – and indeed seems to share some of the stylistic properties of that mode of reflection – might be experienced instead as a contingent recasting (and thereby enlarging) of 'the present field of possible experiences', including those of reading, writing, studying, and teaching in international law (Foucault 1997b: 100).

Conclusion

If Fitzpatrick's interventions in the international legal domain bespeak a 'method', they do so with circumspection. Certainly, immeasurable amounts may be learned from Fitzpatrick's practices of heedful reading and writing with exactitude: the love that he lavishes on words. Nothing emerges, however, that may be applied readily elsewhere. No methodological product is for sale. The ineradicable existence of international law is something, Fitzpatrick suggests, that must be experienced – urgently, vitally, and without mysticism. If this is a 'method', it is one of living in international law, and doing so with ardour, vigilance, and compassion. Fitzpatrick's is a feverish loyalty both to the *fullness* and to the *law* of lawfulness. This loyalty may be relied upon, but it will not reassure.

References

Álvarez, A. (1918–19) 'New conception and new bases of legal philosophy', *Illinois Law Review* 13: 167–82.

Anghie, A. (1999) 'Francisco de Vitoria and the colonial origins of international law', in E. Darian-Smith and P. Fitzpatrick (eds) *Laws of the Postcolonial*, Ann Arbor: University of Michigan Press.

Anghie, A. (2004) *Imperialism, Sovereignty, and the Making of International Law*, Cambridge: Cambridge University Press.

Becker Lorca, A. (2006) 'Alejandro Álvarez situated: Subaltern modernities and modernisms that subvert', *Leiden Journal of International Law* 19: 879–930.

Berman, N. (1999) 'In the wake of empire (Grotius Lecture)', *American University International Law Review* 14: 1515–69.

Bourdieu, P. (1984) *Distinction: A Social Critique of the Judgment of Taste*, trans. R. Nice, Cambridge, MA: Harvard University Press.

Byers, M. and Nolte, G. (eds) (2003) *United States Hegemony and the Foundations of International Law*, Cambridge: Cambridge University Press.

Charlesworth, H. (2002) 'International law: A discipline of crisis', *Modern Law Review* 65: 377–92.

Charlesworth, H. (2004) 'Feminist methods in international law', *Studies in Transnational Legal Policy* 36: 159–83.

Derrida, J. (1987) 'The laws of reflection: Nelson Mandela, in admiration', trans. M. A. Caws and I. Lorenz, in J. Derrida and M. Tlili (eds) *For Nelson Mandela*, New York: Seaver Books.

Dezalay, Y. and Garth, B. G. (1996) *Dealing in Virtue: International Commercial Arbitration and the Construction of a Transnational Legal Order*, Chicago: University of Chicago Press.

Dezalay, Y. and Garth, B. G. (2002a) *The Internationalization of Palace Wars: Lawyers, Economists, and the Contest to Transform Latin American States*, Chicago: University of Chicago Press.

Dezalay, Y. and Garth, B. G. (eds) (2002b) *Global Prescriptions: The Production, Exportation, and Importation of a New Legal Orthodoxy*, Ann Arbor: University of Michigan Press.

Esquirol, J. (2006) 'Alejandro Álvarez's Latin American law: A question of identity', *Leiden Journal of International Law* 19: 931–56.

Fitzpatrick, P. (1992) *The Mythology of Modern Law*, London: Routledge.

Fitzpatrick, P. (2001) *Modernism and the Grounds of Law*, Cambridge: Cambridge University Press.

Fitzpatrick, P. (2003) '"Gods would be needed...": American empire and the rule of (international) law', *Leiden Journal of International Law* 16: 429–66.

Foucault, M. (1977) 'What is an author?', trans. D. F. Bouchard and S. Simon, in D. F. Bouchard (ed.) *Language, Counter-memory, Practice: Selected Essays and Interviews*, Ithaca, NY: Cornell University Press.

Foucault, M. (1997a) 'What is critique?', in S. Lotringer and L. Hochroth (eds) *The Politics of Truth*, New York: Semiotext(e).

Foucault, M. (1997b) 'What is revolution?', in S. Lotringer and L. Hochroth (eds) *The Politics of Truth*, New York: Semiotext(e).

Garth, B. G. (2007) 'Rebuilding international law after the September 11 attack: Contrasting agendas of high priests and legal realists', *Loyola International Law Review* 4: 3–10.

Jameson, F. (1998) 'Notes on globalization as a philosophical issue', in F. Jameson and M. Miyoshi (eds) *The Cultures of Globalization*, Durham, NC: Duke University Press.

Jellinek, G. (1900; 3rd edn 1929) *Allgemeine Staatslehre*, Berlin: Julius Springer.

Kelly, D. (2004) 'Revisiting the rights of man: Georg Jellinek on rights and the state', *Law and History Review* 22: 493–530.

Kennedy, David (1994) 'A New World Order: Yesterday, today and tomorrow', *Transnational Law and Contemporary Problems* 4: 329–76.

Kennedy, David (2000) 'When renewal repeats: Thinking against the box', *New York University Journal of International Law and Politics* 32: 335–498.

Kennedy, Duncan (2006) 'Three globalizations of law and legal thought: 1850–2000', in D. Trubek and A. Santos (eds) *The New Law and Economic Development: A Critical Appraisal*, Cambridge: Cambridge University Press.

Koskenniemi, M. (2004) *The Gentle Civilizer of Nations: The Rise and Fall of International Law 1870–1960*, Cambridge: Cambridge University Press.

Koskenniemi, M. (2006) *From Apology to Utopia: The Structure of International Legal Argument*, rev. edn, Cambridge: Cambridge University Press.

Landauer, C. (2006) 'A Latin American in Paris: Alejandro Álvarez's *Le droit international américain*', *Leiden Journal of International Law*, 19: 957–81.

Lindenfeld, D. F. (1997) *The Practical Imagination: The German Sciences of State in the Nineteenth Century*, Chicago: University of Chicago Press.

Marchart, O. (2007) *Postfoundational Political Thought: Political Difference in Nancy, Lefort, Badiou and Laclau*, Edinburgh: Edinburgh University Press.

Marks, S. (2006) 'State-centrism, international law, and the anxieties of influence', *Leiden Journal of International Law* 19: 339–47.

Mouffe, C. (2005) *On the Political*, London: Routledge.

Musil, R. (1952–3; rev. edn 1978) *Der Mann ohne Eigenschaften*, ed. A. Frisé, Reinbek bei Hamburg: Rowohlt; trans. B. Pike and S. Wilkins (1995) *The Man without Qualities*, New York: Knopf.

Nancy, J.-L. (1991) *The Inoperative Community*, trans. P. Connor, L. Garbus, M. Holland, and S. Sawhney. Minneapolis: University of Minnesota Press.

Nietzsche, F. (2000) *Basic Writings of Nietzsche*, trans. Walter Kaufmann, New York: Random House.

Obama, B. (2009a) 'Inaugural address by President Barack Hussein Obama', Washington, DC, 21 January 2009. Online, available at: www.whitehouse.gov/the_press_office/President_Barack_Obamas_Inaugural_Address/.

Obama, B. (2009b) 'Statement by the President on the budget', Office of the Press Secretary, Washington, DC, 17 March 2009. Online, available at: www.white-house.gov/the_press_office/Statement-by-the-President-on-the-Budget/.

Obama, B. (2009c) 'Statement of President Barack Obama on release of OLC memos', Office of the Press Secretary, Washington, DC, 16 April 2009. Online, available at: www.whitehouse.gov/the_press_office/Statement-of-President-Barack-Obama-on-Release-of-OLC-Memos.

Obregón, L. (2006) 'Noted for dissent: The international life of Alejandro Álvarez', *Leiden Journal of International Law* 19: 983–1016.

Pitkin, H. F. (1998) *The Attack of the Blob: Hannah Arendt's Concept of the Social*, Chicago: University of Chicago Press.

Rancière, J. (1999) *Disagreement: Politics and Philosophy*, Minneapolis: University of Minnesota Press.

Riles, A. (1995) 'The view from the international plane: Perspective and scale in the architecture of colonial international law', *Law and Critique* 6: 39–54.

Sarat, A. (2004) 'Vitality amidst fragmentation: On the emergence of postrealist law and society scholarship', in A. Sarat and M. A. Malden (eds) *The Blackwell Companion to Law and Society*, Oxford: Blackwell.

Weinberger, O. (1991) *Law, Institution, and Legal Politics: Fundamental Problems of Legal Theory and Social Philosophy*, Dordrecht: Kluwer Academic.

Chapter 6

The World Trade Organization and Fitzpatrick's 'new constitutionalism'

Fiona Macmillan

Introduction

This chapter is grounded in Peter Fitzpatrick's pellucid examination and theorization in a number of works, including of course *Modernism and the Grounds of Law* (Fitzpatrick 2001), of the relationship between the national and international, or, more specifically, the mutually constitutive relationship between national and international law. More specifically, the chapter engages with aspects of the argument in '"The new constitutionalism": The global, the postcolonial and the constitution of nations' (Fitzpatrick 2006). As will just about go without saying to Fitzpatrick's devoted readership, the article does not embrace that form of 'new constitutionalism' that might be identified in the putative embryonic juridical world order asserted by Hardt and Negri (2000). Nor, similarly unsurprisingly, is it a cupbearer for the related form of 'new constitutionalism', sometimes identified as emerging from what Richard Peet (2003) has described as the 'unholy trinity' of the international economic organizations: the International Monetary Fund (IMF), the World Bank, and the World Trade Organization (WTO). However, my reading of the article is that an effect of the mutually constitutive relationship between national and international law, has been – precisely as a result of the pretension to constitutionalism at the international level of the 'unholy trinity', and especially the WTO – the seeping into the national constitutional consciousness of economic or market rights: what Fitzpatrick describes as a 'pervasion of economic or, more specifically, market relations' (2006: 9). This is perhaps Fitzpatrick's form of 'new constitutionalism', which he identifies as a consequence of a certain indistinction between the international and the national, 'an indistinction between what is inside and what is outside' (ibid.: 6).

Concepts of distinction, indistinction, and mutual constitution are also the leitmotif of this chapter in another way. All are ways of describing the tapestry of scholarship, not as a product but rather as a process that takes place in the intellectual public domain. Distinct ideas closely associated with particular thinkers or schools of thought are often entwined and woven together so that their provenance develops over time. This process is critical to the vibrancy of intellectual life. And while the process itself relies upon the generous participation of many, including those with whom one finds oneself in disagreement, it is also crucially dependent on foundational thinkers. That is to say, the qualities of the tapestry require not just those who weave discrete and intricate designs – as important as these might be – but also a durable loom and carefully placed warp threads. As this chapter seeks to demonstrate, the great contribution of Fitzpatrick's work is in both the warp and the weft of intellectual life. This chapter adds some embroidery to his foundational work on the relationship between the national and international, but it seeks also to be part of the process of taking forward an aspect of Fitzpatrick's work in a way that, if not mutually constitutive, at least constitutes a productive line of decoration.

Relationship between the national and the international

As Fitzpatrick argues, one constitutive claim is that the international is dependent on the national. In this version, as Tony Carty (quoted by Fitzpatrick) has it, there is 'a *void* at the very heart of international law which is marked by the myth of international legal order' (Carty 1997: 10; Fitzpatrick 2006: 6). As Fitzpatrick himself observes, this would, however, 'involve an impossibly pure plurality, a plurality of singularities' (2006: 6). Instead, international law, using the two branches of its doctrine of recognition, namely constitutive theory and evidentiary theory, has created a system to which a sovereign state must conform in order to be recognized as such. The criteria laid down for such recognition are 'derived from the formation of the modern occidental nation ... peculiarly oriented around an intense attachment to landed territory' (ibid.: 7), but also being 'unitary, autonomous, sovereign, and capable of observing the requirements of international law. So, in recognizing a nation state, in the evocation of its existence in terms shared with other nation states, international law constitutes singular entities having the qualities required to constitute it' (ibid.: 7), thus constituting singular entities as part of a commonality, which, as Fitzpatrick says, must 'be responsive to the singularity' (ibid.: 8). However, this commonality 'cannot be passively responsive ... since that would leave the only available commonality as an entirely commensurable sameness, and this would be to deny singularity' (ibid.: 8). Nation, at the same time, must be illimitably responsive to what is outside. Consequently,

> the pervasive and illimitable quality of nation's responsiveness, as well as nation's constituent relation to the commonalities of the international and the global, result in an indistinction between what is inside

> and what is outside, and we must expect to find the same phenomena on both sides of the border.
>
> (ibid.: 8)

As a consequence of this type of relation, international law pulls off two impressive tricks. First, it effectively constitutes nations, which in their 'illimitable responsiveness' are constantly reshaped by international law; and second, it shapes relations between nations and supranational, international, or, as the WTO would have it, intergovernmental organizations. Since the time of the Washington Consensus, a consequence of both these effects of international law is a pervasion in national constitutions of the language of the market. Fitzpatrick notes that the elbows of the traditional constitutional precepts of democracy, human rights, and the rule of law are rudely jostled by those vulgar newcomers liberalization, deregulation, and privatization. Worse still, the former are instrumentally subordinated to the latter. Notions of 'good governance' bred in the bureaucracies of the IMF and the World Bank drive political organization.

This brief account of a part of Fitzpatrick's argument does it scant justice. I hope, however, that it provides a sufficiently nuanced account of the argument to give some flavour of the way in which its intricacies provide multiple directions for subsequent embroiderers. That said, it is doubtless the case that my account of the argument is affected by the direction in which I wish to take it and the purposes for which I wish to make use of it. (This ineradicable aspect of the scholarly process can be a source of satisfaction, pride, joy, indifference, frustration, and rage, in more or less equal parts, but in a volume like this I hope to have at least avoided the worst of these.) My own needlepoint focuses on the relationship between the political and economic, and the way in which this relationship is refracted in the mutual constitution of national and international law. More specifically, drawing on Fitzpatrick's account I will argue that these 'new' national constitutions have apparently heeded the call for the reintegration of the political and the economic, but something has gone horribly wrong. Instead of this putative reintegration recognizing that the economic is part and parcel of the political, that economic issues are in truth political, the opposite has occurred: the political has become part and parcel of the economic.

Division between the political and the economic at the international level

The current international legal order, which has emerged since the end of the Second World War, embraces a kind of schism between international economic law and public international law. The institutions of international economic law emerged from the Bretton Woods negotiations, which drew up the charters of the IMF, the International Fund for Reconstruction and Development (which became the World Bank), and the International Trade Organization. Despite being the progeny of Franklin D. Roosevelt's 'one-worldism', the International Trade Organization never came into existence. (Its death knell was the intense opposition that it engendered in the United States (Arrighi 2002: 276–7), although the political and business interests ranged against it were not confined to those emanating from the United States (Dunkley 2001: 26–8). However, it metamorphosed into the 1947 version of the General Agreement on Tariffs and Trade (GATT) and was, accordingly, a precursor to the WTO.) The United Nations organizations, which form the framework for public international law, arose from the Dumbarton Oaks negotiations. From the beginning, the mandates of these two systems of international law were distinct. The Bretton Woods institutions were to manage international economic relations, while the Dumbarton Oaks institutions were to manage the international political order. As part of this mandate the Dumbarton Oaks institutions have taken charge of what have been described as 'state-making and war-making' functions (Arrighi 2002: 275). In addition to this, the system of public international law that has been built up around the Dumbarton Oaks institutions has purported to establish international standards in areas such as the protection of human rights and of the environment.

However, the bifurcation of international law along the lines of the putative division between the political and the economic is, I would argue, of greater antiquity and appears to be rooted in the origins of the Westphalia System – one of the more significant moments in what Fitzpatrick calls the 'inconclusive constituent alternation between nation and international law' (2006: 7). The principle that quarrels between sovereigns did not implicate non-combatant civilians was built into the Peace of Westphalia of 1648. As a consequence, the treaties that built upon the Settlement of Westphalia abolished trade barriers and sought to protect the rights of private enterprise to trade across state borders, even during times of war or other political turmoil. Arrighi remarks that '[t]his reorganization of political space in the interest of capital accumulation marks the birth not just of the modern inter-state system, but also of capitalism as world system' (2002: 44; see also Polanyi 2001: 16–17).[1] This is a key point: under the Westphalian system, political space is organized along national lines, revealing Fitzpatrick's 'intense attachment to landed territory' (2006: 7); economic space both recognizes and transcends the boundaries of political space.

It is true that the economic freedoms of Westphalia were not observed during the period of political turmoil and violence marked by the Napoleonic Wars. They were, however, restored in the Settlement of Vienna of 1815 and the Congress of Aix-la-Chapelle of 1818 (Arrighi 2002: 52).

Similarly, after the First and Second World Wars 'the United States first became hegemonic by leading the inter-state system towards the restoration of the principles, norms and rules of the Westphalia System, and then went on to govern and remake the system it had restored' (ibid.: 65). Owing to US protectionism, however, this system did not originally embrace multilateral free trade. Instead, we got the GATT, a framework for negotiations for reductions on restrictions on international trade in goods. Using the GATT, the US government was able to control the process of trade liberalization in ways that benefited US interests. Thus, the period of US dominance has witnessed only a gradual move to a more widely articulated free trade regime.

This gradual movement is closely associated with a major feature of the post-war international landscape. This was the reconstruction of the post-war world markets through the process of direct investment rather than through trade. The engine of the process of direct investment was the vertically integrated multinational or transnational business enterprise, in which the process of international trade was effectively 'internalized' (Arrighi 2002: 72–3; see also Dunkley 2001: 25, citing Wilcox 1949: chs 2–3). Despite many attempts to do so, it is difficult to overstate the significance of this phenomenon. As Arrighi so pithily puts it:

> By about 1970 ... transnational corporations had developed into a world-scale system of production, exchange and accumulation, which was subject to no state authority and had the power to subject to its own 'laws' each and every member of the inter-state system, the United States included ... The emergence of this free enterprise system – free, that is, from the constraints imposed on world-scale processes of capital accumulation by the territorial exclusiveness of states – has been the most distinctive outcome of US hegemony. It marks a decisive new turning point in the process of expansion and supercession of the Westphalia System, and may well have initiated the withering away of the modern inter-state system as the primary locus of world power.
>
> (2002: 74)

The growth of the power of multi- or transnational corporate enterprises was one of the startling features of the twentieth-century landscape. The outcome is a system that is free from any constraints on 'world-scale processes of capital accumulation' that might have been imposed by the territorial exclusivity of states. This involves an autonomy from both political and economic control that, especially when put alongside the changes in the character and constitution of state power, endows multinational enterprises with the capacity to affect the order of things across the putative divide between the economic and the political.

Faux integration?

From their inception, little was provided in the way of legal linkage between the Bretton Woods and the Dumbarton Oaks institutions. Nominally, the Bretton Woods institutions were established within the UN system (Dunkley 2001: 26–7),[2] but the IMF and World Bank have in practice always been independent of it. Interestingly, however, the proposed Charter of the International Trade Organization did allow a member aggrieved by an International Trade Organization decision to seek an advisory opinion from the International Court of Justice, the decision of which would be binding on the International Trade Organization. This attempt at a legal interface between the ordering of the international economic and political systems did not survive the stillbirth of the International Trade Organization. The consequence of this, at least in a technical legal sense, is what I have described as the systemic division between public international law and international economic law.

I should, however, pause here to note that this is not a conclusion to which all, or even the majority, of commentators subscribe. Arguments that the WTO is legally linked to the system of public international law and, indeed, 'is no more than a new branch of public international law' (Hu 2004: 144) abound. To some extent this difference of opinion may be due to differing interpretations of the expression 'public international law'. In this chapter I use this expression to refer to international law operating under the auspices of the UN system. I do not, of course, dispute that WTO law is part of international law.[3] (Indeed, if that were not the case, Fitzpatrick's engagement with these questions would have little relevance for my work in this area.) My argument on this point, addressed at length elsewhere (Macmillan 2004), is (I hope) more nuanced.

One dimension of my attempts at nuance is to note that although the two systems of law are systemically divided, their institutions and activities have a clear, if changing, interrelationship. At the end of the last century, Finger and Tamiotti described some of the permutations of this relationship in terms of institutional development within the two regimes:

> [T]he United Nations, with its multiple agencies, became more and more fragmented and its spread increasingly thin, which appeared particularly problematic when funds became scarce. On the other hand, the Bretton Woods Institutions, especially the World Bank, increasingly invaded UN development territory by subsuming social development and sustainability into its economic development agenda. The GATT finally developed a powerful dynamic of trade liberalisation and, by so doing, somewhat undermined the agendas of both the UN and the Bretton Woods Institutions.... Today we can observe an institutional rearrangement, which makes international

> public institutions regroup around three key issues, all of which are crucial for the management of international public affairs in the years to come. These issues are security, sustainable development, and trade regulation.
>
> (1999: 9)

The Integrated Framework for Trade-Related Technical Assistance to Least Developed Countries, which is a joint venture between the IMF, the World Bank, the WTO, UNCTAD, UNDP, and the International Trade Centre (ITC),[4] provides one useful example of this.

In the first decade of this century, this 'functional' interrelationship has, as Buchanan and Pahuja (2004) have so convincingly argued, evolved towards what might be called *faux* legal integration at the international level. Some of my examples of this are the spineless United Nations Global Compact, the laudable United Nations Norms on the Responsibilities of Transnational Corporations (2003), and, of particular resonance in this context, the instrumental use of human rights by the IMF and the World Bank. These are also, perhaps, examples of Kennedy's observation that 'for all their similarities, the traditions and intellectual styles of public international law and international economic law remain estranged caught in an elaborate pas-de-deux of public and private, metropolitan and cosmopolitan sensibilities' (1995: 671). Of course, the suggestion that this is no more than a form of *faux* integration, that the systems 'remain estranged', may very well be a piece of what in the circumstances will turn out to be ill-judged optimism. Perhaps what we are really witnessing is the creeping subjugation of the political to the economic. If this is so, then, given that this division between the political and the economic has for so long characterized both the international legal system and its mutually constitutive relationship with the nation-state, why are we *now* witnessing an apparent creeping tendency towards some sort of integration at the international level? And while I am asking questions to which I cannot hope to give anything more than a pallid suggestion of an answer,[5] is it the case that this tendency towards integration at the international level is being refracted into the constitutions of states? Or is the process of refraction the other way around?

So far as the matter of the tendency towards integration at the international level is concerned, an approach to the answer might lie in the millennial obsession with the concept of human rights and its consequent rhetorical power when employed instrumentally. This tendency has certainly been stoked by prominent human rights institutions that have urged the three giants of international economic law to take more notice of notions of human rights emerging from the public international law system. These types of injunctions have emanated from, for example, the Committee on Economic Social and Cultural Rights, the Committee on the Rights of the Child, and repeatedly from the UN High Commissioner on Human Rights (see further, for example, Lucke 2005). Most notably in the present context, the last of these has issued a stream of papers examining the human rights implications of the WTO and stressing the need for the WTO to pay more attention to human rights (see, for example, UN Commission on Human Rights 2001, 2002a, b, 2003, 2004; OHCHR 2003). Aside from the obvious fact that the High Commissioner has a legitimate concern, I suspect that the reason for this voluminous flow of words from an institution on one side of the systemic divide to an institution on the other side lies in the High Commissioner's appreciation of the systemic pre-eminence of international economic law over public international law, in which is buried the effective subjugation of the political by the economic.

And how has this systemic pre-eminence been achieved? There is, I think, a good argument for the proposition that it is a consequence of the establishment of the WTO – ironically, the only one of the trinity of international economic law institutions that seems little concerned with the preoccupations and rhetoric of the political; the only one that generally eschews *faux* integration. At the international level this systemic pre-eminence is a consequence of its overwhelmingly effective dispute resolution and enforcement system administered by a quasi (at least) judicial body. Among those concerned with techniques of enforcement at the international level, which is as much (if not more) a diplomatic as a legal question, this system has been regarded as one of the great innovations of the WTO.

This innovation casts an even longer shadow over the well-known problems of enforcement in the public international law arena. That is to say that in the rarefied world of international diplomacy there may be a preference for the use of trade 'leverage' over trade 'sanctions', especially where that leverage is applied by a quasi-judicial body such as the WTO dispute resolution body. There is also a preference in most quarters for trade leverage over war. Perhaps even more than all of this, plenipotentiaries and functionaries operating at the international level like to feel that there is some point to all their frenzied 'legal' activity. In any case, if it is true that international economic law is winning the regulatory competition between the two systems, then it seems reasonable to suggest, as Kennedy has done, that what we are witnessing at the international level is 'economics replacing politics as law's sidekick and nemesis' (1995: 675).

Refraction at the national level: role of the WTO

Is the apparent integration of the political and economic at the national constitutional level, as noted by Fitzpatrick, a direct refraction of the *faux* (or otherwise) integration at the international level? Is it, in fact, a simple instance of that which Fitzpatrick identifies as the 'necessarily illimitable quality of nation's responsiveness' (2006: 8)? Or are developments at the international level refracting those at the national level? Consistently with Fitzpatrick's thesis of mutual constitution, there seems to be some inevitable to-ing and fro-ing between the national and the international.

Assuming that there is some validity to the argument made above that it is the advent of the WTO, in particular, that has been responsible for some degree of integration between the political and the economic at the international level, then we need to remind ourselves that the WTO did not spring into the world spontaneously like some new instance of immaculate conception. It was by the formal agreement of its founding members, seventy-six nation-states, that it was constituted and took its place within the pantheon of international organizations. And it is as a consequence of the sustenance of its now 153 member states that it continues to thrive. It is these members that are responsible not only for putting into place its highly effective dispute-resolution system, but also for the success of this system as a result of their continued participation in, and compliance with, it.

However, in the context of mutual constitution between the national and the international, the WTO is notable also for the fact that, arguably more than any other international organization, it has penetrated the very concept of the national through an exploitation of the permeable quality of the division between the national and the international. The device of the so-called single undertaking under which the price of WTO membership (and its associated trading advantages) is the requirement of adhesion to all the WTO multilateral agreements has sharpened its ability to penetrate law-making at the national level. Requirements for national intellectual property laws under the notably controversial Agreement on Trade-Related Aspects of Intellectual Property Rights, requirements for national sanitary and phyto-sanitary laws under the Agreement on Sanitary and Phytosanitary Measures, and the potential 'liberalization' of national markets for every type of service under the General Agreement on Trade in Services, to name but a few, represent the sort of persistent incursions into the constitution of law at the national level that must figure only in the wildest dreams of the IMF and the World Bank. However, at the same time the thrust of the WTO obligations is the deepening of the internalization of the capitalist system as 'world system', as Arrighi would have it (2002: 44), within the domains of the multinational enterprises.

As Arrighi argues, the growth of capitalism as world system was greatly accelerated after the end of the Second World War as a consequence of its internalization in the domains of the multinational enterprises. It was, therefore, inevitably tied in with the process of decolonization. The effect of decolonization on the world economy has, of course, been profound. In particular, decolonization has called for the development of new techniques for accessing the resources of the so-called developing world on terms that ensure that the dominant position of the former colonial powers in the world economy is maintained. The WTO, with its theoretical roots in the doctrine of comparative advantage and its seat in the engine room of corporate capitalism (see, for example, Charnovitz 1999: 118),[6] has shown itself to be particularly well adapted to this task (see further Macmillan 2010). In particular, the device of the 'single undertaking' has been tied in developing countries to a set of repressive obligations as the price of admission to the world trading system. Thus, it is through the WTO that a handful of nations – at its greatest the thirty members of the Organisation for Economic Co-operation and Development (which, one might note, has a much more static membership than the WTO); at its smallest, the four members of the Quad[7] (with its similarly static membership) – have replicated and strengthened the structural imbalance in world power that emerged in the post-colonial era and had been maintained with decreasing effectiveness by the system of public international law.

This can hardly be regarded as anything other than political. Similarly, the rhetorical commitment of the WTO to a single global market has provoked a range of arguments that cannot be easily compartmentalized as only economic (see, for example, Gray 1998: 23).[8] Yet as has already been noted, the WTO has no overt pretensions to the integration of the political and the economic; indeed, it seems anxious to suppress its political nature. However, if my argument about the effect of the WTO on the constitution of nations is correct, then it has been one of the main instigators of the pervasion of economic and market relations in national constitutions.

Does this mean that the refraction of the international in the national has produced something that is absent at the international level? Has it produced actual integration of the economic and the political in the constitution of nations? The answer to this is, of course, that it has not. And the reason it has not is simply because the persistent internalization of the capitalist system within the domains of the multinational enterprises means that the system exists outside the political/territorial space of nation-states, whatever they might say. Moreover, the very international law organizations responsible for embedding the values of the market in the constitution of nations are, at the same time making it more and more impossible for the occidental nation-state, with its attachment to territory, to capture the economic.

This leads me to conclude that in terms of the relationship between the political and the economic, the mutual constitution of national and international is alive and well. The division between the political and the economic in the constitution of law at the international level is reflected at the national level. The systemic pre-eminence of the international economic law system at the international level has achieved at the national level a *faux* integration of the political and the economic, which only shows its capacity for integration by treating the political as if it were part and parcel of the economic. It has also achieved the willing and expressed subjugation of the political space of the nation to capitalism as world system. Given the apparent subjugation of the political to the economic, unless national constitutions exercising their 'illimitable quality of ... responsiveness' (Fitzpatrick 2006: 8) engage on different terms with international law, they will suppress politics at the level of national constitution-making as effectively as it has been suppressed at the international level.

Conclusion

The suppression of politics in the international economic order is rightly a matter of concern. What gives serious pause for thought, however, is the call for the closer integration of the public international law system with the international economic law system, which might lead to the suppression of politics in both systems, and at both the national and the international levels. Of course, if such integration involved the acknowledgement that the economic is part and parcel of the political, then perhaps that pause would be a lighter matter. However, as the above discussion has sought to show, even the shadow of integration at the international level seems to have led to the ascendancy of the economic at the level of national constitution-making. Given the mutual constitution of law-making at the national and international levels, the spectre of these developments at the national level being re-re-refracted at the international level should not be ignored. I wonder, however, whether this is the only problem with the idea that recognition within international law of the fact that the international economic order is part of the international political order is the key to a more just and democratic reconstitutionalization of power at the international, and subsequently national, level.

At both the general and the more specific levels, such recognition would raise a thorny problem if it were to be realized through the creation of a legal relationship between the systems of international economic law and public international law. This is because the systems share a twofold myopia. First, both systems fail to give any formal or constitutional recognition to so-called 'private actors' in the form of multinational enterprises. Second, neither system appears to be sufficiently concerned about the extent to which power might be exercised outside the cognizance or jurisdiction of the nation-state. It is clear that if one were to recast the law of the world trading system so that it directly intersected with, and was constrained by, the values of public international law, some of the criticisms of the current WTO system in relation to its failure to take on board human rights issues would be on their way to being addressed. However, one overriding concern would remain. This is the issue of the constitutionalization of international corporate or 'private' power – that is, the question of how the power of the multinational corporate sector is to be controlled and regulated within a system of law that both recognizes the existence of that power and is not incapable in the face of it.

The rapid growth of the power and influence of transnational corporations in the twentieth century has shown no signs of abating as we have entered the twenty-first century. The advent of the WTO at the close of the last century is implicated in this phenomenon in the sense that the WTO has a reciprocal relationship with multinational enterprises under which their activities are facilitated through progressive trade liberalization while at the same time they act as instruments of the WTO's (rhetorical, at least) goal of free international trade. This has accelerated the process by which the power of multinational enterprise has become global, while the countervailing political power of the democratic entities has remained trapped within the confines of the nation-state. Thus, multinational enterprises may be regarded as having transcended what Hardt and Negri refer to as 'the constitutional command of the nation states' (2000: 308). It is important to recognize that not only are nation-states politically eclipsed by the power of the international corporate sector, but states have also ceased to resist. They have, in truth, been captured by the ideology of capital. One might even take the argument a step further and say they are controlled by it (see Hirschman 1977).[9] Of course, this goes a little further than the relatively uncontentious observation that in western liberal democracies the relationship between the state and the 'private' sector is very close. On the other hand, it goes some way to explaining the willing cooperation of nation-states with a system of international economic law apparently dedicated to forms of trade and financial market liberalization regardless of their consequences for millions of people (Gray 1998: 18)[10] and regardless of its (selective) insistence on the irrelevance of national borders.

If it is truly the case that multinational enterprises are outside the constitutional command of the nation-state, then, given the myopia of both systems of international law with respect to non-state actors, even laudable initiatives like the United Nations Norms on the Responsibilities of Transnational Corporations are doomed to rather limited effect. What is clear is that, in order to answer some of the most penetrating criticisms of the system of international economic law embodied in the current WTO, any revised system must concern itself not only with regulating the exercise of power between states but also with regulating the exercise of corporate power at the international level. This, of course, raises the question of whether or not it is time to think again about some form of 'one-worldism', in which the political and economic governance of that which now transcends the power of the nation-state is undertaken at a global level. Commentators such as Gray see in global governance not only an antidote to the unpalatable results of global capitalism but also a means to the preservation of the nation-state:

> A regime of global governance is needed in which world markets are managed so as to promote the cohesion of societies and the integrity of states. Only a framework of global regulation – of currencies, capital movements, trade and environmental conservation – can enable the creativity of the world economy to be harnessed in the service of human needs.
>
> (1998: 199)

However, not only is the notion of global governance one that is regarded with suspicion or concern in many quarters, it is also the case that not all commentators share Gray's enthusiasm for a revitalized nation-state. Hardt and Negri, for example, remark:

> We believe, however, that it is a grave mistake to harbor any nostalgia for the powers of the nation-state or to resurrect any politics that celebrates the nation. First of all, these efforts are in vain because the decline of the nation-state is not simply the result of an ideological position that might be reversed by an act of political will: it is a structural and irreversible process.... Second, and more important, even if the nation were still to be an effective weapon, the nation carries with it a whole series of repressive structures and ideologies ... and any strategy that relies on it should be rejected on that basis.
>
> (2000: 336)

Of course, this argument perhaps neglects the mutual constitution between the national and the international, their 'inconclusive constituent alternation' (Fitzpatrick 2006: 7). And I have this sneaking suspicion that in the monumental richness of the Fitzpatrick tapestry it may be possible to find a more direct answer to Hardt and Negri (see, for example, Fitzpatrick 2004). But then that's another story...

Notes

1 Indeed, the putative division between the political and the economic appears to be an essential aspect of the modern system of global capitalism: see, for example, Hirschman (1977), Amin (1998), and Gray (1998).
2 As Dunkley (2001: 27) notes, it was intended that the International Trade Organization would operate under the auspices of the Economic and Social Council of the United Nations.
3 See further Marceau (2002), who suggests that WTO law may be either a 'self-contained regime' (citing Simma 1985) or *lex specialis* under the International Law Commission's Rules on State Responsibility 2001, Art. 55.

4 Itself a joint venture between UNCTAD and the WTO – see *The International Trade Centre*. Online, available at: www.intracen.org.
5 A consequence of word-length restrictions, of course.
6 Charnovitz (1999: 118) writes, '[I]f we peel off the mercantilism from international trade law, which looks at States as trading entities, we discern that the true beneficiaries of GATT are the individual traders.'
7 These are the United States, Canada, the European Union, and Japan.
8 Gray (1998: 23) writes, 'A global single market is very much a late-twentieth-century *political* project' (emphasis in original).
9 Hirschman (1977) shows that it was the emerging system of international financial arbitrage that undermined and controlled the power of the European monarchs and despots from the seventeenth century onwards.
10 Gray (1998: 18) writes of 'economic dislocation, social chaos and political instability in hugely different countries throughout the world'.

References

Amin, S. (1998) *Capitalism in the Age of Globalization*, London: Zed Books.

Arrighi, G. (2002) *The Long Twentieth Century: Money, Power and the Origins of Our Times*, London: Verso.

Buchanan, R. and Pahuja, S. (2004) 'Law, nation and (imagined) international communities', *Law/Text/Culture* 8: 137–66.

Carty, A. (1997) 'Myths of international legal order: Past and present', *Cambridge Review of International Affairs* 10: 3–22.

Charnovitz, S. (1999) 'The globalization of economic human rights', *Brooklyn Journal of International Law* 25: 113–24.

Dunkley, G. (2001) *The Free Trade Adventure: The WTO, the Uruguay Round and Globalism – A Critique*, London: Zed Books.

Finger, M. and Tamiotti, L. (1999) 'New global regulatory mechanisms and the environment: The emerging linkage between the WTO and the ISO', *International Development Studies Bulletin* 30: 8–15.

Fitzpatrick, P. (2001) *Modernism and the Grounds of Law*, Cambridge: Cambridge University Press.

Fitzpatrick, P. (2004) 'The immanence of empire', in P. A. Passavant and J. Dean (eds) *Empire's New Clothes: Reading Hardt and Negri*, New York: Routledge.

Fitzpatrick, P. (2006) '"The new constitutionalism": The global, the postcolonial and the constitution of nations', *Law, Democracy and Development* 10(2): 1–20.

Gray, J. (1998) *False Dawn: The Delusions of Global Capitalism*, New York: New Press.

Hardt, M. and Negri, A. (2000) *Empire*, Cambridge, MA: Harvard University Press.

Hirschman, A. O. (1977, 1997 republished) *The Passions and the Interests: Political Arguments for Capitalism before Its Triumph*, Princeton, NJ: Princeton University Press.

Hu, J. (2004) 'The role of international law in the development of WTO law', *Journal of International Economic Law* 7: 143–67.

Kennedy, D. (1995) 'The international style in postwar law and policy: John Jackson and the field of international economic law', *American University Journal of International Law and Policy* 10: 671–716.

Lucke, K. (2005) 'States' and private actors' obligations under international human rights law and the draft UN Norms', in T. Cottier, J. Pauwelyn, and

E. Bürgi (eds) *Human Rights and International Trade*, Oxford: Oxford University Press.

Macmillan, F. (2004) 'International economic law and public international law: Strangers in the night', *International Trade Law and Regulation* 6: 115–24.

Macmillan, F. (2010) 'The World Trade Organization and the turbulent legacy of international economic law-making in the long twentieth century', in J. Faundez and C. Tan (eds) *International Law, Economic Globalization and Developing Countries*, Cheltenham, UK: Edward Elgar.

Marceau, G. (2002) 'WTO dispute settlement and human rights', *European Journal of International Law* 13: 753–814.

Peet, R. (2003) *Unholy Trinity: The IMF, World Bank and WTO*, London: Zed Books.

Polanyi, K. (2001, republished) *The Great Transformation: The Political and Economic Origins of Our Time*, Boston: Beacon Press.

Office of the High Commissioner for Human Rights (OHCHR) (2003) 'Human Rights and Trade', paper for the Fifth WTO Ministerial Conference, Cancún, Mexico, 10–14 September.

Simma, B. (1985) 'Self-contained regimes', *Netherlands Yearbook of International Law* 16: 111–36.

United Nations Norms on the Responsibilities of Transnational Corporations, UN Doc E/CN.4/Sub.2/2003/12/Rev.2 (2003).

UN Commission on Human Rights (2001) 'The impact of the TRIPs Agreement on the enjoyment of all human rights: Report of the High Commissioner for Human Rights', UN Doc. No. E/CN.4/Sub.2/2001/13.

UN Commission on Human Rights (2002a) 'Globalization and its impact on the full enjoyment of human rights: Report of the High Commissioner for Human Rights', UN Doc. No. E/CN.4/2002/54.

UN Commission on Human Rights (2002b) 'Liberalization of trade in services and human rights: Report of the High Commissioner for Human Rights', UN Doc. No. E/CN.4/Sub.2/2002/9.

UN Commission on Human Rights (2003) 'Human rights, trade and investment: Report of the High Commissioner for Human Rights', UN Doc. No. E/CN.4/Sub.2/2003/9.

UN Commission on Human Rights (2004) 'Analytical study of the High Commissioner for Human Rights on the fundamental principle of non-discrimination in the context of globalization: Report of the High Commissioner for Human Rights', UN Doc. No. E/CN.4/2004/40.

Wilcox, C. (1949) *A Charter for World Trade*, New York: Macmillan.

Chapter 7

Derrida's territorial knowledge of justice

William E. Conklin

Introduction

Peter Fitzpatrick's writings prove once and for all that it is possible for a law professor to write in beautiful English. His work also proves once and for all that the dominating tradition of Anglo-American legal philosophy and of law teaching has been barking up the wrong tree: namely, that the philosopher and professional law teachers can understand justice as nested in empty forms, better known as rules, doctrines, principles, policies, and other standards. The more rigorous our analysis or decomposition of the forms, we have believed, the more closely do we access the identity of laws. Justice has been assumed to be a matter of intellectually accessing such analysed forms. Fitzpatrick's articles and books embody an implicit critique of the analytic view of law and of justice. My entry point into this critique is his preoccupation with Jacques Derrida's theory of laws as universals and with Derrida's theory of justice as an inaccessible immediacy or presence in context-specific or concrete experienced events. Each event is experienced in an official's decision. Such a decision represents what Derrida, Fitzpatrick, and Hegel call 'individuality'.

Derrida's theory of law presents a conundrum. Derrida misses the possibility that law may exist by virtue of its content rather than its form. Derrida misses this possibility because, heavily influenced by Kant (in Derrida's theory of law), Derrida associates law with universals. This is so because Kant (and Derrida) are preoccupied with the identity of what counts as a law (*lois*) rather than with a law's legitimacy. A universal cannot exist unless it is legitimate, and it is legitimate, I claim, by virtue of its content. In his association of law with universals, Derrida presupposes that legal knowledge exists with reference to a territorial-like boundary. The forms are represented or signified by signs (signifiers) within a boundary of the ultimate form (the state, the nation, or humanity). This ultimate form as a universal, like the discrete rules or forms, lacks socially contingent content. A boundary separates knowable universals from the unknowable world on the exteriority of the boundary. The unknowable world is constituted by concrete events experienced in context-specific circumstances. In his legal theory Derrida hones in upon the decision as the experienced event. In a decision, one is present or immediate with the event. Derrida considers such immediacy as justice. The immediacy, however, can only be represented as a sign (sometimes called a signifier). The sign, in turn, represents an empty signifier or form, according to Derrida. Because the immediacy remains a representation rather than a presentation of the experienced event, laws as universals cannot be just. The rupture between the inaccessible immediacy of a decision on the one hand and the represented empty forms on the other is critical to Derrida's theory of law.

I claim that this rupture permeates Derrida's writings about law because Derrida possesses a territorial-like sense of legal knowledge. I shall argue to this effect as follows. In the first section I shall explain the importance of Fitzpatrick's exposure of the vacuity of the foundation of the system or structure of universals. In the second section I shall flesh out two elements of Derrida's legal theory: law as form and the *ipseity* or concrete event that the form excludes from law. This takes me to the third section, where I shall elaborate how Derrida's legal theory presupposes knowledge as territorial. I shall argue in the final section that this very sense of territorial knowledge prevents justice from accessing law and law from accessing justice. I conclude with the hint of a very different sense of law, one that draws from experiential knowledge in contradistinction to territorial knowledge.

The vacuous foundation of law

Permit me to turn to Fitzpatrick's work as my entry point into Derrida's theory of law. When Fitzpatrick seeks the foundation of law in various contexts, including judgments in Canada and Australia, access to justice, and post-colonial thought, he invariably exposes the foundation as nothingness. A foundation must radically differ from the ordinary forms as laws. If the foundation were an ordinary analysable unit or form, there would be no finality in the trace of one unit to another in search of a foundation. So, the foundation, being knowable and yet external to laws as forms, is a mere form without particular content. As Fitzpatrick puts it, the foundation is 'empty', 'vacuous', 'nothingness', 'beleaguered' (2002: 242; 2005: 9–13; 2008a). Relying heavily upon Derrida's 'Force of law' (1990), Fitzpatrick emphasizes that the foundation has a mystical character, in that language (the signifier/signified relation) cannot access it. This mysticism colours the foundation despite the rationalist pretensions of the professional knowers and despite the rhetoric of the rule of law.

I have described the foundation as invisible because of its inaccessibility to legal language.[1] This inacessibility of the foundation has led, ironically, to its construction by legal officials and philosophers. We officials and pedagogues have done so by decomposing concepts into their features or elements on faith that by doing so we would access laws and justice. We have ironically done so in the name of the foundation. Because of this self-generating character of the system of forms and concepts, and because of the need for an externality to the analysis of forms, the ultimate form is not decomposable into further units. The state fulfils this quest for a finality to the analysis of forms.

Because of the emptiness of the ultimate form of the system of legal units, legal philosophers end up concealing the vacuous foundation of law as they analyse theories about the discrete analysable units. Fitzpatrick offers several contexts where such concealment permeates judicial reasoning. In the first context he quotes Kant's oft-forgotten assertion (oft-forgotten even in contemporary readings about ethics and political philosophy) that it is treasonous to question the foundation of the modern legal order (Fitzpatrick 2003b: 436, quoting Kant 1797/1996: 95; see also Fitzpatrick 2006b: 167, 175, 183). In a second context he recalls how the universal truth embedded in law was relied upon by European states in the process of colonizing much of the globe (see, for example, Fitzpatrick 2002: 242). In a third context the impact of the vacuity of the foundation of the system of legal units upon Anglo-American analytical jurisprudence is exposed. Law has been associated with an autonomous system of rules or a coherent narrative structure, both of which are said to depart from the behaviour and the beliefs that a founding rule or a background structure of conceptions represent. Once we are left with the autonomous system of rules or principles, there remains a forgotten 'sub-standard, abnormal case containing within it the threat that the legal system will dissolve' (Hart 1994: 123; Hart's original 1961 edition quoted in Fitzpatrick 1992: 210). In a fourth context, to be discussed later in the chapter as 'being with', the foundation of law is sometimes associated with social bonding. This concern with social bonding as the legitimizing source of the system of rules is also forgotten once officials begin to analyse the chains of rules. Finally, Fitzpatrick turns to the impact of the vacuity of the foundation to international law. Given the vacuity of the state's legitimacy and given that the state is the primary legal person of international law, the legal official needs to address the mystical foundation of the state's domestic legal order before that official can sustain the existence of international law (Fitzpatrick 2003b).

Against the above contexts, law is self-posited and self-determined (Fitzpatrick 2004: 122). The structure of concepts dissolves into the power of state officials. The rule of law becomes a mere rhetorical device to sustain the power of lawyers and judges. The critical aspect of this is that because the concepts themselves are not accessible – always being deferred by the trace of one sign, which represents a signified concept to another representing sign – the power of officials is entangled with their knowledge of legal language. Since professional law schools introduce and protect that language, professional legal education is instrumental in sustaining the power relations of society (see further Conklin 1993, 1998). And legal education does so in the name of the law and access to justice. The consequence is that the foundation is actually constructed by officials as they search for more rigorous lower-levelled forms or concepts in the metaphysical objectivity of higher-ordered forms. The foundation is effectively constructed inside, not outside, the structure of forms as officials aspire to access legal objectivity.

This is the point where Fitzpatrick's work impacts upon the analytic methodology of contemporary jurisprudence, legal teaching materials, and scholarship about the law. What so many contemporary jurisprudes describe as the 'existence conditions' of the legal order – the social facts, the law beyond law, the state of nature, the General Will, the People, the *Grundnorm* – is a myth. In contemporary analytic parlance, concepts are valid if they are reasons for action by officials of the state. The gist of Fitzpatrick's originality might be framed in the language of analytical jurisprudence as follows. The 'existence conditions' of a legal order can be put to the side as not binding reasons for action. Fitzpatrick insists that the philosopher just cannot separate the particular rules of a legal order from the existence conditions that the self-generating and self-defining *Recht* excludes. Further, when one traces a reason for action to another reason for action, one ultimately recognizes that the existence conditions of the legal order are nested in the power relations of state officials. The consequence is that legal forms, so much a part of contemporary legal education in professional law schools, ultimately depend upon the self-defining law itself. Again, the ultimate foundation of law is what Fitzpatrick describes as 'vacuous', 'empty', and a 'layered irony'. The self-defining system of rules and institutions is thereby violently imposed upon inhabitants in the name of the rule of law and objectivity. Fitzpatrick draws from Žižek's reading of Kant to the effect that the origins of the legitimate order are 'lawless origins' that are cancelled by the historico-empirical circumstances that generate the legal order (Žižek 1991: 205). An explanation of the origins of the legal order 'a priori puts us outside'. The myth and mysticism of the origins remain a secret so long as contemporary legal theorists, law teachers, and other officials colour their analyses as the rule of law and objectivity. The secrecy is reinforced by disparaging rhetoric directed towards anyone, whether inside or outside the chains of analysed forms, who attempts to pierce the veil of the invisible foundation. Social bonding among the non-expert knowers of legal forms remains an outside possibility. The very existence of conditions of law – the 'social facts', 'the People', and the like – only depends upon the officials of the territorial state and the power relations internal to the state.

Contemporary Anglo-American legal philosophy, so much a part of and dependent upon the dominance of a state-centred legal order, misses law's inward self-determined and metaphysical construction of the foundation. The quest for the origin of laws in an external source, such as the social facts or a perfect coherent narrative, sustains legal philosophy in an air of naivety and denial. As Hart (1994) described from time to time, he was 'haunted' by the prospect that the existence conditions of the legal order were nested in a social bonding that the analysis of concepts could not access. Such conditions, he admitted, were unrecognized and unrecognizable because they were exterior to the self-conscious writing of the officials of the state. They were 'unstated', prior to the writing of officials. And yet, even that prospect of unstated unrecognized social behaviour remained excluded from legal philosophy. What mattered was power:

> [O]nly officials might accept and use the system's criteria of validity. The society in which this was so might be deplorably sheeplike; the sheep might end in the slaughter-house. But there is little reason for thinking that it could not exist or for denying it the title of a legal system.
>
> (Hart 1994: 117)

But an inquiry beyond the positing and analysis of the elements of a form or concept of recognition or an intellectually coherent narrative in an effort to decompose concepts as reasons for action would amount to 'naïve' beliefs and 'emotion rather than truth', as Matthew Kramer puts it, 'folk theories', 'half-baked', 'intuition-mongering', and 'psychological facts', as Brian Leiter expresses it, or, as Hart asserts, a 'nightmare' that incidentally 'haunts' legal philosophy.[2]

The consequence of the vacuity of the foundation, then, is that power determines law's own legitimacy. Thrasymachus has won out over Socrates' inward voice of inquiry. Fitzpatrick (2006a) examines the ultimate power relations at the foundation of the modern legal order in several contexts. The most obvious one today is the imperial quest of the United States. Another is the failure of international lawyers to address the sovereign's mystical foundation, a mysticism that legitimizes the primary legal persons of international law (Fitzpatrick 2003b). Perhaps the most consistent context of his exposure of the vacuous foundation is his examination of the power of European states as they imposed their concepts upon Australian, African, and North American indigenous inhabitants (Fitzpatrick 1990, 1998, 2001b, 2002, 2008a; Mostert and Fitzpatrick 2004). The signs (or words if we use the latter metaphorically) represent such forms, and such sign/signified relations constitute a language. The language is violent. Raw power and violence, not the rule of law, explain the imposition of forms upon indigenous social life precisely because the origin of the rule of law rests in vacuity. For Fitzpatrick, Derrida's theory of law offers an important explanation as to why this is so.

Fitzpatrick's argument goes like this. When X resists Y, Y's integrity is elevated at the very moment that Y is diminished and parasitic upon X (2008b: xi). In order to maintain its determinacy, law, as form, must *respond* to, as well as *resist*, the diminished and parasitic exteriority of the structure of forms. The latter privileging of the supplemental alien-ness poses an ironic twist. For, although law must resist the individual event, law must also respond to the latter in order for law to be determinate. As a consequence, law, to be law, requires a *relation* between the indeterminate form on the one hand and the determinate particularity on the other. The one cannot exist without the other, and yet the identity of each must remain autonomous of the other. The indeterminacy of pre-legality is 'always' on the other side of the divide. And yet, law needs content – its forms being universal – and this, in turn, requires that law *respond* to the particularities of the indeterminate pre-legality. Pre-legality is indeterminate because legal language, which represents analysed forms, cannot access the non-cognitive determinate experiences. In order to be determinate, law must 'extend beyond, exceed', or respond to what is determinate in a judicial or legislative decision for the time being (ibid.: 440). This responsive relation would lack the character of the 'violent word' or language which is otherwise superimposed upon the concrete, context-specific experiences. The universal forms are superimposed upon the stranger as the voice of such experiences (Fitzpatrick 2001d: 145–6).

Derrida's sense of law

Now I shall take up the relation of universal forms to the individual presence of a particular experiential event, an event that Derrida claims is inaccessible to the forms. This response of the forms to the experienced event, described by Derrida as a decision, faces a formidable problem, namely that so long as we presuppose what I shall call a territorial sense of knowledge, instead of an experiential knowledge, there is an untranslatable rupture between our legal knowledge of universals on the one hand and the immediacy or presence of the identity of utterer and decision on the other. This rupture between territorial knowledge and the outside and pre-existing experiential world raises this prospect: law's response to its antithetical other does not and cannot bring closure to the determinacy of law. This is so because law's response occurs through the configurations of signs with which officials and philosophers are familiar precisely because they are situated in the legal space on the territorial side of the rupture. The best that we can do is picture (or imagine) the identity of the stranger on the other side of the territorial boundary, which defines the outer limit of our knowledge of universals. The best that we can do is translate such an imagined identity into our own familiar language. Derrida especially emphasizes this inevitable need to translate the voice of the stranger into our own language. Again, Derrida understands language as the configuration of the interrelations of signifiers (see Derrida 1985). The consequence is that there is always an extra-ordinary or inaccessible remainder to legal language. Even the rupture between universals and the individuality of a decision cannot be reconciled within the paradigm of legal knowledge, which Derrida takes for granted. Let us gain a closer understanding of Derrida's theory of law in order to appreciate the presupposed rupture that contains law. First, what does Derrida signify by 'law'? Second, what does Derrida signify by 'individuality' or 'singularity'?

Law as form

Derrida takes for granted that law is composed of a system of content-independent forms. It is important in this respect that although Derrida did write about Hegel's logic, Derrida takes Kant for his understanding of the identity of law.[3] In this respect he is especially influenced by Kant's preoccupation with moral law as a conditional or categorical imperative or form (Derrida 1987: 32; 1990: 245, 275; 1992: 191). Conditional and the categorical imperatives intellectually transcend experience. Imperatives are universals because they are purged of social-cultural content. This is so because difference arises from the differentiation of the boundary of one form from the boundary of another. This preoccupation with the boundary of forms is reinforced by our own association of laws with doctrines, rules, principles, tests, and other forms. The consequence is that the interrelation of forms defers to a sameness. A form is important because of its utilitarian relation to another form. A form is stuck in acts of intellectualization. The differences are homogeneous.

Put another way, what might be considered 'difference' is a difference among signified forms in a given disciplinary language. Hegel describes such differentiation as *Verstand*.[4] Although one might literally translate *Verstand* as 'understanding', *Verstand* misses the embodiment of meaning. Gadamer (as did Husserl and Merleau-Ponty) associates understanding with such meaning. Objects can be meant as well as perceived. Meant objects draw from the experiential body so that understanding is lived. Understanding thereby defers to the *prejudicia* or prejudgements and forestructures of the experiential body. *Verstand* lacks such an inquiry into such prejudgements and forestructures of meaning because *Verstand* lifts Gadamer's 'understanding' above lived experiences by distinguishing between the boundaries of signified (and empty) forms. Since law, for Derrida, is composed of signified forms, the justice of legal space – the justice being concrete or immediate (or present) acts of meaning – is inaccessible to such forms. Legal space is highly reified vis-à-vis the *ipseity* of decisions – that is, reified as configurations of signifiers. Signifiers can be intellectually used by officials without ever having to address the experiential content of forms. So, too, the intellectual differentiations of forms miss the immersion of the officials and of the forms in the *prejudicia* of a shared ethos.[5]

The consequence of this sense of a system of laws (*lois*) as forms is that the forms are content independent. If the forms represent social relations as they are or as they ought to be, this is a mere happenstance. And yet the forms are said to be universally applied to all social relationships that fall inside the boundary of the forms. Inhabitants, as subjects, fall 'under' and 'before' the forms. They are 'equal' under and before the boundary within which the familiar knowledge of forms exists. Because the forms are content independent, the forms possess some surpassing *reductive* ability to contain responsiveness, to ensure that 'the aleatory *margin* ... remains *homogenous* with *calculation*, within *the order of the calculable*' (Derrida 1989: 55, quoted in Fitzpatrick 2005: 4, emphasis added). The forms, as universals, assimilate all threatening forms 'out there' beyond their boundaries.

All language is thereby written in the sense of being signifying relations – that is, in the sense that signifiers represent signified forms in terms of other signifiers without ever accessing the forms (see further Conklin 1996). Language, in this context, is thereby public rather than privately thought out inside one's intentional consciousness. Derrida takes Edmund Husserl's theory of meaning to represent a theory of language as private. Husserl (2001: esp. 560–2) claims that a subject may be present or immediate with intended or meant objects. Derrida claims that such an immediacy occurs through speech. Speech itself, however, is nested in the configurations of signifiers, according to Derrida. For Derrida, concepts just do not exist independent of chains of signifiers – that is, of writing. One signifier defers to another signifier, not to the signified forms (see especially Derrida 1974). Indeed, we can never access universals except as signifiers. We are entrapped in the prison-house of language or, as Derrida put it, of *differance*. Joining this early focus of signification to his later works on law, universals (*lois*) are the never-ending configurations of signifiers (or names). Signifiers re-present universals (which we associate with doctrines and rules). We believe that laws are forms but we can never access the forms through language – at least, as Derrida understands language as configurations of signifiers. The inaccessibility of the forms signified by configurations of signifiers leads us to conclude, according to Derrida, that law (*droit*) can never be '*presently* [and] *fully* just' (1990: 253, as quoted in Fitzpatrick 2005: 4). Presence, after all, returns us to Husserl's or embodied experiential language, something which is not possible, Derrida had claimed in his earlier works. As Fitzpatrick emphasizes, the system of forms (*droit*), to be universal (i.e. as forms), 'cannot be contained in its determinate presence' (ibid.: 6).

The consequence for Derrida's own understanding of laws with universal forms is that the forms are nested inside chains of signifiers, not in the constitution of meaning by bodily experiences. Power relations, as a result, determine who is recognized as a legal person. The 'private domain' of the foreigner is recognized as a legal person by the act of officials 'choosing, electing, filtering, selecting their invitees, visitors, or guests, those to whom they [officials of the state] decide to grant asylum, the right of visiting, or hospitality' (Derrida and Dufourmantelle 2000: 55). As Fitzpatrick quotes affirmatively from Derrida, law is 'a system of regulated and coded prescriptions' (Derrida 1990: 250, quoted in Fitzpatrick 2005: 4). And again, law is understood as an 'existing, coded rule' that 'can ... guarantee absolutely' the ultimate decision by a judge or other official (Derrida 1990: 251, quoted in Fitzpatrick 2005: 4). The boundaries of forms are 'coded' by configurations of signifiers. So, legal analysis, in its effort to access legal objectivity, differentiates one signifier in terms of another signifier. The problem is that the discrete laws are never determinate in human experience, at least as long as we assume that laws are content-independent forms. As Derrida (1973: 129–60) emphasizes, the signifier represents a universal (i.e. a form or concept), which in turn is always *deferred* from being accessed. So, the indeterminacy of forms arises from the never-ending trace of one signifier to another. The re-reading of signifiers never accesses the signified forms nor the individual context-specific experiences of meaning-constituting subjects.

This deferring of an immediacy or presence (or embodiment of meaning) to doctrines, rules, tests, and other forms is especially apparent when one re-reads Derrida's reading of Kafka's parable of 'the man from the country'. A castle represents or signifies the Law as a system of forms. The castle does have a door to the exteriority. A sentry, representing the legal official, stands on guard at the door. The guard gazes outward towards the man from the country. The man from the country waits and waits in order to access the Castle through the door. If officials deeper in the Castle decided to admit the man from the country, such a decision would be determinate. Until that moment, the Castle merely represents universals about rights and duties. Because the universals make claims without ever being opened for the man to enter into them, the Law remains indeterminate. The lived experiences of the man are excluded from the Law. The social relations that the man has experienced prior to his lifetime waiting before the Castle represents how the excluded man and his excluded lived experiences were 'before' the Law. They are phenomenologically and analytically before the law. The justice with which we legal officials are familiar – the justice of legal forms – is misdirected because justice rests in the experiential world that Kafka so powerfully describes of K. The universals, which the Castle represents, are inaccessible from the experiential world because an untranslatable rupture is believed to separate the language of the man from the country from the language of the guards of the Castle of Law. The language of the Castle cannot be just:

> To address oneself to the other in the language of the other is both the condition of all possible justice, it seems, but, in all rigor, it appears not only impossible (since I cannot speak the language of the other except to the extent that I appropriate it and assimilate it according to the law [*loi*] of an implicit third) but even excluded by justice as law, inasmuch as justice as law seems to imply an element of universality; the appeal to a third party who suspends the unilaterality or singularity of the idioms.
>
> (Derrida 1990: 245)

Since justice, according to Derrida, dwells in what Husserl describes as lived or experiential meaning, and because such meaning is excluded from writing, justice remains untranslated and untranslatable by the Castle's officials. This is the secret of the Law. This secret is 'an extremely painful thing' (Kafka 1988: 437, as quoted in Fitzpatrick 2005: 13).

Fitzpatrick exemplifies this painful consequence of law with reference to the civilizing mission of the colonialist on the one hand and the indigenous experiences of the aboriginal peoples in North America and Australia on the other. So long as we remain in the illusion that the system (*droit*) of laws (*lois*) has a foundation, we will pursue the colonizing project. Fitzpatrick brilliantly exposes how Chief Justice Lamer of the Canadian Supreme Court defined aboriginality in a way that aboriginal rights could not be defined except within the Enlightenment (i.e. Kantian) philosophical precepts of 'general and universal' (*R. v. van der Peet* [1996] 2 Supreme Court Reports 507, paras 17–19). And Fitzpatrick (2002) explains how the Australian High Court held the concept of *terra nullius* invalid only by the Court's refusal to challenge the concept of colonial acquisition. By inference, indigenous rights are not rights unless they are guided by the universal sameness inside the form(al) legal language of the Europeanized state. Rights are thereby distinguished from each other without addressing the social relations presupposed in the content of the rights as forms. But it is not surprising that Derrida would consider the law, as *Recht*, to be indeterminate. By associating laws (*lois*) with empty forms, Derrida finds it easy to represent justice as the unrepresentable and unsignifiable immediacy of utterer with intended objects, an immediacy that Derrida associates with a decision.

Individuality

Given that laws are understood as forms (or universals), we have to ask, 'What is the exteriority to the system of forms?' Derrida uses the terms *ipseity* and 'individuality' to describe the exteriority to the forms. What does he signify by individuality?

One might respond to this question by returning to the embodiment of meaning by the subject. We have seen, however, that in Derrida's theory of language, all there is is writing, and, as such, there is no subject except as constructed from the configurations of signs. The being is recognized as a legal person with rights and duties. The being is given a place with a name (Derrida and Dufourmantelle 2000: 35). That said, Derrida not infrequently describes the exteriority to law as a heterology of experienced events. Such events crystallize as a decision. There is no doubt, that is, that, in contrast to his early work (*Speech and Phenomena* and *Of Grammatology*), Derrida in later writings recognizes that the experiential meanings *do exist, but* his legal theory claims that they are excluded from the chains of signifiers which represent forms. Indeed, Derrida describes such experienced meanings as justice. Fitzpatrick too associates individuality or *ipseity* with 'the determinate presence' or immediacy upon which 'the universals are dependent' (2005: 4). The experiential meanings become an object of consciousness in a decision. These intended objects render the forms determinate. That is, the forms gain content. Yet the presence or immediacy of author with a decision is only a moment in experiential time. As such, it cannot be signified as a universal inside the border of *Recht* – so long as we understand *Recht* as empty universals or forms.

With this in mind, this may be what the guard of the doorway to the Castle of law meant when he ended the parable with the explanation that the doorway is only for the man from the country and no one else. If the man had been called to enter a doorway, some individual official would have had to make a determinate decision (Derrida and Dufourmantelle 2000: 61). The possibility arises that law would be other than form at that moment of decision (Fitzpatrick 2005: 6). The decision would determine the particular content of the form. Meaning-constituting acts of experiential knowledge would give body to such a determinacy. The determinate decision would be lived. A decision about the forms depends upon this experiential event for its content. This being so, law – as a system of forms – needs to *respond* to the experienced exteriority in order to have determinacy. The experiential meanings of the man from the country incorporate that determinacy. Without the response of codified forms to the context-specific experienced event, we are left with a self-generating and self-defining system of signifiers which construct the deific state and then claim legitimacy by tracing the signifiers to the state as an empty form.

This is the point where Fitzpatrick departs from Derrida. If officials, like the guard of the Castle, can never cross the boundary of the system of forms, the determinate legal decision is an unaccessed remainder to the system of laws as forms. For Fitzpatrick, the remainder is constituted from the individuality of a decision. The individuality, being a determinate decision, concerns a social being-with others (Fitzpatrick 2005: 14–15). It involves *being* because the exterior pre-legality is unreified by the chains of legal signs. It involves being *with*, because the beings only exist with other strangers to the chains of signs. It seems that Fitzpatrick leaves this social relationship as a 'given' in his argument. He is thereby able to locate social relationships in the very justice that is experienced *before* the content-independent forms are analysed (that is, decomposed). But because the forms are so dependent upon the pre-legal social relationships that law craves to enclose in determinate decisions – if only for a fleeting experienced moment – law must respond to unreified social relationships, according to Fitzpatrick. This is difficult for Derrida, because Derrida presupposes a territorial-like boundary that excludes the individuality of a decision (or intuition) as a remainder to laws as a system of forms. Such a boundary stands in the way of Law and of its discrete laws becoming Good. The Good, as a remainder, thereby exceeds the Law and laws (Derrida 1990: 257, quoted in Fitzpatrick 2005: 4).

The territorial sense of legal knowledge

I now wish to ask why it is that violence is considered part and parcel of Derrida's theory of law as a structure of forms. I wish to do so by claiming that the self-defining and self-sustaining system of forms presupposes a special sense of legal knowledge.

Legal knowledge (about *lois*) and knowledge about law (as *droit*) presuppose a territorial-like boundary that separates familiar concepts from an unrecognizable chaos. This territorial knowledge is presupposed about the analysis of laws as empty forms. Such knowledge is ironically preconceptual. It is a priori, or prior to the positivity of concepts, facts, and values. The territorial knowledge assumes a special sense of space and of time. Territorial (as opposed to experiential) space exists as the enclosure of a wild territory by a border. A physical thing exists if it can be located and measured inside the boundary of the space. A thing can be located by objective standards of longitude and latitude. The thing can be measured by a land survey. The thing can be perceived as a physical-chemical mass in territorial space. Even the actions of a human being can be perceived as if locatable on a measurable space within the boundary.

Now, it is a short step from such a sense of space as territorial or physical to a likened knowledge as possessing a territorial-like character. A territorial boundary demarcates an inside from an outside. As Derrida describes the territorial-like knowledge, which pre-censors the foreigner, 'what is at issue ... is once again the trace of a frontier between the public and the non-public, between public or political space and individual or familial home' (Derrida and Dufourmantelle 2000: 49–51). The foreigner on the other side of the frontier of legal knowledge is neither a subject nor an object. Derrida describes this *aporia* in this manner:

> What is a foreigner? What would a foreign woman be?
>
> It is not only the man or woman who keeps abroad of the outside of society, the family, the city. It is not the other, the completely other who is relegated to an absolute outside, savage, barbaric, precultural, and prejuridical, outside and prior to the family, the community, the city, the nation, or the State. The relationship to the foreigner is regulated by law, by the becoming-law of justice. This step would take us back to Greece, close to Oedipus and Socrates, if it wasn't already too late.
>
> (ibid.: 73)

The frontier of legal knowledge dwells in a twilight between the familiar forms inside the boundary of territorial knowledge and the chaos that remains unrecognized beyond the boundary. Subjectivity is believed to be situated in such a chaos. Law must be and remains objective so long as officials analyse the boundaries of forms.

Permit me to suggest several contexts where the common law presupposes territorial knowledge. First, constitutional law is preoccupied with the study of the boundary of legal knowledge. So too, federalism law has accepted territorial knowledge as the key to constitutionality. When constitutional bills of rights address whether to recognize the foreigner, the bills of rights presuppose just such a boundary between the language of rights on the one hand and pre-conceptual experiential knowledge on the other. If legal officials picture the being as outside the boundary of constitutional rights, the being remains nameless and her or his or its voice silent.

Second, territorial knowledge is also manifested in the radical title of the state to territory. Property is private to the state because, as a legal claim, the form of property represents all territory which is possessed and controlled within a territorial boundary. So, too, private property is recognized as legal knowledge because the property is believed to possess a territorial-like boundary, which mirrors the territorial boundary that physically demarcates myself from yourself. Third, even custom is juridified if it can be pinpointed as located on a territorial space and on the calendar date. If so pinpointed, custom is existent with a name (signifier). Both the custom and the culture with which it is identified must have a recognizable name. Interestingly, indigenous cultures began to take on names and on the distinct recognition of a 'tribe' after the Europeans pressed North American inhabitants further and further west, at least to the Rocky Mountains (Albers 1996: 90–118). Territorial knowledge recognizes the identity of beings. As Anne Dufourmantelle writes, '[T]his geography leads throughout the seminar to the revelation of the question

'Where?' as being the question of man' (Derrida and Dufourmantelle 2000: 52). The point that needs emphasis is that time only begins when the claim to knowledge inside a territorial boundary is established and space only exists as a legal condition once there is such a claim to territorial knowledge. Without such a boundary it is difficult for a legal official to speak of knowing the stranger.

The consequence of this territorial sense of time and space is that one knows something if that thing has a name which is recognized inside the 'known' boundary of knowledge. Knowledge is territorial. Officials recognize concepts, including the rule (i.e. concept) of recognition, from inside the territorial-like boundary of knowledge. The official's or philosopher's personal opinion about the content of a concept matters little. Such a personal opinion is something external to the boundary of knowledge. What matters is whether a form is recognizable inside the territorial-like boundary of knowledge. A concept itself is also territorial-like *intra vires* or *ultra vires*. And yet the boundary, being humanly constructed, presupposes a rupture or gap between the inside of legal knowledge and outside the wall. Territorial knowledge is prior to the possibility of the vacuous foundation (*droit*) of the system of forms (*lois*) as a whole.

There is another consequence of the territorial sense of knowledge. If a being inhabits a territory on the other side of territorial space, that being is a foreigner, a stranger, an alien (Conklin 2006a). The being is unrecognized and unrecognizable as a legal person with rights and duties. The being is undefined by statutory or common law rights and duties. Territorial knowledge needs this unrecognizable foreigner in order to maintain the boundary and frontier of legal knowledge. For there to be an inside and an outside, an *intra vires* and *ultra vires*, legal persons and aliens, citizens and non-citizens, familiar rules and unfamiliar rules, law and justice – for there to be such dichotomies, there has to be a territorial-like boundary that severs the inside from the outside. This boundary is so steadfast in our thinking that Derrida describes it and accepts it as 'the law of the law' (Derrida and Dufourmantelle 2000: 65). Derrida ironically seems to accept the boundary as an uncontrollable law – as a natural law, that is.

These two consequences of territorial knowledge are most obviously highlighted in the doctrine of *terra nullius* or 'vacant land', for example. When the Europeans began to settle in Australia, New Zealand, North and South America, and Africa, they brought with them this territorial-like sense of knowledge. Concepts such as the concepts of territorial control and entitlement to property required a fixity in a structure of knowledge. Since the indigenous societies were predominantly nomadic to the west of present-day south-western Ontario and James Bay and east of the Rockies (Albers 1996: 116), it is difficult to invariably describe an indigenous sense of territoriality as associated with a geographical fixity on land. Exclusivity, let alone title to property, hardly characterizes the sense of knowledge of nomadic groups. And yet, without a sense of the fixed and exclusive possession of territory it is difficult to understand how indigenous nomadic societies possessed private property, individual rights, and autonomous nations. Along similar lines, if the indigenous community lacked a semblance of a centrally organized government whose single leader the European military officials could identify with as an equal, treaties with such a community tended to lack a binding character upon the European party to the treaty. Such a territorial view of legal knowledge confers title to territory. The state owns 'ultimate title' or 'underlying title', as property, of all territory that it possesses and symbolically controls. States even extend this knowledge claim, of recent days, to the territorial space of the Arctic Ocean and the moon. The entitlement to the territory includes all resources, land, plants, and animals on, under, and above the territory. The best that strangers, unrecognized inside the territorial-like structure of forms, can claim is an 'inchoate' *usufructory* right to property. Interestingly, the *usufructory* right is a term adopted by Roman lawyers to describe the rights of slaves to possess, but not own, things.[6]

If space can only exist if there is a boundary surrounding a territory, and if indigenous societies did not share such a sense of space or institutionalize their life-worlds in terms of territorial knowledge, the European states could consider the settled lands as *terra nullius* or vacant even though many millions inhabited the territory prior to the transmission of disease and killing by Europeans. With the belief that legal knowledge was constrained by territorial-like boundaries, legal reasoning could even generate what the foreigners looked like as 'social fact'. Legal reasoning could also generate the foundation of the territorial knowledge. This construction of foreigner and of foundation could be maintained as objective fact and as consistent with the rule of law because officials only claimed knowledge within the territorial-like boundary. The boundary of territorial knowledge required that officials imagine the foreigner and the foundation as the inversion of their self-image as officials in a legal order. This inversion underlies Fitzpatrick's comment that civilization imagined itself as 'the kind of society which no longer recognizes any alternative to itself' (2004: 122, quoting Bauman 2001: 99). The consequence is that violence threatens a legal order from within legal language, not from without (Fitzpatrick 2001a: 292). The rule by laws unknowingly disguises violence against the pre-conceptual experiential knowledge as well as against the strangers whom the laws will not recognize with a name. Valid laws are *intra* the *vires*. Invalid laws are *ultra vires*.

This territorial-like knowledge impacts upon contemporary legal reasoning. Like the Law (*droit*) as a whole, each discrete form has a boundary within which the form has a universal scope. The unknowable is preconceptual. What extends beyond the form's boundary is the unknowable world. Each discipline has its own territorial-like boundary. Legal reasoning excludes bodily intuitions, feelings, attitudes, and other 'subjectivist' phenomena as extra-legal, political or moral. Being outside legal knowledge, such extra-legal experiential phenomena are considered arbitrary and chaotic for the legal professional. Such non-legal factors in legal reasoning represent an absence of the possibility of law and of practical reason. We lack names for such a pre-conceptual world. More correctly, we do confer a name on the pre-conceptual world, and that is the name 'power'. Power is juxtaposed with law; the pre-conceptual pre-legal world on the other side of the threshold of knowledge is juxtaposed with the acts of intellectualization inside the threshold. We officials must protect the possibility of a pre-legal world. It is our secret: this has been the social function of the professional North American law school. Officials can, at best, attempt to escape from the prison-house of language by picturing the unreified world on the other side of the frontier by a metaphor. Professional knowers of the familiar signifying relations take the standpoint of the knowable structure, not of the heterology of the voices of strangers on the other side of the border, when picturing the unreified world. The heterologous voices of the stranger, as Derrida (and Merleau-Ponty) emphasize, are silent (Derrida and Dufourmantelle 2000: 25–35). The analysis of forms as laws forgets the language of the foreigner on the other side of the rupture between the familiar and the unknowable, in advance. This pre-censorship of the heterology of voices, as Hart hints in his legal theory and in his private life, causes an 'indefinable anxiety' (Hart 1994: 87; Lacey 2004: 26). The silent voice of the stranger exterior to the threshold of territorial knowledge is 'that terrible thing which opens language to its own beyond' (Derrida 1985: 76).

And so, to take one example, and only as an example, international law presupposes territorial knowledge as a legal space that pre-exists the lawyer and legal critic. The boundary that makes this space possible legitimates the space as well as the rules, doctrines, and other forms, such as the state, which are locatable inside the boundary of legal space as knowable things. This territorial boundary of legal and moral knowledge remains manifested in the international law doctrine of *domaine réservée* whereby the territorial state alone has legitimacy to decide who is a citizen, who may enter its territorial borders, and whom it may expel from its borders. Unless categorized within the boundary of legal knowledge, a being is excluded from legal entitlement of certain rights and duties. One is an 'alien'. This is even so in many judicial decisions if one is habitually resident in the territory of the state for a long period of time. Indeed, the state officials enclose legal space within a structure of concepts such as the concept of property. This prior legitimizing territorial-like boundary was taken for granted in the early modern view of international law: international law existed, according to Fitzpatrick, 'from an already-encompassing scheme of things within which the nations found their existence' (2008a: 279).

This already-existing scheme was attributed to natural law, in the early modern period. Fitzpatrick (ibid.: 289) rightly quotes from Zygmunt Bauman (1989: 53) to describe the more recent colonial world as 'fully and exhaustively divided into national domains ... [with] no space left for internationalism'. This pre-existing division of the globe into legal spaces whose territorial-like boundaries set the limit to legal knowledge continues to the present day. Territorial knowledge prevents any transcendent commonality between the inside and the exteriority. Boundaries have separated legal persons (and therefore legal knowledge) throughout the globe. The boundaries render legal knowledge possible. And human beings invariably fail to be recognized as legal persons inside and outside the territorial boundary of many states.

Aside from the legal recognition of foreigners, territorial knowledge provides the background to our usual sense of freedom as negative. John Stuart Mill recognized this point in the context of his social philosophy as well as in his international legal theory. A boundary protected the territorial-like 'inner sphere of life' of an individual (Mill 1848/1970: 306). Inside the boundary the individual was free to choose and to act unless the individual caused harm by crossing the boundary of familiarity to the incomprehensible world of foreigners. At that point, one's acts were 'other-regarding' and, therefore, open to social scrutiny of the harm caused to other beings (Mill 1859/1962: 129). Mill (1984: 111–24) extended this image of territorial knowledge to the interrelations of the territorial state.

My point for raising this example of territorial knowledge in international law is to emphasize how territorial knowledge reinforces the disguised violence of discrete forms as well as of the ultimate foundation of the forms. The universalist claim of the ultimate foundation of a secular legal order – the state – absorbed the universalism of the medieval Christendom (see especially Fitzpatrick 2006b). Legal philosophers from Bodin to Hart have acknowledged the need both to ground law in something external to knowable legal rules (the state of nature, the general will, the People, social facts) and, at the same time, to describe the system of rules as 'autonomous, enclosed in itself, coherent in itself, and, in a sense above all, self-generating' (Fitzpatrick 2009: 5).

To this end, the rule of law (the rule by law) is an all-or-nothing matter: either self-contained forms or, alternatively, externalized unknowable chaos. In either case, power relations determine the outcome of disputes. Law is juxtaposed to power and power to law. If I am right that territorial knowledge is presupposed in the argument that the foundation of law (*droit*) and the forms (*lois*) of law are vacuous, then violence is part and parcel of the rule by laws – so long, that is, as we retain territoriality as the paradigm of knowledge.

And so, the best that we can do within the boundary of territorial knowledge is to *imagine* the strangeness on the other side of the boundary of familiar concepts. Knowledge of the stranger is a territorial knowledge. The stranger is pictured. And the picture offers a typified form rather than a crossing of the form's boundary to the concrete experienced events of a concrete context-specific being, to the particularity of a decision by an official her- or himself. This ontic character of legal reasoning about strangers is necessary once we accept that knowledge exists within a territorial-like boundary. Anything that does not come within the universal has to be 'utterly antithetical' or of a 'totally different existence' (Fitzpatrick 2003c: 11). One has to *picture* or *imagine* the totally different existence that the self-defining law has failed to enclose. The picture re-presents the stranger in terms that are familiar to officials of the state. One cannot know the non-form, this being the individuality of an experienced event by the stranger or even by the official. The interrelated system of forms, better known as primary and secondary rules, without a picture of the stranger outside the boundary of the system, cannot be known. One cannot know the stranger's language except through our own configurations of signifier and form inside the make-believe wall of territorial knowledge. Nor can one know the rule of law, as a form, without picturing its opposite: rational chaos. Lawyers and judges have to imagine what it would be like without private property, the association of morality with legal rights, the juridification of lived experiences, a secular state, and centralized institutions. Thus, the radical stranger, as antithetical to law, is an optic product because the officials 'perceive' the stranger as inverted to their own self-image as professional knowers of forms. Early common law judgements and authorities (e.g. Blackstone, Adam Smith), contemporary judges (Brennan and Lamer), and legal philosophers (John Austin and Hart) share such an optic vision of the stranger. They are 'undeveloped' or 'primitive'. So, given the theological origin of law in a secularized ideology and given the self-defined universalism of a form, anything outside the boundary of the form has to be included. The universalist aspiration of the form is undermined if the exterior is not included. What is not included within the boundary of knowledge remains alien to the system of forms. The outside offers a challenge for assimilation or conquest. The consequence is that laws are invariably violent against groups and individuals who do not share the content of the forms.

The self-generating and self-regulative legal forms require that law must resist the very possibility of something or someone radically strange to the forms (see Fitzpatrick 2003a: 219–21; 2003b: 438–46; 2003c: 10–16; 2008a: 181–6). Forms enclose everything, and yet can never fully enclose everything. The remainder resists the forms. Fitzpatrick explains the necessary resistance as follows:

> If it [law] were not coherent but contradictory, something else could resolve the contradiction. If it were not closed but open, then something else could enter and rule instead of or along with law. If it were

> incomplete and not a whole *corpus juris* and thence necessarily related to something else, then that something else could share in the ruling with law. Finally, a law which in any of these situations is not going to be dependent upon something else must also be self-originating and self-regulating.
>
> (2003b: 432)

Accordingly, law must either resist or conquer the 'utterly antithetical' chaos and indeterminacy on the other side of law (Fitzpatrick 2003c: 11).[7]

And so, here, we find a paradox. On the one hand, law must *resist* the radical strangeness of individuality in order to sustain its universality. On the other hand, law must *respond* to this radically antithetical strangeness for law to be determinate in content. In the absence of such a response there remains something unrecognized 'out there', far beyond the boundary of the universal legal forms. But this remainder contradicts and undermines the very identity of law as empty forms. The radical strangeness to forms is, drawing from well-known Kafka's parable, *before* the law – 'before' because particular experiences, such as K's, are, as I read Kafka, unreified by the territorial knowledge of the decisions of professional knowers.

The territorial knowledge of justice

Now, once we entertain that forms attempt to assimilate yet forms need the exteriorized justice (as the heterology of meant or embodied objects) in order to be determinate, we must ask whether Derrida's theory of law is well taken. In order to respond to this issue, let us gain a better idea of what is the justice that Derrida considers external to territorial knowledge. To this end, Fitzpatrick offers four contexts.

First, the rule by law conceals the violence that the legal structure perpetuates against infinite individualities that Derrida has associated with justice. Second, so long as professional knowers believe in the deific foundation, the legal structure cannot possibly represent or manifest a social bonding (Fitzpatrick 2001c: 6; 2005: 14). After all, the legal structure is constituted from empty universals and the determinate decision is an individuated decision. There might be 'Being with', as Heidegger and Ben-Dor (Ben-Dor 2007) claim, but such a Being is inexpressible and inaccessible if we are limited to our ontic picture of the Being on the other side of the territorial boundary between law and the stranger. Such an idealized 'Being-with', however, is hardly what Fitzpatrick has in mind when he uses the term 'being with' as the remainder of law. Third, forms, as universals, lack an incorporation of the pre-conceptual objects, which the third (the judge) means (in Husserl's sense of meant objects in his *Logical Investigations*).[8] This absence of meant objects also characterizes the languages of beings who lack legal recognition. Although the Greeks used the term *nomos* to represent the drawing of a territorial boundary in the sand, *nomos* also represented the emotions and beliefs experienced by a group (Fitzpatrick 2001c: 211–12, 221). In a fourth context, Kafka's parable of the man from the country raises the prospect of the individuality of the one's experiences and the inability of the guard to the castle of law to allow the man to enter the universals of law through the doorway especially made for him (see Derrida 1992: 191, discussed in Fitzpatrick 2005: 9). Further, as I have already observed of H. L. A. Hart (1994: 87), a dread overcomes the jurist and philosopher who faces the prospect that concepts do not control decisions (see also Lacey 2004). Today, philosophers describe this dread of individuality as idiosyncratic, subjective, arbitrary, and the like.

Now, what is interesting is that for Derrida, justice is the very presence or immediacy, which in his earlier works he had argued was inaccessible to language (Derrida 1973). For Derrida, forms lack an immediate bonding or presence of the individual with the forms (see especially Fitzpatrick 2005: 6). Yet Husserl had claimed that just such a bonding of utterer with signifiers characterizes acts of embodied meaning. The bonding is manifested in an intuition. This intuition characterizes a decision. Because experience, expressed as meaning rather than as signification (the signifier/signified relation), determines a decision, law, as signified forms, excludes the 'distinctiveness' of 'the singularity of lived experience' (Fitzpatrick 2009). This excluded, yet necessary, determinacy ironically begs that we study the role of phenomenology in *le droit* as well as in *des lois*. We cannot know law without knowing the experiential pre-conceptual world that territorial knowledge has excluded as unknowable. Fitzpatrick has a different name for this phenomenology: the 'sociologic' or 'meta-ethics' (2003b: 444).[9] Territorial knowledge has so far presupposed a rupture between the forms of territorial knowledge and the experiential meanings best manifested in intuition or a decision. The question I raise is whether there is another sense of legal knowledge, one that does not require a leap from *Verstand* to phenomena or from phenomena to *Verstand*. After all, as von Uexküll urged, 'the secret of the world is to be sought not behind objects [such as indeterminate forms], but behind subjects' (1926: 29). Such subjects embody determinate meant objects.

My point bears repeating. As legal officials we tend to recognize the stranger by assimilating the stranger into the metaphysical boundaries of concepts, the concepts being rights, duties, and rules. This act of juridification leaves the language of the stranger unassimilated. The sociability of the stranger remains uncodified. I have elaborated the complexity of this uncodified sociability elsewhere (Conklin 1998: 222–48).[10] This social bonding is experienced as immediacy without the intervention of concepts. A determinate decision cannot represent what is not enclosed within its concepts. Accordingly, sociability characterizes the presence of unreified beings that the coded rules, representing forms, do not and cannot access inside the boundary of territorial knowledge. Legality depends upon this sociability because, contrary to the whole thrust of contemporary analytical jurisprudence that concepts can be and are reasons for action, 'in law' '"no existing, coded rule can or ought to guarantee absolutely" in advance [of] the outcome of any decision' (Derrida 1990: 251, quoted in Fitzpatrick 2009: 17). That Derrida even acknowledges presence or immediacy as important for an understanding of law is interesting, given his claim that just such a presence lies at the core to the philosophy of metaphysics. One needs to be mindful of Derrida's critique of presence throughout his works about language. The unrepresented presence of sociability is really 'a law of originary sociability, prior to all *determined* law, *qua* natural law or positive law, but not prior to law *in general*' (Derrida 1997: 231, quoted in Fitzpatrick 2005: 7, emphasis in original). The 'law in general', of course, is composed of the empty universals. Of course, once the foundation is exposed as vacuous, we are left with the social belonging that is other than transcendent, content-independent forms. Derrida understands justice as otherwise than content-independent forms. Justice, for Derrida, is excised from the metaphysics of forms (Fitzpatrick 2005: 6).

Fitzpatrick makes an analytic argument as to why law must respond to justice in Derrida's sense of justice. First, Fitzpatrick restates Nancy's point that an excluded singularity cannot be *with* another singularity without the pre-existence of both the included and excluded singularities. An ontological community thereby exists in a far deeper sense than 'man as a social being' (Nancy 1991: 28).[11] Next, Fitzpatrick draws from Davidson, who explains that different entities can only be distinct and yet have a relation with each other 'if there is a common coordinate system on which to plot them' (Davidson 1985: 130, quoted in Fitzpatrick 2008a: 289). Fitzpatrick reverses this idea by suggesting that if different entities are things-in-themselves and yet are being-with each other, then the only commonality possible is external to sameness. Thus, a community 'as a continuate being-with cannot be contained within any existent realization of it ... it must ever extend receptively beyond present existence, otherwise it will not be able to continue "in being"' (ibid.: 289). So, law forever responds to the excluded 'being-with' that remains unrealized in empty universals at any one determinate moment. A law, considered an empty form, depends upon what is excluded from it for its determinate content. For example, both the universal and general laws of the colonial states and the universal *ius gentium* of international law are empty of content by virtue of their claim to universality. And yet they are dependent upon the absent infinite individualities of aboriginal peoples and of the particular *ethe* of nations for their content. This being so, 'this vertiginous alternation' between the (posited formal) law on the one hand and then its determinate response to the 'existently singular' of 'being-with' on the other is the 'pointed place for [justice as] access' (Fitzpatrick 2005: 14).

This argument holds only so long as we share Derrida's sense of laws as empty forms, however. Given the universal as a metaphysical construct, given the emptiness of such a universal, and given that the universal is signified in writing, these three conditions necessitate that singularity be excluded upon the positing of the legal decision. Justice is thereby derived from the exteriority on the other side of the territorial-like boundary of law. But such formalist law presupposes the territorial sense of knowledge. What is recognized as a universal is signified *inside* the territorial boundary of the familiar. The walled construction is signified in writing vis-à-vis speech. Such a view of legal knowledge reinforces the territorial sense of law and, accordingly, of justice. What remains unrecognized is excluded as non-law. The experiential body of the third is also excluded. But if lived experiences remain untouched by legal forms, does not this raise the need to reconsider the identity of laws as discrete, content-independent universals? Is not experiential knowledge important in understanding 'what is a determinate law'? And if this is so, is there some sense of law otherwise than universal forms?

Regrettably, space (territorial space) prevents me from elaborating a theory of law as social content (see Conklin 2008). Derrida, it bears reminding, relies heavily upon Kant's moral and legal works for Derrida's own understanding of the identity of law. For Kant, again, a universal transcends social phenomena by virtue of its emptiness of social-cultural content. A universal, however, is a norm whose content is shared in an ethos. The function of the decision-maker is to identify the presupposed reciprocal social relations in the content of a form and then to address whether those reciprocal relations are coherent with the said relations in the ethos of which formal laws are only one element (see Conklin 2008: 83–112, 156–87). Hegel argues, rightly, that the critical issue is not 'what is law?' but 'what identified form is legitimate?' A determinate decision does not exist as a legally binding decision unless the meant, as opposed to signified, objects of its content manifests a reciprocal recognition of beings. This view of the legitimacy of law undermines Derrida's legal formalism. More, this view of the legitimacy of Law and of laws explains on my terms (rather than Fitzpatrick's) why Law and laws must respond to justice as Derrida (and Fitzpatrick) understand justice.

Discrete determinate decisions (including Derrida's concern for determinacy in a decision) cannot exist without such a determinate decision being legitimate. And the legitimacy of a law, in turn, depends upon the reciprocal recognition of individuals as presupposed in the content of a discrete form. Laws do not exist, that is, without the very content that Kant excludes from the universal form of *das Recht* and that Derrida believes only arrives on the scene in the decidability of an official's reasoning about empty forms. If Hegel's understanding of discrete laws is compelling, then the antithetical chaos, savagery, and feminine – the locus of experiential time and space – is not dependent upon the universal form of the foundation such as the state or humanism. Rather, determinate laws are nested in the experiential and shared meanings of a pre-legality. This pre-legality has heretofore been excluded from 'the law' and from the study of law in the analytic tradition. This is so both analytically and phenomenologically before universal forms are ever posited as the starting point of the philosophy about the nature of law. Accordingly, the secret of determinate laws lies in the subject's constitution and fulfilment of meanings. The exposure of such a secret, though, begs that one inquire into the legitimacy of universals. If inquiry proceeds behind such forms to the subject's constitution and fulfilment of embodied meaning, it may be that such meaning provides the determinacy that has heretofore been excluded from law.

Once we reconsider Derrida's understanding of law and of laws as empty forms, a whole series of issues is begged. Most importantly, 'does the judge as "the third" address justice, as lived experiences, when the third makes a determinate decision?' And if so, 'are determinate decisions rendered with reference to standards that are not posited but rather are constituted from the intentional acts of the third (that is, of the lived acts of meaning according to Husserl)?' A phenomenology of the pre-legal world undermines Derrida's theory of law. As a consequence, the phenomenology of the pre-legal world is the call for justice.

The contemporary professional knower of 'legal' signs has been satisfied with the positing of social facts or with the justification of forms nested in posited beliefs and values. Until the rich writings of Fitzpatrick are recognized, jurists and philosophers will continue to bury their heads in the sand and to close their eyes as if blind to the vacuity of the foundation of a legal structure. The problem is especially critical because of the risk that we forget that we have even forgotten the vacuity of the foundation of a modern legal order and thereby the excision of the pre-legality from legal recognition. If one forgets an experience, one can remember it (sometimes with the aid of a therapist). But if one forgets that one ever forgot the experience, one can never remember it. We have claimed to be lawyers and legal philosophers who know how to imagine the outside but we do not know what we have been talking about. We have been content with the decomposition of concepts as signified by the analytic methodology. And yet, 'There is still here a primary assertion of the bounded to which a ranging beyond remains tethered. There has to be yet more. Nomos cannot be positioned only in the bounded but must somehow extend intrinsically to an "outside"' (Fitzpatrick 2001c: 221). The outside is inside – that is, the officials and philosophers of the state themselves posit who is outside, a foreigner, to a legal order, and the outside is derived from the inside of territorial knowledge.

A phenomenology of the pre-legal world has been introduced elsewhere (Conklin 1998, 2006a, b, 2008). What I need to emphasize at this point is that experiential knowledge raises the prospect that the identity of law radically differs from the empty forms with which Derrida derives his understanding of laws. For just as lived meanings embody the stranger's, as K's, individuality upon which legal forms depend, so too the professional knower incorporates meant or experienced objects that determine one's decisions. Such meant objects radically differ from the posited determinate standards that officials and legal philosophers have heretofore taken for granted as objectivity. Such determinate standards are meant. And meant objects are shared in the collective memories of an ethos. Meant objects are not the same as perceived or posited objects. Meant objects are concealed inside the forms that Derrida takes for granted as the essence of law. Such meant objects draw from bodily experiences rather than from the objectivity of the signifier/form relations with which Derrida identifies *le droit* and *les lois*.

The issue is whether embodied meanings in an ethos play a role in the identity of law and of laws. Are the objects of experiential knowledge shared in such a deep and self-conscious way that one can speak about social bonding and a social ethos as integral parts of laws? And if a form's content is determinate – that is, if the phenomenology of meaning constitutes determinate forms – does sociability still dwell exterior to the law? Justice is access, just as Fitzpatrick claimed. But the access is directed towards the intentional acts of the official, just as access also addresses the intentional acts of non-officials. Shared intentional meanings constitute the social bonding that legitimizes the content of determinate decisions. Derrida's sense of law sets out such bonding as somehow another law that differs from the Kantian empty universals. But such formalism is hardly recognizable as a system of laws precisely because forms are not legal units if their content lacks legitimacy and if legitimacy addresses the reciprocal relations of individuals in an ethos presupposed by the content of a form's boundaries. Territorial knowledge fails to address such a possibility because territorial knowledge posits a boundary between the inside and outside, formalism and social-cultural ethos, universal and individuality, law and justice. Without an inquiry into the content of the inside – of the forms and universals – the territorial-like boundary misdirects what is law and, therefore, of law's call for justice.

Notes

1 I explain this point in more detail in Conklin (2001: 37–55).
2 See, for example, Kramer (2007: 16, 75) and Leiter (2007: 55, 101, 133, 258). For Hart's view, see Hart (1977: 969). According to Hart, the pre-legal experience of social bonding 'haunts much legal thought' (1994: 87) as if it were 'a chain binding those who have obligations so that they are not free to do what they want'. Hart acknowledged that pre-theoretical differences might well have explained why Hart and Fuller saw the world so differently: 'I am haunted by

the fear that our starting-points and interests in jurisprudence are so different that the author and I are fated never to understand each other's work' (1983: 343). Nicola Lacey (2004) describes how Hart dreaded the intervention of experience into rationality in his day-to-day life.

3 On this point, see, for example, Derrida (1990: 233, 245, 254, 275; 1992: 191, 194; 1994: 28, 190; 2002: 3–18) and Derrida and Dufourmantelle (2000: 69–73, 147–51). Fitzpatrick incorporates the problematic as Kant's in many of his writings (see, for example, Fitzpatrick 2005: 11).

4 This notion is generally explained in Conklin (2008: 95–9).

5 This is explained in more detail in Conklin (2008: 99–112, 162–87).

6 Although the slave could use the *peculium* as a source of capital income and, over time, could amass sufficient funds, the slave could not own property (see Borkowski and du Plessis 2005: 96–7).

7 Here, the resistance is not *to* law nor *against* law but *of* law. Modern law must *resist* its antithetical alien, the experience of individuality.

8 A meant object is generated from the act of meaning of the individual's experiential body. This contrasts with an object that is posited by a source external to such an act of meaning. Edmund Husserl explains this distinction in his *Logical Investigations* (1970), and the distinction is elaborated in Conklin (1998: 30, 103, 207).

9 The possibility of understanding law as such ethicality in the content of legal forms is addressed in further detail in Conklin (2008: 169–87).

10 This sociability arises because an individual, by her- or himself, does not exist unless she or he relates to other beings, according to Fitzpatrick (2006b: 82).

11 Fitzpatrick cites Nancy's analysis on several occasions.

References

Albers, P. C. (1996) 'Changing patterns of ethnicity in the northeastern plains', in J. D. Hill (ed.) *History, Power and Identity: Ethnogenesis in the Americas, 1492–1992*, Iowa City: University of Iowa Press.

Bauman, Z. (1989) *Modernity and the Holocaust*, Cambridge: Cambridge University Press.

Bauman, Z. (2001) *The Individualized Society*, Cambridge: Polity Press.

Ben-Dor, O. (2007) *Thinking about Law: In Silence with Heidegger*, Oxford: Hart.

Borkowski, A. and du Plessis, P. (2005) *Textbook on Roman Law*, 3rd edn, Oxford: Oxford University Press.

Conklin, W. (1993) 'Teaching critically within a modern legal genre', *Canadian Journal of Law and Society* 8: 33–57.

Conklin, W. (1996) 'The trace of legal idealism in Derrida's grammatology of law', *Philosophy and Social Criticism* 22: 17–42.

Conklin, W. (1998) *Phenomenology of Modern Legal Discourse*, Aldershot, UK: Dartmouth.

Conklin, W. (2001) *Invisible Origins of Legal Positivism*, Dordrecht: Kluwer.

Conklin, W. (2006a) 'A phenomenological theory of the human rights of the alien', *Ethical Perspectives* 13: 245–301.

Conklin, W. (2006b) 'Lon Fuller's phenomenology of language', *International Journal for Semiotics of Law* 19: 93–125.

Conklin, W. (2008) *Hegel's Laws: The Legitimacy of a Modern Legal Order*, Stanford, CA: Stanford University Press.

Davidson, D. (1985) 'On the very idea of a conceptual scheme', in J. Rajchman and C. West (eds) *Post-analytic Philosophy*, New York: Columbia University Press.

Derrida, J. (1973) 'Differance', in *Speech and Phenomena and Other Essays on Husserl's Theory of Signs*, trans. D. B. Allison, Evanston, IL: Northwestern University Press.

Derrida, J. (1974) *Of Grammatology*, trans. G. Chakravorty Spivak, Baltimore: Johns Hopkins University Press.

Derrida, J. (1985) *The Ear of the Other: Otobiography, Transference, Translation*, trans. P. Kamuf, ed. C. McDonald, Lincoln: University of Nebraska Press.

Derrida, J. (1987) 'The laws of reflection: Nelson Mandela, in admiration', in J. Derrida (ed.) *For Nelson Mandela*, New York: Saver Books.

Derrida, J. (1989) 'Psychic inventions of the other', in L. Waters and W. Godzich (eds) *Reading de Man Reading*, trans. C. Porter, Minneapolis: University of Minnesota Press.

Derrida, J. (1990) 'Force of law: The "mystical foundation of authority"', trans. M. Quaintance, *Cardozo Law Review* 11: 919–1045; reprinted in J. Derrida (2002) *Acts of Religion*, ed. Gil Anidjar, New York: Routledge [citations are to the latter translation].

Derrida, J. (1992) 'Before the law', in D. Attridge (ed.) *Acts of Literature*, New York: Routledge.

Derrida, J. (1994) *Specters of Marx*, New York: Routledge.

Derrida, J. (1997) *Politics of Friendship*, trans. G. Collins, London: Verso.

Derrida, J. (2002) *Ethics, Institutions, and the Right to Philosophy*, trans. and ed. P. Trifonas, Lanham, MD: Rowman & Littlefield.

Derrida, J. and Dufourmantelle, A. (2000) *Of Hospitality*, trans. R. Bowlby, Stanford, CA: Stanford University Press.

Fitzpatrick, P. (1990) 'Custom as imperialism', in J. M. Abun-Nasr, U. Spellenberg, and U. Wanitzek (eds) *Law, Society and National Identity*, Hamburg: Helmut Buske Verlag.

Fitzpatrick, P. (1992) *Mythology of Modern Law*, London: Routledge.

Fitzpatrick, P. (1998) 'Traversing *terra nullius*: Legal origins and Freudian fictions', *Law, Text, Culture* 4: 18–47.

Fitzpatrick, P. (2001a) 'Consolations of the law: Jurisprudence and the constitution of deliberative politics', *Ratio Juris* 14: 281–97.

Fitzpatrick, P. (2001b) 'Magnified features: The underdevelopment of law and legitimation', in I. Pardo (ed.) *Morals of Legitimacy: Between Agency and System*, Oxford: Berghahn Books.

Fitzpatrick, P. (2001c) *Modernism and the Grounds of Law*, Cambridge: Cambridge University Press.

Fitzpatrick, P. (2001d) 'Why the law is also nonviolent', in A. Sarat (ed.) *Law, Violence and the Possibility of Justice*, Princeton, NJ: Princeton University Press.

Fitzpatrick, P. (2002) '"No higher duty": *Mabo* and the failure of legal foundation', *Law and Critique* 13: 233–52.

Fitzpatrick, P. (2003a) 'Breaking the unity of the world: Savage sources and feminine law', *Australian Feminist Law Journal* 19: 47–60, reprinted in P. Fitzpatrick, *Law as Resistance: Modernism, Imperialism, Legalism*, Burlington, VT: Ashgate [citations are to the latter reprint].

Fitzpatrick, P. (2003b) '"Gods would be needed...": American empire and the rule of (international) law', *Leiden Journal of International Law* 16: 429–66.

Fitzpatrick, P. (2003c) '"In God we trust" can relieve us of trusting each other', *The Believer* 3: 63–72, reprinted in P. Fitzpatrick, *Law as Resistance: Modernism, Imperialism, Legalism*, Burlington, VT: Ashgate [citations are to latter reprint].

Fitzpatrick, P. (2004) 'Terminal legality? Human rights and critical being', in P. Fitzpatrick and P. Tuitt (eds) *Critical Beings: Law, Nation and the Global Subject*, Aldershot, UK: Ashgate.

Fitzpatrick, P. (2005) 'Justice as access', *Windsor Yearbook of Access to Justice* 23: 3–16.

Fitzpatrick, P. (2006a) 'Righteous empire', *Unbound: Harvard Journal of the Legal Left* 2: 1–18. Online, available at: www.law.harvard.edu/students/orgs/unbound/articles/2UNB001-Fitzpatrick.pdf.

Fitzpatrick, P. (2006b) '"What are the Gods to us now?": Secular theology and the modernity of law', *Theoretical Inquiries in Law* 8: 161–90.

Fitzpatrick, P. (2008a) 'Latin roots: Imperialism and the making of modern law', *Clave: Counterdisciplinary Notes on Race, Power and the State.* Online, available at: www.clave.org/latinroots.pdf; reprinted in P. Fitzpatrick, *Law as Resistance: Modernism, Imperialism, Legalism*, Burlington, VT: Ashgate [citations are to the latter reprint].

Fitzpatrick, P. (2008b) *Law as Resistance: Modernism, Imperialism, Legalism*, Burlington, VT: Ashgate.

Fitzpatrick, P. (2009) 'Law as theory: Constitutive thought in the formation of (legal) practice', *Socio-Legal Review* 5: 1–20.

Hart, H. L. A. (1977) 'American jurisprudence through English eyes: The nightmare and the dream', *Georgia Law Review* 11: 969–89.

Hart, H. L. A. (1983) 'Lon L. Fuller: The morality of law', in H. L. A. Hart, *Essays in Jurisprudence and Philosophy*, Oxford: Clarendon.

Hart, H. L. A. (1994) *Concept of Law*, 2nd edn, Oxford: Clarendon.

Husserl, E. (1970) *Logical Investigations*, trans. J. N. Finley, vol. 2, London: Routledge & Kegan Paul.

Husserl, E. (2001) *Logical Investigations*, vol. 2, trans. J. N. Findlay, London: Routledge [first published in German in 1900–1].

Kafka, F. (1988) 'The problem of our laws', in *Collected Short Stories of Franz Kafka*, trans. W. Muir and E. Muir, London: Penguin.

Kant, I. (1797/1996) *Metaphysics of Morals*, trans. M. Gregor, Cambridge: Cambridge University Press.

Kramer, M. H. (2007) *Objectivity and the Rule of Law*, Cambridge: Cambridge University Press.

Lacey, N. (2004) *A Life of H. L. A. Hart: The Nightmare and the Noble Dream*, Oxford: Oxford University Press.

Leiter, B. (2007) *Naturalizing Jurisprudence: Essays on American Legal Realism and Naturalism in Legal Philosophy*, Oxford: Oxford University Press.

Mill, J. S. (1859/1962) *On Liberty*, ed. M. Warnock, Glasgow: William Collins.

Mill, J. S. (1848/1970) *Principles of Political Economy*, ed. D. Winch, London: Penguin Books.

Mill, J. S. (1984) 'A few words on non-intervention', in J. Robson (ed.) *Essays on Equality, Law and Education – Collected Works of J. S. Mill*, vol. 2, Toronto: University of Toronto Press.

Mostert, H. and Fitzpatrick, P. (2004a) '"Living in the margins of history on the edge of the country": Legal foundation and the Richterveld community's title to land', *Journal of South African Law* 2: 309–23.

Nancy, J. L. (1991) *The Inoperative Community*, ed. P. Connor, Minneapolis: University of Minnesota.

R. v. van der Peet [1996] 2 Supreme Court Reports 507.

Uexküll, J. von (1926) *Theoretical Biology*, trans. D. L. Mackinnon, London: Kegan Paul.

Žižek, S. (1991) *For They Know Not What They Do: Enjoyment as a Political Factor*, London: Verso.

Chapter 8

Reading Luther

Law, modernity, and psychoanalysis

Judith Grbich

> After eight years my release day came.... We were given our sealed files, some small change and our tickets to Sydney. After many hours the train finally pulled in at Central Station and I walked into my new life, the last words of Mr Worthington still beating in my brain: 'Remember, 33, black people are the scum of the earth.'
>
> (Simon, Montgomerie, and Tuscano 2009)

The invitation of Fitzpatrick's *Mythology of Modern Law*

Bill Simon's story of being an indigenous child in Australia in the middle of the twentieth century, stolen from his parents' home by state officials in New South Wales at age ten and incarcerated for eight years in a 'boys home' in which each boy was a number, beaten, humiliated, and emotionally abused, has added to my questions about how to research and write law in ways that seek to understand law's role in institutional racism and its supports in everyday racism. The gratuitous insult of Mr Worthington, employed by the Kinchela Boys Home to care for indigenous children, is both strange and ordinary.

My story here is one of reflecting upon 'reading modern law' in a way that reveals methods and rationales and also one of acknowledging how the work of Peter Fitzpatrick has contributed to my reading of modern law. My research has a focus on power and money, sexism, racism, and colonialism. Trying to understand the legal and cultural supports of racism remains its focus. Ian Duncanson's early historical critique of legal theory had pointed to the worlds of science, history, and politics within which contemporary jurisprudence seemed embedded. The 'legitimacy and validity' of law were 'a kind of *gestalt*' (Duncanson 1984: 159), and in jurisprudence, law became 'a *séance* of self-designating officials, gazing at a space and materializing a supreme rule' (Duncanson 1982: 18). The languages of Irigaray (1985) and Spivak (1989) on embodiment and power opened up the intellectual histories of the *gestalt* and the *séance*, in one form or another (Grbich 1992).

The 1970 English translation of Foucault's *The Order of Things* drew many English-speaking Anglo academics into researching the poetic forms and pictures within which one lived and breathed the disciplinary relations of the human sciences. Biology, economics, and the sciences of language were tracked by Foucault back from their heydays in nineteenth-century facticities and positive epistemologies, to their eighteenth-century lives in the European Enlightenment concerns with life, labour, and language. In Foucault's consummate creation, and dismantling, of man as an 'analytic of finitude', as a 'strange empirico-transcendental doublet', the research bearings of the Anglo academic community changed. Foucault (1970: 203) had led us through early modern philology, grammars, taxonomies, natural sciences, and wealth sciences, and had proposed that we could understand the domain of wealth as being like a domain of words. Order in the domain of wealth had the same mode of being as the order of representation as manifested by words. Theories of money acted like functions of language: there were moments in each of 'attribution, articulation, designation, derivation'. Foucault linked the theory of money and the theory of value with a general grammar (ibid.: 73). Money and value were both sciences of 'signs that authorize exchange and permit the establishment of equivalency between men's needs and desires', and in his 'general grammar' there flourished 'the science of signs by means of which men group together their individual perceptions and pattern the continuous flow of their thoughts' (ibid.: 73). Foucault ventured tentatively into the order of things in psychoanalysis, preferring to stop short with mention of Freud's achievements in *Totem and Taboo*, of bringing psychoanalysis and ethnology into a common field, and the establishment of the possibility of 'a discourse that could move from one to the other without discontinuity, the double articulation of the history of individuals upon the unconscious of culture, and of the historicity of those cultures upon the unconscious of individuals' (ibid.: 379). Foucault stopped short at that point of recognizing that as man 'has killed God, it is he himself who must answer for his own finitude: but since it is in the death of God that he speaks, thinks, and exists, his murder itself is doomed to die'. He brings us to Nietzsche and 'the explosion of man's face in laughter, and the return of masks' (ibid.: 385).

In Peter Fitzpatrick's writing in *The Mythology of Modern Law* (1992), Foucault's picturing of the character and order of representation was taken up with a focus on law's own jurisprudential prehistory, law's archive, law's archaeology. Peter's questions were of modernity, and of law as a kind of mythology, a mythology of Genesis in which a creationist God of the Hebrews makes things and man with names, and dwells within the modern self as an origin story of law. Peter's research sought to 'subvert

Western rationalities from within by heightening the contradictions and suppressions involved in their construction ... [in] an attempt at internal decolonization' (ibid.: 13–14). Following his questions and methods, I began to ask, what is the character of this God, which dwells as a colonizer within, and who or what aspect of ourselves has this God colonized? Peter located his study of modern law as having mythic foundations in a focus upon objects of the modern world; where Enlightenment and modernity rejected mythology, it was returned, in Peter's writing, in the occidental form of a kind of property whose absence was a sign of savagery: 'where it is absent there can only be its precursors or savagery' (ibid.: 50). He raised the paradox of the casting out of the savage from the Christian light by Enlightenment belief, and Enlightenment use of Judaeo-Christian mythologies to make the European identity and law in a comparison with what it was not: the savage. In Peter's writing on the 'mythic consolidation of modern law' in nineteenth-century jurisprudence he never quite names the figure of the savage as the New Testament Christ, never quite names the subject of the analytic of finitude as the industrial labourer sacrificed on the altar of a national currency, and never quite names the universal industrial worker as the new savage of a financial colonialism as old as Luther. At this threshold my own research methodologies from Duncanson, Foucault, and Fitzpatrick ventured into those disciplinary boundaries of legal theory, political economy, property law, and poetics. In his *Modernism and the Grounds of Law*, Peter brought 'Freud's alluring tale' in *Totem and Taboo* (Freud 1990) into service 'to situate the analysis of law's grounds' (Fitzpatrick 2001: 1). Critical legal theory in the Anglo world could no longer ignore how psychoanalysis might play a role in law's story of authority, rule, and justice, or how the legal subject appeared to be gendered male and always accompanied by images of a feminized and abject other.

In that serendipitous way of most legal academic research, I found my research plans for a critique of taxation law during a 'study leave' programme in Edinburgh somewhat dampened on finding that the university library held no legal judgments from Australian courts. Those were the days before electronic archives. As my political economy of taxation had been developed upon Australian case law and readings of Foucault, a change of plan was needed. Walking past the First of May bookshop in Edinburgh, which was closing down, I was invited to take what I needed. So Marx became my new study leave programme for the next six months, and Marx's 'Revenue and Its Sources: Vulgar Political Economy' (1972), with its focus on fetishisms, the fictions of capital and property, and the insights of Luther, became my research methodologies. I read for its poetics of generation. Marx, born a Jew and raised a Lutheran, named the revenue returns from financial property as fetishism, and as transubstantiation. He used the already critical language of his Lutheran upbringing in which the wine and bread of the Catholic Mass became the blood and body of Christ to theorize, or perhaps simply to describe, how the illusions of financial revenue remained aloft, how one substance was transformed into another (ibid.: 494). For Lutherans, and other Protestants, the wine and bread were instead memorials of Christ's sacrifice rather than matter as if magically transformed.

Teaching and researching revenue law in Australia in the 1980s made the gendered archive of monetary discourse far too explicit for a woman not to pursue a critical legal methodology. Historically speaking, 'hands are the father of wealth' and 'lands are the mother of wealth' (Petty 1964: 68), provided one had an economy based on hands, or labour, and land. With the introduction of a monetary 'factor of production', Marx argued that we now inhabit a 'bewitched, distorted and upside-down world haunted by *Monsieur Le Capital* and *Madame La Terre*' (1981: 969).[1] This gendered archive was too explicit, in that indexes of taxation textbooks, case collections, professional commentaries, and even indexes of scholarly articles contained an entry named 'husband and wife'. It usually included every conceivable area of taxation law and practice, being a listing of any instance in a text in which the words 'husband and wife' were used. While it was obvious that the word 'wife' was the sign that meant a practice of a male person of transferring a monetary sum to a person presumed incapable of having any earning capacity (i.e. a wife), it was not so obvious to any woman reading these texts why the numerous kinds of capacities and activities described in these cases should be read so clearly as meaning an avoidance of tax on the part of a 'husband', as meaning that her labour in a business partnership was insignificant. Why was a female person a sign of 'nothing', a limit to his activities, a limit that facilitated the calculation of what he 'really' did? How did her labour signal only the presence of him (Grbich 1987)? And also, how did the figure of the taxpayer come to complement, or is it supplement, the fantastic exploits of *Monsieur Le Capital*? Did *Monsieur* always appear on the page with the taxpayer whose labour signified suffering, or would any suffering figure complement the exploits of *Monsieur*? Nineteenth-century economists were content to pair *Monsieur* with Crusoe's Friday, as labourer, as a person of race. Crusoe was an eighteenth-century creation of Defoe in which *Monsieur* as Crusoe traversed the globe, travelling from his plantations in South America to England and back. The closer one reads political economy to the time of Luther, the more Christ-like becomes the suffering of the companion to his maker. These figures become both more godly, in a Christology of suffering and redemption, of gifts, death, longing, and salvation; and also more explicitly a coded form of the imitation of God's power to write the names of things, and to create life and things with words. In early modern biblical poetics one moves easily between Christ as the Word, and language as a practice of coining things.

Reading Lacan reading Luther

The 'wife' as the sign of 'nothing' limiting the pursuits of the 'husband' of the twentieth-century tax lawyers was a 'black' in the discourse of nineteenth-century political economists, who used the story of Crusoe and Friday to explain the particular and higher value of a white man's labour, or rather why a managerial type had a labour that returned a higher revenue than a worker's. In Luther's early-sixteenth-century *Treatise on Good Works*, any person who took more than his labour fairly warranted was figured as a Jew. Luther had three 'special, distinct works all rulers might do in our times': 'first, to make an end of the horrible gluttony and drunkenness' because of its expense; '[s]econdly, to forbid the excessive cost of clothing, whereby so much wealth is wasted, and yet only the world and the flesh are served'; and '[t]hirdly, to drive out the usurious buying of rent-charges, which in the whole world ruins, consumes and troubles all lands, peoples and cities through its cunning form, by which it appears not be usury, while in truth it is worse than usury, because men are not on their guard against it as against open usury'. Luther named these 'the three Jews, as men say, who suck the whole world dry' (1943b: 266–7). In Luther's sixteenth-century writings the European wealthy are all Jews, who can only hope to give a good account of themselves to God by limiting their wealth-taking in relation to the returns of a 'day labourer'. The peasant and his labour or suffering are to be brought into a calculation of the rightfulness of the returns due to the wealth-takers. Luther's anti-Semitism in the *Treatise on Good Works* is symbolic in the sense that it repeats the narrative of the Jews as the killers of Christ; the wealth-takers of whatever religious beliefs are responsible for the ruination of the peasants.

Lacan (1992: 97) has placed Luther at the period in the early sixteenth century when 'God's eternal hatred of man' was written about, and has ventured into how we might read the significance of these events in European and theological history within Freud's theorization of a European trauma. Whether Freud adequately captured, or created, a mythological rendering of the death of the Old Man of the Mosaic texts in his *Moses and Monotheism* is given considerable focus in Lacanian psychoanalysis (ibid.: 181). How the killing off of Moses, the father figure of the Mosaic Law in the Old Testament of the Bible, was repeated in the Christologies of European Protestantism in the focus on Christ's death can be read as the historical form of Freud's mythological *Totem and Taboo*. In Freud's eyes, *Moses* far surpassed what he had hoped to achieve in *Totem*, and of course he gave a fantastical form to this cultural development, or malaise, which he so subtly traced in *Civilization and Its Discontents*. Freud hoped that his *Moses* story, with its two Moses, could provide the cultural tools to divide and alienate some parts of the cultural malaise and enhance other, more creative parts. Lacan's readings of Freud's fictions, his European mythologies, give a method for reading the other ways in which God has been historically killed off, and sublimated. The way in which early modern European cultural practices were understood as killing off God is in its infancy, so to speak, in law. It has been culturally buried, erased, and repressed. Luther gives us some access to these ways in which God was understood as being killed off, and how he imagined life could nevertheless go on.

Luther was quite explicit that the wealth-takers of all kinds were 'Jews', as it were, who condemned the poor and destitute to an early death. The day labourer struggled for life; the excesses of the gluttonous, the well robed, and the buyers of the rights to income from rental lands killed off this labourer, quite literally, in Luther's commentaries. As food prices soared, the labourer and his family starved to death. In Luther's mind, humankind lived from the produce of the land, a providence from God. To the extent that men claimed the produce of the land to be within their power to sell, and claimed the full benefits of the use of this potentiality of life before the soil had even had a chance to produce, one had killed off God. One had taken the grounds for life in the future as one's own. Luther was railing against the new forms of commerce and finance, which he considered usurious, or worse than usurious where they pretended to be something else.

In the case of trading in foreign goods, such as silks, gold work, and spices, these were simply evil as they 'serve no useful purpose, and ... drain away the wealth of land and people' (Luther 1943d: 13). There was also the sin of selling goods as dear as possible, of looking to one's own greed and caring nothing for the needs of one's neighbour. Because of this greed,

> the wares must have a price proportioned to his neighbour's need.... Is not that selling a poor man his own poverty?... Selling ought not to be a work that is entirely within your own power, and will, without law or limit, as though you were a god and beholden to no one.

How much to charge a neighbour should be calculated according to the time of your own labour in acquiring and selling the wares, using the earnings of a day labourer at another occupation as a comparison, and allowing some calculation of the loss that might have been suffered in payment of your work if the wares had not sold:

> How am I to get at what is fair and right so as not to overreach or overcharge my neighbor?...
>
> In deciding how much profit you ought to take on your business and your labor, there is no better way to reckon it than by estimating the amount of time and labor you have put on it and comparing it

> with that of a day laborer, who works at another occupation, and seeing how much he earns in a day. On that basis reckon how many days you have spent in getting your wares and bringing them to your place of business, how great the labor has been and how much risk you have run, for great labor and much time ought to have so much the greater returns.
>
> (Luther 1943d: 15–17)

But where one is dealing in money, Luther says that 'the trade is based on nothing'. If a particular piece of ground is specified from which the income of the rents is derived, one could imagine that it produces profit out of the earth, but where the great merchants place money on ground in general without specification, they ascribe to the nature of money a power which is only accidental to it, God's power (Luther 1943c: 61).

In Lacan's readings of Freud, these themes of Luther circulate around what Lacan named as the discourse of the master; authority, life, and its proper use, which are played out in the language of commerce, trade, finance, and state, take up a position in the unconscious as each person enters into cultural life and into language. Reading between Lacan on Luther and Luther's own texts, one can trace a certain sexed and familial relation between merchants, money, the earth, and God long before the arrival of *Monsieur Le Capital* and *Madame La Terre* in Marx. As Luther explained, usurers sell a power which is not theirs to sell; they say money might buy income from a piece of ground, but

> it does not do so yet, and perhaps it never will. Hans can take a Gretchen, but he has her not yet, and so he is not yet married.
>
> Your money can buy income; that is half of it, but the deal depends on the rest of it – the acceptance and the other half.
>
> (Luther 1943c: 62)

Where the great merchants place money on ground in general without specification, where the deal to buy income is not linked with a specific piece of ground, one cannot know what the land might produce, or might not produce.

Lacan finally settled his account of law in 1972 in *Encore* (Ragland 1997) as one beginning with Aristotle's search for the Good as a process of each being orienting itself towards the greatest being 'by confounding its good, its own good, with that with which the Supreme Being shines' (Lacan 1999: 84). Aristotle's theory of politics, knowledge, and ethics follows a fantasy of the making of knowledge as like a procreation, or a conception, in which the masculine is the activating of a life, the feminine an inert material, and the soul or spirit a dwelling within that activation. As Lacan explained it:

> The strange thing is that in this crude polarity that makes matter passive and form the agent that animates it, something, albeit something ambiguous, nevertheless got through, namely, that this animation is nothing other than the *a* with which the agent animates what? He animates nothing – he takes the other as his soul.
>
> (ibid.: 82)

Can we say that little *a* which Lacan says is related to the imaginary follows the tracks of the Aristotelian soul, a kind of a priori thing or aspect of the Supreme Being, of a God? For Lacan, this Aristotelian soul represented 'the possibility of a bond of love between two of these beings', but it could also be understood as 'manifesting the tension toward the Supreme Being' (ibid.: 85).

In Lacan's account of law by the time of his 1972 Seminars, *On Feminine Sexuality: The Limits of Love and Knowledge: Encore*, Plato, Aristotle, and a Platonic Christianity have simply left us with a God who recognizes the beloved as the same, as like a soul within from the beginning, or a Son who sees in God's image himself as divine. The cultural accretion of these classical and Judaeo-Christian codes of love forms the relation of language, signification, and affects that constitute those social links which Lacan calls the unconscious. In the earlier and middle years of Lacan's writing, his focus on the practices of love bore some resemblance to the discourse on the types of love in Plato's *Symposium*. Reinhard has pointed out how Lacan

> in his [1960] Seminar VIII on transference … presses the encomium of love in Plato's *Symposium* into the service of his argument that love is an act of metaphoric 'substitution'. In Phaedrus' discourse on the hierarchy of types of love, this substitution occurs in its more conventional form when it is the lover who takes the place of (or sacrifices him or herself for) the beloved.
>
> (1995: 788)

In his 1953 *Seminar I: Freud's Papers on Technique*, Lacan had used the schema of two mirrors to set out specular lines of love, and presented love as 'one's own ego that one loves in love, one's own ego made real on the imaginary level' (1991: 142). In this early work, Lacan was tracing Freud's idea of the development of the child's identification with a parent as a model of the person he would like to become, and how this 'earliest and original form of emotional tie' (Freud 1991: 136) can provide some understanding of the psychology of groups, whether the Church, army, or the 'primal horde'. Freud had argued that 'the subsequent history of this identification with the father may easily be lost sight of'. At the same time as this identification with his father, the child may develop an object relation with a mother; the two may subsist side by side, although in time the little boy notices that his father stands in his way with his mother. Freud names this conflict between a boy's identification with his father as model or ideal, and what he would like to have – his mother – as the Oedipus complex. Freud had positioned love as that process where the ego assumes the characteristics of the object. In the idealization of lovers, 'the object is being treated in the same way as our own ego ... the object serves as a substitute for some unattained ego ideal of our own' (ibid.: 143).

Lacan goes on to develop further Freud's concept of the ego ideal, identification, and its constitutent processes of separation and alienation into a theorization of discourse as the social link in which, in Ragland's words, 'the agent of speech addresses the other from a place of lack' (Ragland 1997: 1092). As a child's fantasy of being at one with the mother are experienced as a loss, or lack, the traits or marks of this imaginary locate a place and experience of lack, which gives a sense to language. It is this process of experiencing a fullness in being in the image or mirror of the carer, the child's subsequent sense of loss at awareness of its separation from the mother, and the introduction of the father's no, or name, which Lacan positions at the place of the early imaginary, the earliest fantasy for making up for the loss. Whether it is a theme of love or of identification in Lacan, the effect is to be the same: fantasy images of loved ones and the condensation and substitution of one for oneself are like the processes of language, and like the conflict and displacement of affect that the young child experiences in the early years of life and language acquisition. Where Freud gave to these processes and personae of separation and alienation the names of mother, father, the family romance drama, and Oedipal complex, Lacan transforms this sexed and conflicted imagery to one more culturally condensed and fixed around Aristotle's theologically based politics. The Lacanian move in psychoanalysis has shown how the already sexed and theologically loaded fantasies embedded in the jurisprudential archive have a central place in the ways the subject in modernity is conceived.

The question of the neighbour in reading modern law

Lacan's transformation of Freud's family romance drama, with its later version as the 'Moses family drama' of *Moses and Monotheism*, into the Aristotelian–Platonic–Christian schema of love in *Encore*, is easier to recognize in its sixteenth-century forms in the writings of Luther, Erasmus, and perhaps More. My reading of Lacan reading Luther has produced a way of engaging with that onto-theology of Luther which continues to be reproduced in contemporary forms of thinking, being, doing, and reflection. As one writes, one renews the Father's name as author of a life, and as one reads the images and objects imagined as animating the text, one usurps the procreative powers of female bodies, an imaginative practice at least as old as Aristotle. Figuring cognition as a masculine making is how minds metaphorize conceptions of things.

The difference of the sexes set out in Aristotle's *On the Generation of Animals* (1941) and its model of the father who sees the origin of his offspring in his own soul, a reflection of himself writ large as a divisible part of a Supreme Being, is faithfully reproduced in Luther and Lacan, as well as the countless jurisprudes who metaphorize the actors of commercial life as playing out a 'family romance'. Lacanian psychoanalysis is like an archaeology of the European Renaissance in which the fossils of classicism lie close to the surface, close enough to recognize Aristotle's model of the difference of the sexes repeated in the sexed personification of the players in the poetic forms of key juridical logics such as the common law's *usufruct* and the *chose* in action, and as Luther's characters of financial property playing out their scenarios as Hans and Gretchen.

Turning then to early modern texts, whether theological, humanist, or simply fanciful, provides a politics of how contemporary fantasies that animate nations, peoples, and currencies in the twenty-first century might be engaged at different levels. How do these fantasies animate and sustain beliefs that play out as the violence of states or the violence of institutions, and in whose name are these enjoyments distributed? Always in hindsight, the prior deployment of a fantasy can reveal whose enjoyment was at stake and who was made to bear the fictions of subjecthood.

Lacan argued that Freud's *Civilization and Its Discontents* was, throughout, a confrontation with the commandment to love thy neighbour as thyself: 'that is where he begins, where he remains throughout, and where he ends up' (Lacan 1992: 179). Following on from his focus on the specular or imaginary relations of love, Lacan poses the question of transgression, *jouissance*, or enjoyment and the Lutheran moment in the early sixteenth century when, for Luther, good works meant nothing. Lacan locates the commandment as 'the conservation of something destroyed at a different level'. He says that

> [t]he two notions, the death of God and the love of one's neighbour, are historically linked ... through the drama of the passion ... Christianity, in effect, offers a drama that literally incarnates that death of God. It is also Christianity that associates that death with what happened to the Law; namely, that without destroying that Law, we are told, but in substituting itself for it, in summarizing it, and raising it up in the very movement that abolishes it – thus offering the first weighty historical example of the German notion of *Aufhebung*, i.e., the conservation of something destroyed at a different level – the only commandment is henceforth 'Thou shalt love thy neighbor as thyself.' (ibid.: 193)

The historical moment of the passion of Christ as incarnation, as the substitution of the new law of love for the old Mosaic prohibitions, can be tracked to Luther's 1520 text *The Treatise on the New Testament That Is the Holy Mass.* Luther transformed the meaning of the Eucharist – the rituals performed by the Catholic clergy – from the bread and wine being a repetition of the sacrifice of Christ's body on the Cross, a sacrifice to God, to another meaning in which the bread and wine incorporated by the faithful was to repeat the experience of the sealing of a gift from God. In Luther's 'new' reading of the words of Christ from Matthew 26: 28 and Luke 22: 20, 'This is the cup of a new eternal testament in My blood, that is shed for you and for many for the remission of sin', it is, said Luther,

> [a]s though He said: 'Behold, man, in these words I promise and bequeath thee forgiveness of all thy sin and eternal life. And in order that thou mayest be certain and know that such promise remains irrevocably thine, I will die for it, and will give My body and blood for it, and will leave them both to thee as sign and seal, that by them thou mayest remember Me.'
>
> (1943a: 300)

Luther argued that a testament or bequest was performed, under which the testator, Christ, bequeathed to his heirs, the Christians, eternal life – that is, remission of sin and entry to the eternal Kingdom of God. The bequest is the eternal life,

> the seal or token, the sacrament, bread and wine, and under them His true body and blood. For everything that is in this sacrament must live; therefore He did not put it in dead writ and seal, but in living words and signs which we use from day to day.
>
> (ibid.: 302)

In the preface to Luther's own translation of the New Testament of the Bible into German in 1522 he warned the reader to

> beware lest you make Christ into a Moses, and the gospel into a book of law or doctrine ... the gospel demands no works to make us holy and to redeem us. Indeed, it condemns such works, and demands only faith in Christ ... Thus it is not by our own works, but by His work, His passion and death, that He makes us righteous, and gives us life and salvation.
>
> (1962: 17)

Luther advised the reader that

> [i]f he have faith ... his whole life and all his effort are directed towards the benefit of his neighbour ... he employs his strength, uses

> his goods, and stakes his reputation, as he sees Christ did for him, and therefore follows His example. Christ never gave any other commandment than that of love, because He intended that commandment to be the test of His disciples and of true believers
>
> (ibid.: 18)

Can we say that Lacan has positioned Luther's new reading of the Eucharist, the words of Christ of thanks at the Last Supper, and its performance by the Protestant faithful as a gift of life to be used for the neighbour as his central model for those psychoanalytic links he names as the imaginary, the symbolic, and the real? Lacan says he is following Freud's example on this. But can we say that when Luther positioned Christ as an ego ideal, his bequest or gift of eternal life for others as a model to follow, in the form of love of one's neighbour, he abandoned sacrifice altogether? His interpretation of *Paul* suggests he did not. In his 1522 preface to his own German translation of the Epistle of St Paul to the Romans, Luther gave an interpretation of *Paul* in which the Mosaic Law is 'silenced and put out of action; it makes no further demands. It is as if you were in debt to a lender and unable to pay'. While there would be two ways of settling the matter and setting you free, the first, of simply ruling off the debt in the account in the ledger, is wrong, says Luther. Rather, he supports the second meaning, that of Christ having paid off the debt on our account, and 'this is how Christ has set us free from the law' (1962: 18). Luther says we must follow 'the example of Christ, who has done for us what we too must do in following him'.

Luther's interpretation of Christ's words as a testament or gift is ambiguous, in the sense that it is a gift, but one which has to be repaid – as if it were a loan of money, paid off by Christ. It is ambiguous in the sense it preserves the structure of the Mosaic Laws on the transgression of law being a sin for which the sinner is not absolved. Hence Lacan's analysis that there is a substitution which is 'the conservation of something destroyed at a different level', the conservation of a debt or obligation under Mosaic Law, and its settlement with the Lutheran doctrine of faith, or at least in the performance of the mass as the experience of an inheritance of life by the supplicant.

In the godly writing of a life as if it were a gift, the settlement of the loan begins to look remarkably like the signature of a financier, or the sign of financial property. Numerous cultural commentators as well as biblical translators and authors have made these same links. The writing of a life and the ambiguity of its use and return, a use that separates out enjoyment, limitation, and negation, has provided a structural logic, in language as the linking of metaphor and metonymy, and in philosophy as the symbolic of Hegel's master and slave. In political economy and critical legal theory, *Monsieur Le Capital* and *Madame La Terre* take up their parts.

In Lacan's venture into the 'seamy side of psychoanalysis' – politics – he gives numerous instances of this same structural logic, most readily identified with political economy paradigms: Smith's *Wealth of Nations* and Marx's *Capital* (Lacan 2007: 79). Lacan comes close to including the poetical form of revenue law logics, the logics of lakes and streams, although he terms them dams and ponds. Lacan makes clear that the truth hidden within the master's discourse, something 'compressed' that needs to be unfolded, does not become less so for being noticed. Nor, he emphasizes, does it change anything to find out at what point in history Luther or Calvin was responsible for a change in the structure of the logic of the signifier, 'for the important point is that on a certain day surplus jouissance became calculable, could be counted, totalized. This is where what is called the accumulation of capital begins' (ibid.: 177).

The problem which Luther's interpretation of the Mass poses is that the gift logic of the Eucharist positions the Christian as having inherited an entitlement to freedom at the same time as having to follow the example of Christ in loving his neighbour as himself – that is, giving up his life and freedom, as Christ did. There is an indeterminacy of the subject in Christianity in the place between the inheritance of a gift and the imaginary of the neighbour, or is it the neighbour's neighbour? One must love the neighbour as one loves the neighbour's neighbour – that is, as oneself. But how is one to love oneself, within the meanings of the Judaeo-Christian archive or its Lacanian manifestation? It seems that if the neighbour is imagined as abject, such as a woman, one has inherited a freedom. If the neighbour is imagined as having an entitlement to a full life, one is sacrificed and becomes abject, in the sense of there being an abject subject. The conditions of any perceived freedom seems contingent upon these logics of the details of Christ's life, although these are repressed or hidden from the discourse of the gift, Luther's Protestant and Christian discourse of the gift.

Luther seems to have articulated these layers of subjectivity and cultural coding of political life in his 1520 essay on the evils of commercial life, his 'Treatise on usury'. He struggles with the proper Christian way of dealing in business, and 'the right use of temporal goods', even where canon law has made concessions to usurious practices. He railed against the current 'avoidance' of usury practices where money received from another for the use of your finance could be characterized as a compensation for the loss you had forgone on not having your money fixed in land or crops:

> Let us imagine, then, or dream, or force ourselves to think that this business is right, as it is now conducted: nevertheless, it deserves that pope, bishops, emperor, princes and everybody else endeavor to have it abolished, and it is the duty of everyone who can prevent it to do so,

> if only on account of its wicked and damnable fruits, which burden and ruin the whole world.
>
> (1943c: 58)

What kind of dream could allow him to imagine that the commercial practices against which he railed, and which he saw as sucking the life out of his neighbours, could be right? It must be a dream in which the usurous practices have been removed, or where there are no practices of standing surety for another, which he thought akin to usurping the power of God, 'an invasion of God's rights' (Luther 1943d: 19). He seems to suggest that if Hans *had* married Gretchen, if married love had produced an offspring, Hans could rightfully claim the offspring as his own; it would be an offspring or gain grounded in the land, in God's providence, in God (Luther 1943c: 62). The financial practices to which Luther referred in this poetic phraseology would not be usurious, because, looking through the fantasy of Aristotelian generation, the father makes the offspring himself as he carried this little soul inside himself from the beginning; he sees his reflection in this soul and knows he is a father. Looking through his Aristotelian glasses, Luther could picture how practices that sucked the life out of his neighbours could be made to look right. Or can we say a Lacanian analysis of his dream explains how Hans' claims to the exclusive parentage of his gains are simply the madness of a modernity long used to thinking in these terms, of origins as autochthonous, as single-parented?

Critical legal theory has provided a critique of the logic of proper use and rightful actions in which the claims to plunder, destruction, and genocide in the name of sovereignty have been shown to be a base colonialism, of both the nation and the spirit. In Australia's native title law these claims to rightful plunder as simply an act of state and therefore beyond question have long been removed of any ethical or equitable stance. How we read the lives of children removed from their parents and raised in institutions in the twentieth century in Australia, children addressed as a number and described as 'the scum of the earth', is an issue that has not gone away. We live with these children, now adults, as our neighbours. Understanding how the state continues to imagine it can be right to remove whole townships of indigenous peoples from their lands, or remove schools, medical services, water, and power from these townships in the name of progress, in 2009, remains.[2]

Notes

1 Curiously, the personae of *Monsieur* and *Madame* are present in the 1981 Fernbach translation in Penguin but absent from the 1972 Lawrence & Wishart republication of the Moscow-based Progress publication, prepared in 1964 by the Institute of Marxism-Leninism in Moscow.

2 See Murdoch (2009) for a recent account of the plans of the Australian Northern Territory Government on the removal of services from some Indigenous peoples in the Northern Territory.

References

Aristotle (1941) *The Basic Works of Aristotle*, New York: Random House.

Duncanson, I. (1982) 'Jurisprudence and politics', *Northern Ireland Legal Quarterly* 33: 1–19.

Duncanson, I. (1984) 'Moral outrage and technical questions: Civil liberties, law and politics', *Northern Ireland Legal Quarterly* 35: 153–79.

Fitzpatrick, P. (1992) *The Mythology of Modern Law*, London: Routledge.

Fitzpatrick, P. (2001) *Modernism and the Grounds of Law*, Cambridge: Cambridge University Press.

Foucault, M. (1970) *The Order of Things: An Archaeology of the Human Sciences*, London: Tavistock.

Freud, S. (1990) 'Totem and Taboo', in *The Origins of Religion*, vol. 13, London: Penguin.

Freud, S. (1991) 'Group psychology and the analysis of the ego', in *Civilization, Society and Religion*, vol. 12, London: Penguin.

Grbich, J. (1987) 'The position of women in family dealing: The Australian case', *International Journal of the Sociology of Law* 15: 309–32.

Grbich, J. (1992) 'The body in legal theory', *University of Tasmania Law Review* 11: 26–58; abridged version in M. Fineman and N. Thomadsen (eds) (1991) *At the Boundaries of Law: Feminism and Legal Theory*, New York: Routledge.

Irigaray, L. (1985) *Speculum of the Other Woman*, trans. G. Gill, New York: Cornell University Press.

Lacan, J. (1991) *Freud's Papers on Technique, 1953–1954, The Seminar of Jacques Lacan, Book I*, trans. J. Forrester, ed. J.-A. Miller, New York: W. W. Norton.

Lacan, J. (1992) *The Seminar of Jacques Lacan*, Book VII, *The Ethics of Psychoanalysis, 1959–1960*, trans. D. Porter, ed. J.-A. Miller, London: Routledge.

Lacan, J. (1999) *The Seminar of Jacques Lacan*, Book XX, *On Feminine Sexuality: The Limits of Love and Knowledge, 1972–73, Encore*, trans. B. Fink, ed. J.-A. Miller, New York: Norton.

Lacan, J. (2007) *The Seminar of Jacques Lacan*, Book XVII, *The Other Side of Psychoanalysis*, trans. R. Grigg, ed. J.-A. Miller, New York: Norton.

Luther, M. (1943a) 'A treatise on the New Testament, that is, the Holy Mass' [1519], trans. J. J. Schindel, *Works of Martin Luther*, vol. 1, The Philadelphia Edition, Philadelphia: Muhlenberg Press.

Luther, M. (1943b) 'Treatise on good works' [1520], trans. W. A. Lambert, *Works of Martin Luther*, vol. 1, The Philadelphia Edition, Philadelphia: Muhlenberg Press.

Luther, M. (1943c) 'Treatise on usury' [1520]', trans. C. M. Jacobs, *Works of Martin Luther*, vol. 4, Philadelphia: Muhlenberg Press.

Luther, M. (1943d) 'On trading and usury [1524]', trans. C. M. Jacobs, *Works of Martin Luther*, vol. 4, Philadelphia: Muhlenberg Press.

Luther, M. (1962) *Martin Luther: Selections from His Writings*, ed. J. Dillenberger, New York: Anchor.

Marx, K. (1972) 'Revenue and its sources: Vulgar political economy', in *Theories of Surplus Value, Part III*, London: Lawrence & Wishart.

Marx, K. (1981) 'The revenues and their sources', in *Capital*, vol. 3, trans. D. Fernbach, Harmondsworth, UK: Penguin.

Murdoch, L. (2009) 'Death knell for homelands: Aborigines forced to move to regional hubs', *The Age*, Melbourne, 19 May.

Petty, W. (1964) 'A treatise of taxes and contributions [1662]', in C. Hull (ed.) *The Economic Writings of Sir William Petty*, vol. 1, New York: Kelley.

Ragland, E. (1997) 'Lacan and the subject of law: Sexuation and discourse in the mapping of subject positions that give the ur-form of law', *Washington and Lee Law Review* 54: 1091–118.

Reinhard, K. (1995) 'Kant with Sade, Lacan with Levinas', *Modern Language Notes* 110: 785–808.

Simon, B., Montgomerie, D., and Tuscano, J. (2009) *Back on the Block: Bill Simon's Story*, Canberra: Aboriginal Studies Press.

Spivak, G. (1989) 'Feminism and deconstruction, again: Negotiating with unacknowledged masculinism', in T. Brennan (ed.) *Between Feminism and Psychoanalysis*, London: Routledge.

Chapter 9

Totemic immimanence

Peter Fitzpatrick's liminal contemplation of law

Johan van der Walt

Introduction

> Time that is always gone stays still
> A moment in this quiet room.

These lines are from Rosemary Dobson's poem 'The Mirror: Jan Vermeer Speaks' (1972).

They are also from Peter Fitzpatrick's book *Modernism and the Grounds of Law* (2001: 85, 224).

The lines invite one to contemplate the temporal structure of a human abode, a room. Fitzpatrick's work, and not only in this book, responds to this invitation by contemplating the temporal structure of another human abode, the law.

Is the decision that lays down law felicitously, be it a judicial or legislative decision, comparable to the temporal stillness of a Vermeer interior? I shall argue in this chapter that it is, but to the extent that it is, one would have to distinguish the stillness at issue here from all notions of 'stilled content'. The stillness of Vermeer's room strikes Dobson, strikes us not as 'stilled content', certainly not as stilled time. Time, for a moment, stays still, is yet not stilled. The stillness of the room prevails precisely because of quiet echoes of time 'that is [again] gone', of time or times that could not and cannot be retained or contained. The temporal stillness of the room is the quiet but, however still and silent, also disquiet remainder of someone who has left or someone who was expected but never arrived. The stillness of a room thus has an external relation to itself.

This, I shall argue, is also how Peter Fitzpatrick understands the law when he writes:

> Even at its most settled, or especially at its most settled, law could not 'be' otherwise than in a responsiveness to what was beyond its determinate content 'for the time being'. If that content could be perfectly stilled, there could be no call for decision, for determination, for law.

> And it is in the very response to this call, in the making and sustaining of its distinct content, that law 'finds itself' integrally tied to, and incipiently encompassing of, its exteriority.
>
> (2008: 219)

This is not just a reminder of what is always excluded by the law, as facile renditions of a Derridean non-equivalence of law and justice might move us to think. At issue is an encompassing of exteriority. The law, even and especially *settled* or felicitous law, invites the outside into the room, living space, or momentary stillness that it creates. As Fitzpatrick puts it, 'law has somehow to be conceived of, not just in a potential relation to what is outside what it may be "for the time being", but as having that outside with-in itself' (ibid.: 220).

I shall elaborate this understanding of law in Fitzpatrick's work to the structure or structuration of law that I have in recent papers begun to describe in terms of the irreducible immanence and imminence of law, the immanence and imminence of law that can for the sake of economy be called the *immimanence* of law. But much ground needs to be covered before we can move towards an understanding of immimanence. This is so because the meaning of immanence itself is not altogether clear in contemporary thinking. Anyone who has come to understand both Nancy's and Deleuze and Guattari's engagements with or invocations of immanence would have realized that immanence does not mean the same thing or non-thing for them. I shall therefore begin in what follows with two short explorations of the word 'immanence' in the work of Nancy and Deleuze and Guattari and then move on to reflect the outcome of these explorations on a number of key concerns in the work of Peter Fitzpatrick, namely *the totemic*; *sacrifice*; *breaking up the unity of the world*; *non-violent law*; *the return of the gods.*

Immanence in Nancy and Deleuze and Guattari

Deleuze and Guattari write about a plane of immanence that is immanent to nothing but itself. When immanence invokes the notion of an immanence *to* something, it immediately invokes transcendence. It invokes a being or moment that transcends the plane of immanence. Immanence thus understood does not relate or refer to the plane of immanence that Deleuze and Guattari bring to bear on the thinking of our time. Let me quote extensively in order to be precise:

> Whenever immanence is interpreted as immanent 'to' something a confusion of plane and concept results, so that the concept becomes a transcendent universal and the plane becomes an attribute of the concept. When misunderstood in this way, the plane of immanence revives the transcendent again: it is a simple field of phenomena that

> now only possesses in a secondary way that which first of all is attributed to the transcendent unity.
>
> (1994: 44–5)[1]

> Immanence is immanent only to itself and consequently captures everything, absorbs All-One, and leaves nothing remaining to which it can be immanent. In any case, whenever immanence is interpreted as immanent *to* Something, we can be sure that this Something reintroduces the transcendent.
>
> (ibid.: 45)[2]

One has to take utmost care to understand accurately what Deleuze and Guattari are saying when they say 'immanence is immanent only to itself'. It is important to understand that the 'immanence *to* immanence' that is at stake here does also not raise immanence on the second count to the status of a universal concept and thus to something that somehow conceptually transcends itself, conceptually transcends and thus limits, constrains, or contains itself. Concepts, Deleuze and Guattari make clear from the beginning of their 'description' of the plane of immanence, operate within this plane. Concepts and plane relate to one another, but must also be clearly distinguished from one another:

> Concepts and plane [of immanence] are strictly correlative, but nevertheless the two should not be confused. The plane of immanence is neither a concept nor the concept of all concepts. If one were to be confused with the other there would be nothing to stop concepts from forming a single one or becoming universals and losing their singularity, and the plane would also lose its openness.
>
> (ibid.: 35)[3]

There are remarkable points in this passage that must be noted.

First, concepts are not to become or form a single one if they are not to lose their singularity. In other words: they need to remain plural to remain singular. The resonance that this thought would find in Nancy (1996) is well known.

Second, what keeps concepts from becoming one and thus preserves their plurality is the non-conceptual plane of immanence that prevails or remains apart from the concepts that form or figure on this plane. If this non-conceptual plane were to get reduced to conceptuality, it would become one or One. It would, as a concept, become not just a, but *the* universal. And it is exactly this one universal or universal oneness from which we must take care to distinguish the second 'immanence' in the phrase 'immanence to immanence' that is at stake when Deleuze and Guattari say 'immanence is immanent only to itself'. They make this abundantly clear, but a small slippage in one's reading can make one miss the point. Immanence is not 'All-One, it '*absorbs* All-One' (emphasis added). At one point they do seem to commit some slippage themselves here, but only to retract almost forthwith, or within the span of half a page:

> Diverse movements of the infinite are so mixed in with each other that, far from breaking up the One-All of the plane of immanence, they constitute its variable curvature, its concavities and convexities, its fractal nature as it were.
>
> (Deleuze and Guattari 1994: 38–9)[4]

But then, half a page later:

> The plane [of immanence] is, therefore, the object of an infinite specification so that it seems to be a One-All only in cases specified by the selection of movement.
>
> (ibid.: 38–9)[5]

Thus do Deleuze and Guattari quickly revoke the One-All of the plane of immanence and replace it with a plane of immanence that *only seems* to be a One-All in the unitary swing or sway of a selected or selecting movement. One should suspect a Freudian slip here, and we shall indeed return to this suspicion shortly. But it is important to note, before we do so, that there is now a dissonance instead of resonance with Nancy that has clearly come to the fore here. When Nancy invokes the word 'immanence', he does so precisely to denote the All-One that would, if it could, absorb all otherness; the oneness that would, if it could, absorb its own exterior or exteriority; the oneness that would, if it could, ingest its relatedness or exposure to an outside and thus destroy the singularity that issues only from plurality – destroy the singularity, the *this one not that one*, that only comes about in the co-appearance or *comparution* of more than one (Nancy 1986: 35–8, 68–76).

Deleuze and Guattari and Nancy obviously have different if not indeed opposite things or non-things in mind when they invoke the word 'immanence'. There is in fact reason to believe that Deleuze and Guattari denote by 'immanence' exactly that which Nancy denotes by 'exteriority', namely the double-gossamer interface of the self's exposure to otherness, the inside's exposure to outsides. They write:

> Perhaps this is the supreme act of philosophy: not so much to think *THE* plane of immanence as to show that it is there, unthought in every plane, and to think it in this way as the outside and inside of thought, as the not-external outside and the not-internal inside.
>
> (Deleuze and Guattari 1994: 59–60)

I have dwelled long here on immanence in Deleuze and Guattari's thought, on the one hand, and in Nancy's, on the other, in order to prepare the way for a question that issues from Fitzpatrick's work, a question that Fitzpatrick can be argued to pose to Deleuze and Guattari and to Nancy. Is a contemplation of an immanence that would not collapse into the All-One, but would in fact absorb the All-One and thus set free the singularity of concepts on a plane of infinite immanence, sufficient to think through the 'breaking up of the unity of the world' that is so central to Fitzpatrick's concerns? Let us not lose sight of the slippage that prompted us above to suspect a Freudian slip in Deleuze and Guattari's description of immanence: '[F]ar from breaking up the One-All of the plane of immanence, [concepts] constitute its variable curvature, its concavities and convexities, its fractal nature as it were.' Let us keep this slippage or slip between the *unbroken unity* and *fractal nature* of the One-All in mind when we read their description of the plane of immanence in terms of an infinite but fractal expanse of singular conceptual or intensive ordinates. They write:

> Spinoza was the philosopher who knew full well that immanence was only immanent to itself and therefore that it was a plane traversed by movements of the infinite, filled with intensive ordinates.
>
> (Deleuze and Guattari 1994: 48)[6]

> [E]lements of the plane are *diagrammatic features*, whereas concepts are *intensive features*. The former are movements of the infinite, whereas the latter are intensive ordinates of these movements, like original sections or differential positions: finite movements in which the infinite is now only speed and each of which constitutes a surface or a volume, an irregular contour marking a halt in the degree of proliferation. The former are *directions* that are fractal in nature, whereas the latter are absolute *dimensions*, intensively defined, always fragmentary surfaces or volumes. The former are *intuitions*, and the latter *intensions*. The grandiose Leibnizian or Bergsonian perspective that every philosophy depends upon an intuition that its concepts constantly develop through slight differences of intensity is justified if intuition is thought of as the envelopment of infinite movements of thought that constantly pass through a plane of immanence.
>
> (ibid.: 39–40)[7]

Is the unity of the world really breaking up with these fractal and fragmentary halts in the degrees of proliferation that mark the infinite movement of immanence? Or is the absorption of the All-One that takes place with these movements a matter of fatal consumption that turns it inside out or belly-up, thus in fact turning the silent Bergsonian intuitions that bring it forth into surreptitious conceptualizations? Do these intuitions not in the final analysis conceptually grasp (*greifen sie nicht begrifflich*, one would say in German) and hold together in unity a world that is beautifully multifaceted but ultimately ONE, albeit rather diffusedly ONE? Is the brief slippage in Deleuze and Guattari's text pointed out above not all too Freudian, not all too telling of an unconscious or at least poorly scrutinized desire for an infinite unity? And all too un-Freudian in the same breath, for is it not from Freud that we learn that the unity of the world is broken up by crime and sacrifice, crime from which sacrifice removes the criminal stains and stigmata or, if not quite removing them, makes them sacred (*sacer facere*)? And is it not from Fitzpatrick that we have in recent years received the clearest invitation to think through again this Freudian insight (Fitzpatrick 2001: 40; 2008: 208, both referring to Freud 1960: 153)?

Where, then, is the place of sacrificial blood and sacrifice in the kaleidoscopic intuitions of the infinite and the immanent in Deleuze and Guattari's work, the sacrificial blood required for 'breaking up the unity of the world'? It should not be surprising if it is largely or completely absent from their thoughts. Is their thought not after all by design and aspiration an articulation of an anti-Oedipal and hence non-sacrificial myth (Deleuze and Guattari 1973: 325–458; 1980: 38–93)?[8] And is this not where Fitzpatrick's work respectfully and silently parts company (without, of course, terminating the incircumventible engagement) with them?

The same questions must be directed to Nancy. The singular plural existence that Nancy contemplates does not issue from sacrifice. It is an existence that cannot be sacrificed, he maintains (1990: 105).[9] And one must assume that it is this singular plural existence that is finally in the offing for humanity, now that, according to Nancy (ibid.: 105), we in fact stand on the eve of a non-sacrificial experience of community.[10] Here too we can clearly see the anti-Oedipal thrust of Nancy's breathtaking thought. When he turns to Freud, it is to a note that Freud wrote shortly before his death – that is, to a real fragment in the face of ultimate infraction or fracture: 'Psyche ist ausgedehnt, weiss nichts davon' (Psyche is extension, knows nothing thereof). From this note, Nancy (ibid.: 87) draws evidence of a late-Freudian insight into an extended corporality liberated from gaping wounds. Perhaps quite correctly so. Perhaps Freud indeed took an anti-Oedipal turn in the face of death. It may just be that the excruciating insights of his work became too much for him to carry towards the end of his life. We shall never know.

From this fragment of Freud, Nancy derives a description of a body of law clearly reminiscent of Deleuze and Guattari's rhizomatic thinking in *Mille plateaux*, a body of law surely marked by injuries (*les blessures*) and pain (*le douleur*) (cf. Nancy 2000: 87), but no longer split in any way by a gaping wound (*la plaïe*) (ibid.: 67–71).

> The model of the body (*corpus*) is the *Corpus Juris*, collection or compilation of the Institutions, the Digestes and other Codes of all the articles of Roman Law. It is neither chaos nor an organism: the body bears itself, not really between the two, but rather elsewhere. It is the prose of an other space, not abyssal, not systematic, neither collapsing [without foundations], nor founded. This is the space of the law: its foundation steals away to find its place (*son fondement s'y dérobe à sa place*), the law of the law is itself always without law. The law oversees (literally: overhangs, *surplombe*) all cases, but it is itself the cases of its institution, as strange to God as it is to nature. The body obeys the rule that goes from case to case, discrete continuity of principle and exception, of exactitude and flexibility (*de l'exigence et de la dérogation*). Pronouncing the law (*juridiction*) consists less in announcing the absoluteness of the law, deriving therefrom the reasons [for the decision] than in saying what the law can be *here*, there, for now, in this case, in this place ... local pronouncement, spaced, horizontal.[11]
>
> (ibid.: 48)

It should be clear now that there is an obvious difference between the ways in which Deleuze and Guattari, on the one hand, and Nancy, on the other, invoke the word 'immanence'. They obviously attach inverse meanings to the word. It should nevertheless also have become clear now that they all think on the same or very similar anti-Oedipal planes of thought. And my intuition is that, despite all the disavowals of immanence in Nancy's work, he is in fact thinking on the plane of immanence that Deleuze and Guattari describe. *They are all thinkers of immanence for reasons of not being thinkers of imminence.* This is so because, notwithstanding their respective claims to be thinkers of the event,[12] they fail to acknowledge or contemplate seriously the significant or deep disruptiveness and enormous risk that mark the eventfulness of the significant event. And it is this failure that allows them to only acknowledge surmountable injuries (remember Hegel?[13]), but not the abyssal wound that marks all things human so unforgivingly (Nancy); allows them to invoke notions of the unbroken unity of the infinite, despite its fractal nature (Deleuze and Guattari). It is this failure that moves them to only discern rhizomatic intensions (Deleuze and Guattari) or extensions (Nancy) in the unfolding body of life and law. Hence the absence of a clear regard for the inevitability of sacrificial violence in the passage or passages of the infinite in which humanity participates. For a consistent regard for the inevitability of sacrifice stems only from a regard for the abyssal wound that marks the impossible passages of the infinite from its here to its there, and its now to its then. Sacrificial violence is humanity's way of grafting and forging and coping with these impossible passages in the passage of the infinite. But we need to cover more ground before this will become sufficiently clear, and we shall have to take Fitzpatrick as our guide to make further headway in this regard.

Totemic immimanence

Fitzpatrick's *Modernism and the Grounds of Law* provides us with an extensive engagement with Freud's narrative regarding the origin of human society as related especially in *Totem and Taboo.* The essential elements of the narrative are these:

1 A primordial state of group existence – the primal horde – in which the father enjoys exclusive possession and sexual enjoyment of the women in the group.
2 An intermediary phase in which the brothers in the group revolt against the father, kill him, and consume him in a meal, and subsequently have free access to and enjoyment of the women in the horde.
3 A third stage during which the brothers, ridden by guilt, identify and institutionalize an animal that may not be killed and consumed, the totem, except in specific ritual re-enactments of the original killing of the father, the totemic feast. Concomitant to the institution of the totem takes place a self-imposition of the sexual repression formerly imposed on them by the father by developing the laws regulating the prohibition of incest.

The three phases of the narrative, but especially the second and third ones, reflect Freud's view of the origin of society. The first stage is one of 'utter fixity', the fixity of the absolute order imposed by the father on the horde (Fitzpatrick 2001: 1). The second stage ushers in a non-state of boundless freedom among the brothers to compete for the possession of the women through which new possibilities of social coexistence or orderings constantly and savagely replace those already established. Constant '[p]ossibility [thus] enter[s] the world' (Fitzpatrick 2001: 2). But constant possibility offers no stable abode and the brothers, on the eve of society, find themselves split by two seemingly irreconcilable concerns, the concern with a stability reminiscent to some degree of the fixity formerly imposed by the father, on the one hand, and a freedom to take leave of this order when the exigencies of desire and circumstance require this leave-taking. Driven by the need to reconcile these irreconcilable concerns, or by their guilt trip (Freud does not make it clear which economy, that of remorse or that of practicality, is the essential force here), the brothers institute an order that allows for fixed law that exacts general compliance as well as the freedom of occasional non-compliance with the fixed demands of law. They do so by the institution of the totem, the killing of which the law generally proscribes but occasionally allows in the form of the ritual feast. The totem thus reconciles or at least connects or combines the diverging concerns with fixity and freedom from fixity that mark the minds of the brothers after the killing of the father. Thus ensues the 'first form of law', which is, *at least in aspiration*, neither a mere function of forceful repression regardless of circumstance, nor one of boundless or savage circumstantial freedom. Fitzpatrick writes:

> The totem is for Freud the first form of law. The killing of the father initiated law, and the killing of the father surrogate, the totem animal, *wondrously concentrates its dimensions.* Here is a force to law's deathly claim to determine finally, to fix and hold life, denying its protean possibility. Yet death also dissolves the determinant and opens to what is unknowable beyond. So, the totemic death determines, yet it also clears the ground of existing determination and invites newness into the world. With the savage totem, these two dimensions are quite *unmediated*, but with civilization the prospect of a return to savagery is advanced to sustain a predominance of the determinant.
>
> (2001: 3, emphasis added)

> Freud, in short, produces an allegory of law. He situates law's *two extremities*, one in the completely determined position of the primal horde and the other in the ensuing chaos where anything can responsively be other than what it is, and he intimates how they *are to be combined.* This he does in his quasi-ethnographic elevation of the totem.
>
> (Fitzpatrick 2001: 3, emphasis added)

In view of these passages, the core of the totem's characteristics can be described in terms of a *wondrous* and *unmediated concentration* and *combination* of its two *dimensions* or *extremities.* The two terms that Fitzpatrick employs to denote the two dimensions or extremities at issue here are *determination* and *responsiveness* (see Fitzpatrick 2001: 2–3). But these dimensions or extremities can as well be described in terms of two homonyms that allow us to contemplate and trace further their *wondrous* and *unmediated* concentration and *combination.* The homonyms at issue here are *immanence* and *imminence.*

The concern with determined law or legal *determination* is a concern with law that is *immanent* to itself. *Immanent to itself*, however, not in terms of Deleuze and Guattari's aspiration or failed aspiration highlighted above. It is immanent to itself not in terms of a plane of immanence that allows for conceptual ordinates and intensities, on the one hand, and absorbs and exceeds them, on the other. It is *immanent to itself* in terms of an immanence to its fundamental concepts; *immanent to itself* in terms of the ideal pursued by Kelsen; *immanent to itself* in terms of the sovereign aspiration resisted by Nancy; *immanent to itself*, indeed, in terms of what Deleuze and Guattari would describe as conceptual transcendence.

The concern with responsiveness and responsive law is a concern with *imminence* – that is, with law that is irreducibly imminent. It is a concern with law that is never fixed but always to come, always to be assessed anew in response to what comes and is always again about to come. Responsive law is imminent in the way the rhizomatic extensions in the non-conceptual body of law that Nancy describes in *Corpus* are always imminent (quoted below at note 11). Responsiveness and responsive law also invoke the regard for imminence, latency, and historicity that Derrida highlights as the mark of responsibility in *Spectres du Marx* (1993: 62–3, 266). But Nancy, we have seen, underplays or underestimates or ignores the drama and trauma of the imminence and thus of responsiveness. In Derrida we find a relentless regard for the drama and trauma and risk of the imminent and therefore also of the responsibility and responsiveness, legal or otherwise, through which humanity negotiates the passage between immanence and imminence.[14] Derrida does not bypass the disruptive and traumatic eventfulness of the event. Real acknowledgement and affirmation of the event – that is, real hospitality to the event – is for him therefore always a mourning hospitality, a hospitality that is inevitably deeply struck by the incircumventible ruins of the event, the ruins of the event that are, in fact, our only access to the event.[15] Hence also his recognition of the inevitability of sacrifice in the eventful passage of the infinite (van der Walt 2005). Hence also the insights we can draw from him regarding the sacrificial violence of the link between immanence and imminence or determination and responsiveness. And it is from the precipice of this acute Derridean recognition of sacrifice in the affairs of humanity that the abyssal depths of the 'wondrous' and 'unmediated concentration' and 'combination' of determination and responsiveness in the work of Freud and Fitzpatrick become clear.

If it is really a wondrous concentration and unmediated combination that are to be understood here, one can indeed invoke the homonymic economy between *immanence* and *imminence* to guide us towards the full complexity of what is at stake. In the same way that Derrida invoked the term *différance* to invoke a wondrous concentration and unmediated combination of difference and postponement, the misleading homonymic play between immanence and imminence can in fact lead us to hear imminence when we hear immanence and vice versa, or lead us to hear both simultaneously and leave us to first think and *listen to* what is to be heard before we can respond aptly. The problem is, however, that we are bound *not* to be misled and startled thus. The reason for this is a dominant and determining context of law and legal thought that will invariably prompt us to hear immanence whenever either imminence or immanence may have been invoked. The last line of the second-last passage quoted above makes clear that civilization as such has much at stake to mislead us thus: 'with civilization the prospect of a return to savagery is advanced to sustain a predominance of the determinant'. This predominance of the determinant and thus of immanence, Fitzpatrick makes clear, reaches its apex with modern law and modern legal thought: 'The modern rule of law, with its avowal of assured stability and ultimacy of determination, seems closer to the condition of the primal horde' (2001: 2). With modern rule of law, in other words, we come close to returning to the utterly fixed and unitary world of the primal horde. High (court) civilization reverts to primitive barbarism. It is but a different kind of savagery that is coming to our attention here. The 'savage' is indeed also subject to a certain slippage and reversal in Freud and Fitzpatrick. It not only refers to its primary or preferred manifestation of 'breaking up the unity of the world' and allowing for the new and the possible to enter it, but also sometimes refers to the savagery of the primal father's relentless rule (ibid.: 2, 24–32).[16] If there is something to be learned from this crossing of signals, it is surely that utter fixity and utter responsiveness are interchangeable savage responses, both of which return us to a unitary world.

This conundrum of the savage – its vacillation between utter fixity and utter responsiveness – casts considerable light on the conundrum of immanence and imminence in the work of Deleuze and Guattari and Nancy. For the utter reversibility of the savage points to the utter reversibility of immanence and imminence in any thinking that would move to understand them *apart* from one another. If more chapters are to be written towards a post-apartheid theory of law and politics, they would do well to begin with the *post-apartheid* of immanence and imminence – that is, with the inevitability of a *wondrous concentration* of immanence and imminence. Sheer or total immanence devoid of imminence is also sheer imminence. Immanence that is not a temporal delimitation or respite from imminence would be the absolute event that does not cease to happen. If there is one thing that the histories of totalitarianism have proved abundantly, it is surely the fact that nothing is certain and safe under its capricious reign. Total immanence cannot be but an absolute exposure to a cataclysmic eventfulness. The same would be inversely true of sheer imminence. The absolute exposure to a cataclysmic eventfulness cannot but constitute a fully immanent scheme.

The conundrum of the savage thus also explains why Deleuze and Guattari's concern with a plane of immanence that absorbs and surpasses all inclinations to conceptual transcendence surreptitiously reinstates conceptual transcendence; and why Nancy's concern with an exteriority that no longer takes seriously the trauma of interiority, or the trauma of the split or wound between interiority and exteriority, reinstates the very immanence that he sets out to resist by invoking sheer exteriority.

Kept completely apart, immanence and imminence become indistinguishable mirror images of one another. A post-apartheid theory of imminence and immanence would, in bringing them together, nevertheless not simply fuse them, for that would only complete their cataclysmic mirroring. To be thought is indeed their *wondrous* concentration and combination.

It is no wonder that one thinker of our time hears and talks about immanence when the other hears and talks about imminence and vice versa, for in keeping them fully apart (Nancy) or in fusing them (Deleuze and Guattari), they fall into the conundrum of an absolute difference and an absolute sameness that cannot be distinguished from one another. As is the case with modern law (recall Fitzpatrick: 'The modern rule of law, with its avowal of assured stability and ultimacy of determination…'), modern philosophy largely fails to hear and observe the *relative* or *relating* difference *between* imminence and immanence, and predominantly subsumes the former under the latter. In order to break up the unity of the world we also have to break up the homonymic unity of the word. We have to break up the homonymic unity that fuses immanence and imminence and renders inaudible their impossible and therefore *wondrous* (*wondrous* because impossible) concentration. We need to disrupt this homonymic fusion with a tongue-tripping interpellation for thinking to sit up and discern incisively the impossibility of any interchangeability between or unmediated combination of immanence and imminence. We need the impossibility that renders their concentration *wondrous* to stumble on the ear. It is for this purpose that I employ the neologism *immimanence* in what follows.

Between immanence and imminence is an infinitesimally small but always hugely impossible step, namely the step between the now and not-now, the step between time that is still for a moment and time that is always gone. The totem was devised to traverse this impossible step and embody this impossible threshold. And it is the consistent focus on this impossible step or threshold between the here and there and the now and then of law that renders Fitzpatrick's work so relentlessly liminal – that is, first philosophy or first theory of law in the most fundamental sense of the word 'first'. Fitzpatrick's work is consistently concerned with the impossible threshold of the law.

The totemic concentration of immanence and imminence, however wondrous, is an impossible feat that calls for infinite repetition. The crime from which society originates has to be repeated without end (Fitzpatrick 2001: 25). This originating crime may sometimes be accompanied by moral failure, but it does not have moral failure as an essential ingredient. *Essentially* at issue in this crime is much rather the fate of having to constitute a *more* or *less* convincing engagement with the Sisyphean task of traversing the aporetic split or wound between immanence and imminence. The degree of law's persuasiveness in its passage from what it was to what it is to what we believe it should be in future lies not in obfuscating appeals to smooth switches. Nor does it lie, as we shall see shortly, in anonymous 'agency shifts' that somehow extract the bitter sting (or blunt stab) from the very non-passage or aporia at the core of these temporal passages, namely the aporia or non-passage between articulating and enforcing the law; between the word and the violence of the law (no passage between the then and the now and the not yet of the law passes without passing through this non-passage between the language and the violence of the law).

That the law has somehow but indeed muddled through again becomes clear with the recognition that the blood on its records has dried. Fitzpatrick's passing comment regarding Cover's histrionics would surely also be apt here, but let us not forget what is at issue: the coming or bringing to consciousness of deep disturbances with regard to which the law and legal theory have hitherto remained largely unconscious (Fitzpatrick 2008: 115). A degree of histrionics may therefore well be an apt way of debriefing the real risk of hysteria that legal theory should be facing here. Hence the insistence: the traversal of the impossible *split* between immanence and imminence consists not in a passage, but through recognition of the *spilt* – spilt blood, spilt opportunities, spilt lives; the *spilt* with regard to which lamentation is futile but sober recognition essential for an incisive understanding of law.

The regard for the impossible traversal of the threshold between immanence and imminence is the regard for the *split and spilt* in all human affairs, the *split* that cannot be crossed (or crucified) without turning it into the *spilt.* This is the ancient regard for the inevitability of sacrifice in the affairs of mankind. All human *facere* is *sacer facere,* as Agamben (1999: 135) reminds us poignantly. The engagement with the irreducible and repetitive totemic origin (or lack of origin) of the social in *Modernism and the Grounds of Law* provides us with another consistent reminder in this regard (Fitzpatrick 2001: 23–5). A respect for the responsiveness of the law, writes Fitzpatrick (ibid.: 105), 'could orient and even impel' us towards the recognition of the legal decision as 'the denial and sacrifice of the other'.[17]

Non-violent law?

It is against the background of this clear regard for the sacrificial essence of law in Fitzpatrick's writings that one must question his suggestion that the law can also be non-violent. Having masterfully deconstructed the separation between the non-violence of the word and the violence of law enforcement that Cover seeks to effect with the notion of an 'agency shift', and having thus masterfully exposed the violence of the law as inhering also in its very words or wording, Fitzpatrick nevertheless suggests, 'in sympathy with Cover now', that the law is or can also be non-violent. And this non-violence of the law, he suggests, relates to the very responsiveness of law that in *Modernism and the Grounds of Law* guides us to the sacrificial essence of law. Fitzpatrick writes:

> In stark contrast [with Cover], my analysis held violence and nonviolence joined and integral to each other; but, in sympathy with Cover now, that very connectedness required that they also be apart. This entailed a different conception of violence – not one confined to the painful infliction of physical force, and not one that destroyed the word, but instead one constituent of the word itself. Such a violence also provided force and sustained focus as the word moved, as it always had to move, beyond the confines of its determined 'completeness'. This movement meant that the word had to be not just violently determining *but also nonviolently responsive to what lay beyond it 'for the time being,' and that nonviolent responsiveness* in its turn could not have effect except in the violence of determination. On these voyages, the word is neither simply destroyed nor simply conserved but is ever being destroyed and conserved – destroyed in its responsiveness and conserved in its being repeatedly determined. This was not a matter of 'compromise' or of any other encompassing combining of these two imperatives. They were instead distinctly coexistent, existing in apposition, yet integral to each other – 'neither one nor two.'
>
> (Fitzpatrick 2001: 140, emphasis added)

It is arguable that the law, sacrificial as it irreducibly is, is simultaneously violent and non-violent: violent in relation to the party sacrificed and non-violent in relation to the beneficiaries of this sacrifice. It is doubtful, however, that the non-violence of law can be related to its responsiveness – that is, to its ground-breaking imminence. The violence of law is not restricted to its need for determination. The violence of the law also relates to its need for innovation, to its undetermined openness towards otherness, which also cannot avoid frustrating and sacrificing the expectations and aspirations of some. The distinction between the violence and non-violence of the law that separates this violence and non-violence effects or reflects a disregard for either imminence or immanence, for a thinking that maintains a regard for both immanence and imminence cannot avoid marking the violence of the relation between them, the violence that links them and holds them apart. It is the impossible and violent-because-impossible threshold between imminence and immanence that I wish to denote with the non-word *immimanence.* An acute regard for the irreducible *immimanence* of law renders any remainder of the distinction between the violence and non-violence of the law deeply questionable.

A concern with the responsiveness of law nevertheless remains a concern with a softening of law's violence through 'sharing it out' between its beneficiaries and victims. The notion of the responsiveness of the law raises the promise and hope that the defining boundaries between victims and beneficiaries of legal violence are not foregone and fixed conclusions, but temporal limits that bear witness to those currently (most) excluded. The law thus understood is therefore never a matter of stilled content. To the extent that it does create for a moment, perhaps felicitously but certainly not justly and not without violence, a liveable human abode, it is but a quiet room, the stillness of which always evokes a disturbing disquiet regarding the 'always gone' that it appears to arrest. Has there ever been a quiet room devoid of reminders, of traces, of ghosts, devoid of a disturbing disquiet, however silent?[18] It is, for better or for worse, not to Vermeer but to the ghost of Vermeer that we have to address this question.

Notes

1 The argument that follows will be based on a close reading of Deleuze and Guattari's text. It is therefore important to corroborate the reading with a consideration of the original French. Deleuze and Guattari (2005: 47; see under Deleuze and Guattari 1994) reads: 'Chaque fois qu'on interprète l'immanence comme "à" quelque chose, il se produit une confusion du plan et du concept, telle que le concept devient un universel transcendant, et le plan, un attribut dans le concept. Ainsi méconnu, le plan d'immanence relance le transcendant: c'est un simple champ du phénomènes qui ne possède plus qu'en second ce qui s'attribue d'abord à l'unité transcendante'.

2 The original reads: 'L'immanence ne l'est qu'à soi-même, et dès lors prend tout, absorbe Tout-Un, et ne laisse rien subsister à quoi elle pourrait être immanente. En tout cas, chaque fois qu'on interprète l'immanence comme immanente à Quelque chose, on peut être sûr que ce Quelque chose réintroduit le transcendant' (Deleuze and Guattari 2005: 47).

3 The original reads: 'Les concepts et le plan sont strictement corrélatifs, mais doivent d'autant moins être confondus. Le plan d'immanence n'est pas un concept, ni le concept de tous les concepts. Si on les confondait, rien n'empêcherait les concepts de fair un, ou de devenir des universaux et de perdre leur singularité, mais aussi le plan de perdre son ouverture' (Deleuze and Guattari 2005: 38).

4 The original reads: 'Divers mouvements de l'infini sont tellement mêlés les uns aux autres que, loin de rompre l'Un-Tout du plan d'immanence, ils en constituent la courbure variable, les concavités et les convexités, la nature fractale en quelque sorte' (Deleuze and Guattari 2005: 41).

5 The original reads: 'Le plan est donc l'objet d'une spécification infinie, qui fait qu'il ne semble être l'Un-Tout que dans chaque cas spécificié par la sélection du mouvement' (Deleuze and Guattari 2005: 41–2).

6 The original reads: 'Celui qui savait pleinement que l'immanence n'était qu'a soi-même, et ainsi qu'elle était un plan parcouru par les mouvements de l'infini, rempli par les ordonnées intensives, c'est Spinoza' (Deleuze and Guattari 2005: 49).

7 The original reads: '[L]es éléments du plan sont des *traits diagrammatiques*, tandis que les concepts sont des *traits intensifs*. Les premiers sont des mouvements de l'infini, tandis que les secondes sont les ordonnées intensives des ces mouvements, comme des coupes originales ou des positions différentielles:

mouvements finis dont l'infini n'est plus que des vitesse, et qui constituent chaque fois une surface ou un volume, un contour irrégulier marquant un arrêt dans le degré de prolifération. Les premiers sont des *directions* absolues de nature fractale, tandis que les seconds sont des *dimensions* absolues, surfaces ou volumes toujours fragmentaires, définies intensivement. Les premiers sont des *intuitions*, les seconds, des *intensions*. Que toute philosophie dépende d'une intuition que ses concepts ne cessent de développer aux différences d'intensité près, cette grandiose perspective leibnizienne ou bergsonienne est fondée si l'on considère l'intuition comme l'enveloppement des mouvements infinis de pensée qui parcourent sans cesse un plan d'immanence' (Deleuze and Guattari 2005: 42).

8 The recurring thought on these pages is the shift from psychoanalysis to schizoanalysis which articulates the reproach that Freud reduced the cries of multiple wolves to the one wolf imposed on the Wolfman, namely the father. See especially Deleuze and Guattari (1980: 51): 'On reproche à la psychanalyse de s'être servie de l'énonciation oedipienne pour faire croire au patient qu'il allait tenir des énoncés personnels, individuels, qu'il allait enfin parler en son nom'.

9 'L'existence n'est pas à sacrifier, et on ne peut pas la sacrifier. On ne peut que la détruire, ou la partager' (Nancy 1990: 105).

10 'C'est l'existence insacrificiable et finie qui est offerte à partager: la *methexis* se propose désormais ainsi, comme le partage de cela même qui partage: à la fois la limite de la finitude, et le respect de l'insacrifiable. Effacement du sacrifice, effacement de la communion, effacement de l'Occident: cela ne veut pas dire que l'Occident reviendrait à ce qui l'a précédé, ni que le sacrifice occidental reviendrait aux rites qu'il était censé spiritualiser. Cela voudrait dire que nous sommes au bord d'une autre communauté, d'une autre *methexis*, où la *mimesis* du partage effacerait la mimique sacrificielle d'une appropriation de l'Autre' (Nancy 1990: 105).

11 Translated from: 'Le modèle du *corpus* est le *Corpus Juris*, collection ou compilation des Institutiones, Digestes et autres Codices de tous les articles du droit romain. Ce n'est ni un chaos, ni un organisme: le *corpus* se tient, non pas exactement entre les deux, mais plutôt ailleurs. Il est la prose d'un autre espace, ni abyssal, ni systématique, ni effondré, ni fondé. Tel est l'espace du droit: son fondement s'y dérobe à sa place, le droit du droit lui-même est toujours sans droit. Le droit surplombe tous les case, mais il est lui-même le *cas* de son institution, étranger à Dieu comme à la nature. Le *corpus* obéit à la règle qui va de cas en cas, continuité discrète du principe et de l'exception, de l'exigence et de la dérogation. La *juridiction* consiste moins à énoncer l'absolu du Droit, à en dérouler les raisons, qu'à dire *ce que* peut être le droit *ici*, là, maintenant, dans ce cas, en ce lieu ... diction locale, espacée, horizontale, et moins diction de l'être du droit que de son faire, de son savoir-faire et de son pouvoir-faire *dans ce cas*' (Nancy 2000: 48).

12 For Deleuze and Guattari, every distinction or differentiation, every this- or here-ness (*heccéité*) is an event of intensification. Cf. Deleuze and Guatari (1980: 310): 'Qu'est-ce l'individualité d'un jour, d'une saison, ou d'un événement?... Un degré, une intensité, est un individu, *Heccéité*, qui se compose avec d'autres degrés, d'autres intensités pour former un autre individu.... Bref, entre les formes substantielles et les sujets determines, *entre les deux*, il n'y a pas seulement tout un exercice des transports locaux démoniaques, mais un jeu naturel d'heccéités, degrés, intensités, événements, accidents, qui composent des individuations, tout à fait differentes de celle des sujets bien formés qui les reçoivent.' Everything in the end, then, is some or other event of intensification that throws up this hereness or that thereness. From this rather aerial perspective

on the plane of immanence, a perspective that could easily have been Hegel's, the instance of membranization without which *heccéité* cannot commence, is little more than a hiccup. From a more horizontal or mortal perspective, however, the frailty of an individual membrane begins to register – the frailty of the membrane that halts or hesitates the flux so that *heccéité* can commence (or the hesitation of the flux that brings forth the *heccéité* of the membrane, as Deleuze and Guattari might want to say in order to stress that the membrane is not first). From the experience of this frail register, *heccéité* is more than a hiccup, more than a reflux in the flux of continuous existence. It is the constituting and deconstituting individualizing event of which the experience must always be cataclysmic and traumatic (also orgiastic, of course). On this horizontal and mortal plane, the many wolves (yes, also the *chevreaux* – see *Mille plateaux* 52) become one wolf, big enough at that to be called the father, as Freud understood well. Nancy, who claims to take us onto the plane of horizontal mortality/mortal horizontality, *l'horizontalité des morts* (cf. Nancy 2000: 49), must and does concede that the event comes as a surprise – *la surprise, le saut dans l'espace-temps, coupe et chiasme d'origine* (cf. the essay *Surprise de l'événement* in *Être singulier pluriel* (Nancy 1996: 185–202, especially at 199). Cf. also Nancy (1988: 147): '*La surprise [ouvre] le temps.*' The surprise opens time. And the surprise may inflict some injuries (*des blessures*) but never as much as a wound (*une plaie*). Only sacrificial Christianism and sacrificial sovereignty wound (cf. Nancy 2000: 67–71), not existence as such. The latter cannot be sacrificed and therefore does also not sacrifice itself, as we saw above (see notes 9 and 10 above). Indeed, the event brings hours of good and bad fortune (*malheur/bonheur* – cf. Nancy 1993: 219) but in the hour of the opening there is ultimately no real lack; everything is complete: 'Rien ne manque au monde: le monde est la totalité, et la totalité s'accomplit comme l'ouvert, comme la non-totalisation de l'ouvert ou de l'*heur*' (see Nancy 1993: 230). In the serene hour of this courageous stoicism, in the hour of this equanimity-in-orbit for which the world, from afar, becomes whole, total, and beautiful, Nancy moves very close to Deleuze and Guattari's aerial survey of the plane of immanence. His concern with exteriority and exposure in *La Communauté désœuvrée* now also seems to come from a different planet.

13 'Die Wunden des Geistes heilen, ohne daß Narben bleiben' (Hegel 1970: 492).

14 On Derrida's responsibility as a negotiation of the abyssal tension between immanence and imminence, see van der Walt (2009).

15 On this mourning hospitality and the love for ruins, see van der Walt (2005).

16 According to Fitzpatrick, the 'savage holds the place of irresolution' and thus of a 'protean' non-fixity in society (2001: 28, 30) that allows newness or 'circumstance and possibility into the world' (ibid.: 32) and thus breaks up the 'brute savagery' (ibid.: 24) and '"sameness" of savagery' (ibid.: 32) and 'utter fixity' (ibid.: 1) of the father's rule. But the slippages and reversals go further: the savagery of the brothers not only brings circumstance and possibility into the world, but ultimately also repeats the utter fixity of the father's rule in the different format of utter unfixity. Where the father 'eliminate[d] individuality' (ibid.: 28) and therefore 'all circumstance and possibility', the brothers, 'unceasingly pitted against each another' in a 'world without determination' (ibid.: 32), produce 'nothing but individuality' (ibid.: 28), a world determined or fixed by individuality, one might say. Thus do the rebellious brothers represent in Freud's myth the wild and savage or ur-savage heart of the feminine in Cixous (Fitzpatrick 2008: 205, 210, 214, 220) and repeat the masculine fixity or sameness of the father's savagery.

17 See also Fitzpatrick (2001: 57) with reference to Eliade: '[B]ringing into being involves the sacrifice, the making sacred, of what is rejected in so doing.'

18 See Derrida (1994: xix): 'If I am getting ready to speak at length about ghosts, inheritance, and generations, and generations of ghosts, which is to say about certain *others* who are not present, not presently living, either to us, in us, or outside us, it is in the name of justice. Of justice where it is not yet, not yet *there*, where it is no longer, let us understand where it is no longer *present*, and where it will never be, no more than the law, reducible to laws or rights. It is necessary to speak *of the* ghost, indeed *to the* ghost and *with* it, from the moment that no ethics, no politics, whether revolutionary or not, seems possible and thinkable and *just* that does not recognize in its principle the respect for those others who are no longer or for those who are not yet *there*, presently living, whether they are already dead or not yet born. No justice – let us say no law and once again we are not speaking here of laws – seems possible or thinkable without the principle of some *responsibility*, beyond all living present, within that which disjoins the living present, before the ghosts of those who are not yet born or who are already dead, be they victims of wars, political or other kinds of violence, nationalist, racist, colonialist, sexist, or other kinds of exterminations, victims of the oppressions of capitalist imperialism or any of the forms of totalitarianism. Without this *non-contemporaneity with itself of the living present*, without that which secretly unhinges it, without this responsibility and this respect for justice concerning those who *are not there*, of those who are no longer or who are not yet *present and living*, what sense would there be to ask the question "where?" "where tomorrow?" "whither?"'

References

Agamben, G. (1999) *Potentialities*, trans. D. Heller-Roazen, Stanford, CA: Stanford University Press.

Deleuze, G. and Guattari, F. (1973) *Capitalisme et schizophrénie 1: L'Anti-Œdipe*, Paris: Les Éditions de Minuit.

Deleuze, G. and Guattari, F. (1980) *Capitalisme et schizophrénie 2: Mille plateaux*, Paris: Les Éditions de Minuit.

Deleuze, G. and Guattari, F. (1994) *What Is Philosophy?*, London: Verso; (2005) *Qu'est-ce que la philosophie?*, Paris: Les Éditions de Minuit.

Derrida, J. (1993) *Spectres du Marx*, Paris: Éditions Galilée; (1994) *Specters of Marx*, New York: Routledge.

Dobson, R. (1972) 'The mirror: Jan Vermeer speaks', in H. Heseltine (ed.) *The Penguin Book of Australian Verse*, Ringwood, Victoria: Penguin Books.

Fitzpatrick, P. (2001) *Modernism and the Grounds of Law*, Cambridge: Cambridge University Press.

Fitzpatrick, P. (2008) *Law as Resistance*, Farnham, UK: Ashgate.

Freud, S. (1960) *Totem and Taboo*, trans. J. Strachey, London: Routledge & Kegan Paul.

Hegel, G. W. F. (1970) *Werke in 20 Bänden*, vol. 3: *Phänomenologie des Geistes*, Frankfurt: Suhrkamp.

Nancy, J.-L. (1986, 1999 edn) *La Communauté désœuvrée*, Paris: Christian Bourgois.

Nancy, J.-L. (1988) *L'Expérience de la liberté*, Paris: Galilée.

Nancy, J.-L. (1990) *Une pensée finie*, Paris: Galilée.

Nancy, J.-L. (1993) *Le Sens du monde*, Paris: Galilée.

Nancy, J.-L. (1996) *Être singulier pluriel*, Paris: Galilée.

Nancy, J.-L. (2000) *Corpus*, Paris: Métailié.
van der Walt, J. W. G. (2005) *Law and Sacrifice: Towards a Post-apartheid Theory of Law*, London: Birkbeck Law Press/Johannesburg: Wits University Press.
van der Walt, J. W. G. (2009) 'Rawls and Derrida on the historicity of constitutional democracy and international justice', *Constellations* 16: 23–43.

Chapter 10

'The obliging etymology of "nomos"'

Peter Fitzpatrick and the aesthetics of law

Carrol Clarkson

Introduction

In *Modernism and the Grounds of Law*, Peter Fitzpatrick speaks of the '*spatial* locating of law's range via the obliging etymology of "nomos"' (Fitzpatrick 2001b: 91, my emphasis). He goes on to cite Cornelia Vismann's essay 'Starting from scratch: Concepts of order in no man's land', which describes the 'initial scene of the law':

> The primordial scene of the *nomos* opens with a drawing of a line in the soil. This very act initiates a specific concept of law, which derives order from the notion of space. The plough draws lines – furrows in the field – to mark the space of one's own. As such, as ownership, the demarcating plough touches the juridical sphere. [...] The primordial act as described here brings together land and law, cultivation and order, space and *nomos*.
>
> (Vismann 1997: 46–7, cited in Fitzpatrick 2001b: 91–2)

Vismann's paper constitutes a reading ('an enthralling account and analysis', in Fitzpatrick's terms (Fitzpatrick 2001b: 225)) of Carl Schmitt's *The Nomos of the Earth*. In this chapter I begin to suggest ways in which Fitzpatrick's nuanced discussion of *nomos* in *Modernism and the Grounds of Law* takes further Vismann's critique of Schmitt's relentlessly spatial account of the law, even while Fitzpatrick's engagement takes the 'obliging etymology' of *nomos* on board. More specifically, I elaborate on what Fitzpatrick calls 'the other, responsive dimension of space' (2001b: 93), a concept that offers provocative commentary on Schmitt's understanding of the relation between *nomos* and the law defined as spatial orientation. My discussion then opens onto my central argument: that Peter Fitzpatrick's work can be read as forging a new kind of discourse, what I like to think of as an aesthetics of law. More specifically put: in contrast to the insular spatial determinism that Schmitt identifies with common law, and would like to apply to law more generally, Fitzpatrick develops the idea that law, like poetry, is intrinsically responsive to its other.

A distinctive feature of Fitzpatrick's own writing style is his extensive and creative use of quotations from a range of other sources. Literary, philosophical, psychoanalytic, anthropological, and critical-legal texts become the colourful and tightly woven-in threads that make up the fabrics of his own arguments. The sustained – even foregrounded – device of quoting and alluding to other works is characteristic, too, of several of the modernist literary texts to which Fitzpatrick himself refers with such insight. My chapter plays up Fitzpatrick's allusiveness; in fact, I would go so far as to say that my essay is inspired by thoughts about the aesthetic and ethical implications of Fitzpatrick's use of citation in his own critical legal discourse. In his insistent responsiveness to – and incorporation of – the writings of others in his texts, Fitzpatrick not only speaks about but *performs* what he might call the disruptive ambivalence of instantiating a conceptual field that depends upon what is ever beyond, but at the same time incipient within, it.

Finally, I would like to set Fitzpatrick's practice of responsiveness to other writers alongside a central ethical preoccupation in the writing of Nobel prize-winning author J. M. Coetzee. 'Writing is not free expression', says Coetzee:

> There is a true sense in which writing is dialogic: a matter of awakening the countervoices in oneself and embarking upon speech with them. It is some measure of a writer's seriousness whether he does evoke/invoke those countervoices in himself, that is, step down from the position of what Lacan calls 'the subject supposed to know.'
>
> (1992: 65)

Carl Schmitt and the *jus publicum Europaeum*

I begin by picking out and following back to its source one of the citation-threads in *Modernism and the Grounds of Law.* The passage quoted from Cornelia Vismann's essay at the outset of my chapter – and quoted in Fitzpatrick's *Modernism and the Grounds of Law* – in its turn alludes to Carl Schmitt's extended reflection on the *nomos,* a reflection that brings *nomos* into the field of a philosophical, historical, and politically charged discourse. In the foreword to *The* Nomos *of the Earth in the International Law of the Jus Publicum Europaeum,* Carl Schmitt presents the concept of *nomos* as having a primordial, foundational, and even chthonic quality. 'Human thinking again must be directed to the elemental orders of terrestrial being here and now', writes Schmitt. 'We seek to understand the normative order of the earth' (2003: 39). *Nomos,* in Schmitt, links order and orientation: '*Nomos* comes from *nemein* – a [Greek] word that means both "to divide" and "to pasture." Thus, *nomos* is the immediate form in which the political and social order of a people becomes spatially visible' (ibid.: 70).

The boundary line, or fence, or wall, for Schmitt takes on an unequivocally positive and spatially visible relation to that which is enclosed, and hence, to the law:

> [T]he solid ground of the earth is delineated by fences, enclosures, boundaries, walls, houses, and other constructs. Then, the orders and orientations of human social life become apparent. Then, obviously, families, clans, tribes, estates, forms of ownership and human proximity, also forms of power and domination, become visible.
>
> (2003: 42)

Further, and importantly in Schmitt, the concrete historical event of land appropriation is intrinsically bound up in the concept of law. Schmitt speaks of land appropriation as being the 'archetype of a constitutive legal process'; it 'creates the most radical legal title, in the full and comprehensive sense of the term *radical title*' (ibid.: 47). Even further still, it is the historical act of land appropriation that grants conceptual legitimacy to the law: 'we must take heed that the word not lose its connection to a historical process – to a constitutive act of spatial ordering' (ibid.: 71); 'it is a constitutive historical event – an act of *legitimacy*, whereby the legality of a mere law first is made meaningful' (ibid.: 73). Carl Schmitt approvingly cites the German linguist Jost Trier: 'In the beginning was the fence', says Trier:

> Fence, enclosure, and border are deeply interwoven in the world formed by men, determining its concepts. The enclosure gave birth to the shrine by removing it from the ordinary, placing it under its own laws, and entrusting it to the divine.
>
> (Trier 1942: 232, cited in Schmitt 2003: 74)

Thus, *nomos* 'is a fence-word' (Schmitt 2003: 75), and '[e]very *nomos* consists of what is within its own bounds' (Trier 1942: 232, cited in Schmitt 2003: 75).

Schmitt sees the action of the *nomos* as having three stages: appropriation, division, and cultivation (2003: 351), and the emphasis of his inquiry is on what is inside the boundary, what the fence tells about the enclosed field it delineates. Hence, 'this is the original meaning of *nomos*', writes Fitzpatrick, citing Dudley Young, 'that portion of food-bearing land (we still call it "keep") through which my sheep may safely graze' (Young 1992: 317, cited in Fitzpatrick 2001b: 92). Schmitt notes that from the sixteenth to the twentieth century, the cultivated, and – by extension – the civilized field demarcated by European international law was taken to be representative of an order applicable to the whole earth. Further, '*Civilization* was synonymous with *European* civilization' (Schmitt 2003: 86), and the new world was considered not as enemy territory but as free space, open to European occupation. But the presumed spatial certainty of that which is bounded, unequivocally circumscribed by the *nomos*, becomes more complex with colonial expansion in Africa. The 'crucial distinction between European and non-European or colonial soil', writes Schmitt's translator, G. L. Ulmen, 'was lost in Africa, and with it the meaning of the legal distinction of "beyond the line," which separated the reach of European public law from the sphere of lawlessness' (2003: 26–7). The question of what is legitimately European in colonial soil demands a separate essay of its own.[1] But what is pertinent for the argument in this chapter is that the complexity of our understanding of the spatial range of the *nomos* intensifies the moment we undertake further serious thinking about the *logic* of the limit. In thinking the boundary, or the limit, or the fence, one is often led to think foremost of what is supposedly *excluded* or beyond the range of that limit. The 'philosophy of the limit' (to use Drucilla Cornell's name-phrase for deconstruction), with reference to Derrida's '"logic of parergonality," demonstrates how the very establishment of a system as a system implies a *beyond* to it, precisely by virtue of what it excludes' (Cornell 1992: 1). Moving away from Schmitt's resolutely spatially determined legal interiors, Fitzpatrick, with reference to Jorge Luis Borges' *Dreamtigers* (1964) and Lewis Carroll's 'The Hunting of the Snark' (1976) (in turn, examples both discussed by Boaventura de Sousa Santos (1995), to whom Fitzpatrick also refers), speaks of the irresolution of law's spatial determinations: '[W]hilst determination can never be completely spatially formed, responsiveness cannot be ever completely unformed' (Fitzpatrick 2001b: 90–1).

In the work of both Fitzpatrick and Cornell, the *irresolution* of what is inside the supposed boundary, thanks to its responsive relation to what is beyond it, takes on an ethical resonance. For Cornell reading Derrida, the 'project is not only to show us why and how there is always the Other to the system; it is also to indicate the ethical aspiration behind that demonstration' (Cornell 1992: 2). Further, and more specifically, Cornell's undertaking is to 'show the significance for legal interpretation of Derrida's own understanding of justice as an aporia that inevitably serves as the limit to any attempt to collapse justice into positive law' (ibid.: 2). By way of a thinking through of this philosophy of the limit in relation to the tensions and suspensions between justice and the law, both Fitzpatrick and Cornell offer a challenge to Schmitt's materially spatial conceptions. Fitzpatrick takes this even further: the content of the law is not only irresolute but vacuous.

Law's vacuity: law and law's other

In his nuanced discussion in *Modernism and the Grounds of Law*, Fitzpatrick demonstrates the ways in which the common law, 'despite its vaunted and supposedly exceptional grounding, provides no alternative to law's vacuity' (2001b: 93). This passage reminds me of Heidegger's discussion of art in his essay 'The origin of the work of art'. In this section of my chapter I bring aspects of Heidegger's aesthetic theory into conversation with Fitzpatrick's theory of law. The discussion ultimately brings Heidegger's use of the word '*Riss*' (a rift, a fissure, a scratch, and also a draft, a plan, a sketch, according to the *Langenscheidt Standard Dictionary*) into juxtaposition with the concept of *nomos* and the philosophy of the limit, as I have been sketching it out thus far. But first let us consider the idea of law's vacuity in relation to Heidegger's discussion of art. What is the origin of the work of art, Heidegger asks. Is it the artist, or the work?

> The artist is the origin of the work. The work is the origin of the artist. Neither is without the other. Nevertheless, neither is the sole support of the other. In themselves and in their interrelations artist and work *are* each of them by virtue of a third thing which is prior to both, namely ... art.... But can art be an origin at all? Where and how does art occur? *Art – this is nothing more than a word to which nothing actual any longer corresponds.*
>
> (1993: 143, my emphasis)

Perhaps both the artist and the work have been vaunted as art's grounding, but just as Fitzpatrick registers law's vacuity, Heidegger draws attention to art's correspondence to 'nothing actual'. For Heidegger, 'Art is truth setting itself to work' (ibid.: 167) – and he goes on to discuss this idea in some detail with specific reference to the building of a Greek temple. I track this example here at least in part because of the kinetic relation Heidegger establishes between what he calls 'world' and 'earth' – which will bring me back to the concept of the *nomos* (recall Schmitt's *Nomos of the Earth*) – via the multivalency of Heidegger's term *Riss*.

First to the temple: we are perhaps tempted to think that the temple is built as an act of portraying the prior existence of the gods in that place, and that the ground there is already holy. However, in Heidegger's subtle account a 'building, a Greek temple, portrays nothing. It simply stands there in the middle of the rock-cleft valley', and yet, '[b]y means of the temple, the god is present in the temple. This presence of the god is in itself the extension and delimitation of the precinct as a holy precinct' (Heidegger 1993: 167). Thus, even while it portrays nothing, it is the temple building that signifies the ground as sacred, that creates within it the shape of meaning and human destiny in acts of nature (birth, death, and other natural phenomena, such as the existence of other animals, or the weather) which in themselves are void and heedless of any meaning that humans might attribute to them. This, in turn, makes me think of a conversation between two characters in Anne Michaels' novel *The Winter Vault*:

> A temple was the first power station. Think of the formulas invented, the physical achievement of thousands of men moving a mountain, hewing and hauling stone tonne by tonne, often hundreds of kilometres, to a site of precise coordinates – all in an attempt to capture spirits.
>
> To define space [...] No. Not to give shape to space, but to give shape to ... emptiness.
>
> (2009: 9)

The temple in Heidegger gives shape not only to the abstract emptiness of a human world with respect to the gods, but also to the physical earth surrounding the building. The presence of a work of art, for Heidegger, is not simply a 'bare placing'; it instantiates a site for human dedication to, and consecration of, a meaningful world where truth finds its opening. 'Towering up within itself, the work opens up a *world* and keeps it abidingly in force' (Heidegger 1993: 169, emphasis in original) and 'To be a work means to set up a world' (ibid.: 170). At the same time, the ground upon which the temple is built *becomes* 'earth' – in Heidegger's special sense. The temple gives definition to the rocks upon which it is built as sturdy foundation, say. It makes manifest the violence of the storm raging above it, or the radiance of the light of day when the sun glints off its stones. In the natural phenomena that arise, thanks to the building of the temple, 'earth occurs essentially as the sheltering agent', and thus the 'temple-work, standing there, opens up a world and at the same time sets this world back again on earth, which itself only thus emerges as native ground' (ibid.: 168).

What gradually comes into focus in Heidegger's essay is a vertiginous relation between 'world' and 'earth' – both of which are called forth in the creation of a work of art. What interests me here is the metaphor Heidegger uses to describe this relation – that is, the image of *Riss*. The German word *Riss* (as I have mentioned) designates a fissure, rift, or scratch, but it is also a design, draft, or drawing, and it is worth noting that it is also a cognate of the English word 'writing' (see editor's note, Heidegger 1993: 188). In Albert Hofstadter's translation of Heidegger's essay, *Riss* is often rendered as 'rift-design' in English, and it is clear that Heidegger himself is playing up the multivalency of the term. 'For in truth', writes Heidegger, 'art lies hidden within nature; he who can wrest it from her, has it.' Heidegger goes on to provide a gloss on his use of the word 'wrest' – '*Reissen*': '"Reissen" heisst hier Herausholen des Risses und den Riss reissen mit der Reissfeder auf dem Reissbrett' – in Hofstadter's translation: '"Wrest" here means to draw out the rift and to draw the design with the drawing-pen on the drawing-board' (Heidegger 1993, and translator's footnote: 195). This rift, or design, for Heidegger, thus *puts into relation* what is simultaneously separated and joined on either side of the *Riss* – world and earth, or, even more crudely put, art and nature: 'This rift does not let the opponents break apart; it brings what opposes measure and boundary into its common outline' – and even further still, 'The rift is the drawing together, into a unity, of sketch and basic design, breach and outline' (Heidegger 1993: 188). Thus, the world of art is responsive to the earthly forms in nature; in fact, art discloses those forms – it neither excludes them nor does it abstract or reduce them to the supposedly determinate limits of its own world.

Now, the last sentence of the previous paragraph purposely carries verbal echoes of Peter Fitzpatrick's own way of writing about law. The alignment I am beginning to suggest between a philosophy of law and a philosophy of art may seem far-fetched – but it is an alignment obligingly provided by Fitzpatrick himself (as we shall see in a moment), and also by Heidegger, in volume 1 of *Nietzsche: The Will to Power as Art*: 'The artistic states are those which place themselves under the supreme command of measure and law, taking themselves beyond themselves in order to advance' (Heidegger 1991: 130). And further, 'Such states are what they essentially are when, willing out beyond themselves, they are more than they are' (ibid.: 130). I read close parallels here in Fitzpatrick's accounts of the law in *Modernism and the Grounds of Law*: 'Determination itself depends integrally on law's responsiveness and this responsive dimension is always beyond the determinant' (Fitzpatrick 2001b: 107). And: 'Even at its most settled, or especially at its most settled, law could not "be" otherwise than responsive to what was beyond its determinate content "for the time being", but neither could it dissipate in a pure responsiveness' (ibid.: 104). What this amounts to, finally, is 'the irresolution of law's dimensions' (ibid.: 107), to the extent that law's capacity for responsiveness, in Fitzpatrick's philosophy of law, is indeed part of what constitutes it in the first place. Bringing this finally back to the *nomos*, in Fitzpatrick's inimitable style:

> A return to that obliging etymology of nomos can now extend beyond the fixing of law in the bounded earth and unfold more of how the responsive may be 'placed' in law: 'with a supremely judicious sense of metaphor, the Greeks also used "*nomos*" to designate song or melody, that portion of structured time through which my emotions ... may safely range in search of nourishment without fear of being ecstatically carried away'.
>
> (ibid.: 101, citing Young 1992: 317–18)

There is a certain sense in Heidegger's work, as well as in Fitzpatrick's, that art/law does not simply exclude but in fact makes possible, and even brings forth that other to which law is intrinsically responsive; the *nomos*, *Riss*, or outline evokes thoughts of what lies beyond it, unsettling complacent preconceptions of what is supposedly stabilized within its border.

Further still, if part of what constitutes the law is its responsiveness to this other, then what is 'other' to the law is not dispensable but a structural condition for law's being what it is. Within the specific context of Schmitt's rigidly spatial conception of *nomos*, and other 'talismanic spatial metaphors of inside and outside – of boundaries, terrain and atemporal demarcation' to posit the idea of autonomous law, Fitzpatrick's concern is 'to show how the very effort at such determinant positing calls forth, or at least indicates the need of, the other, responsive dimension of space' (ibid.: 93, with reference to Davies 1996: 18; 1998: 155–6; Derrida 1992: 6).

Towards an aesthetics of law

Ever since Plato's *Republic*, poetry has been presented as law's other. In the dialogue, Socrates, Glaucon, Adeimantus, and others sketch out their vision of a just state, and they reach the conclusion that poetry and the dramatic arts ought to be banished from it. Once you admit 'the sweet lyric or epic muse', says Socrates, 'pleasure and pain become your rulers instead of law and the rational principles commonly accepted as best' (§607a); the poet

> wakens and encourages and strengthens the lower elements in the mind to the detriment of reason, which is like giving power and political control to the worst elements in the state and ruining the better elements. The dramatic poet produces a similarly bad state of affairs in the mind of the individual, by encouraging the unreasoning part of it.
>
> (Plato 2003: §605b–c)

If philosophy identifies the just state and its laws as being on the side of reason, and poetry and the arts generally as being on the side of 'feelings' (§605d), 'instinctive desires' (§606a), and 'desires and feelings of pleasure and pain' (§606d), then the logical conclusion is that the arts have no place within the domain of the law.

Nevertheless, I would argue that the very core of Fitzpatrick's oeuvre consists in a sustained critique of the kind of mutually exclusive dualisms that are easy to find in Plato's dialogue.[2] In two recent papers, Fitzpatrick challenges a Manichaean approach to law and its other with specific reference to law and poetry. In 'Law like poetry: "Burnt Norton"' (2001a) and 'Juris-fiction: Literature and the law of the law' (2004), Fitzpatrick argues that the logic at work in both law and literature is a responsiveness to what is supposedly beyond the limit of the respective discipline. In 'Juris-fiction', Fitzpatrick states this explicitly: 'Law and literature [...] share the same ambivalence between existent instantiation and what is ever beyond yet incipient in it' (2004: 222). Even more radically, the 'disruptive ambivalence' that constitutes the law 'can be derived from a quality of literature' (ibid.: 215). In its call for a *decision* in each legal case (the outcome of a case is not absolutely foreseeable in advance), '[w]hat is always involved with the law ... is the creative reaching out to a possibility beyond its determinate existence, a beyond where law "finds itself" in being integrally tied to, and incipiently encompassing of, its exteriority' (ibid.: 221). Throughout his work, Fitzpatrick links law and literature through their utter responsiveness to what is yet to come as a possible constituent of it – which leads us to question complacent assumptions about where the borderlines of those disciplines really are. In his essays specifically focused on law and literature, Fitzpatrick's argument develops by way of philosophical reflections on – and incisive and sensitive close readings of – fiction and poetry, perhaps most notably the work of Modernist and other twentieth-century poets: T. S. Eliot, Wallace Stevens, and W. H. Auden, to name just a few.

But increasingly what has come to interest me is not only what Fitzpatrick *says about* law and literature in his work, but what he *does* in his own writing. A characteristic feature of Fitzpatrick's stylistic and conceptual approach (this is a feature I have foregrounded in this chapter) is an insistence on quoting, citing (that is, 'to summon officially in a court of law', the *Oxford English Dictionary* tells us), invoking, drawing on, alluding to, borrowing from, referencing and cross-referencing the innumerable other texts that are thereby threaded through the present piece of writing. The cumulative effect of these quotations is that in reading Fitzpatrick's work one develops a sense of not simply reading a monologic text in isolation. Instead, the words become gateways onto a multivoiced philosophical conversation – a conversation that goes as far back as Plato and that includes voices such as those of Hobbes, Heidegger, T. S. Eliot, Wallace Stevens, Freud, Blanchot, Foucault, Derrida, and Beethoven, among countless others. The impact of all these references and quotations is that Fitzpatrick's own writing, like the law he writes about, *performs* the utter responsiveness that gives it such a profoundly ethical orientation. Fitzpatrick's work is thus the product not simply of one who writes, but of one who listens, intently, to the voice of the other.

I would like to discuss this in detail; I restrict myself to just one example – that is, the first sentence of *Modernism and the Grounds of Law*.... Actually, now that I come to it, let me cite the first two sentences, but I shall speak about the first sentence; even more specifically, my emphasis is on the first word. Here are the opening sentences of the introduction:

> Extravagant as it may seem, this whole work is initially encapsulated in Freud's attempt to locate the origin of society in the primal parricide of *Totem and Taboo* (Freud 1960). Here Freud turned to 'the originary question of grounds', to borrow the phrase (Derrida 1989: 60).
>
> (Fitzpatrick 2001b: 1)

At the back of my mind as I read this is the opening sentence of E. M. Foster's *A Passage to India*: 'Except for the Marabar Caves – and they are twenty miles off – the city of Chandrapore presents nothing extraordinary' (Foster 1982: 31) – but to return to *Modernism and the Grounds of Law*, 'extravagant' also has an 'obliging etymology', as *The Shorter Oxford English Dictionary* tells us:

> **Extravagant** (ekstræ·văgănt). ME. [-*extravagant-*, pres. ppl. stem of med.L. *extravagari*, f. *extra* EXTRA + *vagari* wander [...] That wanders out of bounds; vagrant; keeping no fixed place [...] 'Roving beyond just limits or prescribed methods'
>
> (J.)

The first two sentences of *Modernism and the Grounds of Law*, with their reference to Freud as the impetus for the project and a borrowed phrase from Derrida, certainly are extravagant in their roving beyond the prescribed methods one would expect from a book on legal philosophy. The book announces itself as a response to Freud's *Totem and Taboo* – and thus the effect of 'seem' (in 'Extravagant as it may seem...') gains its semantic force: what are the 'bounds' of *Modernism and the Grounds of Law* if it is explicitly cast as having its origins in the work of Freud? Is Freud's 'attempt' then not incipiently *within* the arguments of *Modernism and the Grounds of Law*, and Fitzpatrick's supposed vagrancy in citing it not really a wandering out of bounds at all? Yet if the arguments of *Modernism and the Grounds of Law* are only 'initially encapsulated' in Freud, then the book is not entirely in that keep either. Thus, the citation in the very first sentence already raises unsettling questions in a thematic way, but, perhaps more importantly, it *performs* the 'disruptive ambivalence' that Fitzpatrick locates in the responsiveness of law. Like the law of which it speaks, the book itself is only questionably contained within determinations one might traditionally set for a monograph written by a single author, as we shall see in the concluding section.

But first let me reiterate that my interest in Fitzpatrick's work has to do not only with the ideas expressed but also with the implications of his stylistic approach. I would argue that, far from being an irrelevant if idiosyncratic feature of his writing, Fitzpatrick's strategy of referencing, which is to say, his giving voice to the other, enacts the ethic of responsiveness that underwrites his legal philosophy.

Conclusion

In the previous section I spoke about what I called 'the first sentence of *Modernism and the Grounds of Law*' – but of course this is not strictly the first sentence. The real first sentence, after the list of contents, appears under the heading 'Acknowledgements', and *this* first sentence reads, 'Rarely can the arrogations of authorship have been so sorely tested' (Fitzpatrick 2001b: ix). The acknowledgements elaborate on this idea: the 'infinity of influence cannot be encompassed', Fitzpatrick writes, and at a more radical level any supposed containment of the book itself is open to question: 'Its spurious self-sufficiency is also greatly challenged by the creative readings of previous drafts, or a chunk of them offered by....' A litany of names follows, each linked to an item in an enchanting list that includes 'exuberance', 'research on globalism', 'poetry', 'red pens', 'intellectual companionship', an 'exemplary index', 'sustaining joy', a 'Kentish-Brazilian garden', and 'much everything' (Fitzpatrick 2001b: ix).

To return specifically to the idea of the tested arrogations of authorship: the entire project of *Modernism and the Grounds of Law* is ostensively acknowledged and introduced by its author as being intimately engaged in conversation with other voices in creatively different ways. This brings me back to the passage that I cited from Coetzee at the outset. For Coetzee, '[w]riting is not free expression'; it is intrinsically 'dialogic: a matter of awakening the countervoices in oneself' (1992: 65). In a moment of the writer's utter responsiveness to the other, for Coetzee – and I would say that this holds for Fitzpatrick as well – one's authorship cedes ground to an internal dialogue that questions ideas about the writer's presumptive occupation of sites of authority and knowledge. What all of this leads to is an argument that Fitzpatrick's sustained literary device of citation throughout his writing can be understood to take effect in the *Riss*, the fault line, the in-between (a word that Fitzpatrick often uses) that both separates and joins speaker and listener, writer and reader, *I* and *you*. A book like *Modernism and the Grounds of Law* is thus the work not simply of a single author, but of an *interlocutor* – that is to say, one who carries the ethical freight of participating in a conversation, of listening and responding, of questioning the grounds of one's authority, of rethinking and perhaps revising one's initial position. The ethical charge is activated, and measures a higher voltage, when the interlocutor assumes responsibility as the writer.

The performative effect of writing-as-response, even before the subsumptive themes and ideas are opened for analysis, is of particular interest to J. M. Coetzee. 'Ideas are certainly important – who would deny that?', Coetzee writes, and then goes on to say:

> [A] style, an attitude to the world, as it soaks in, becomes part of the personality, part of the self, ultimately indistinguishable from the self. To put it another way: in the process of responding to the writers one intuitively chooses to respond to, one makes oneself into the person whom in the most intractable but also perhaps the most deeply ethical sense one wants to be.
>
> (1993: 7)

In *this* book, *Reading Modern Law*, we, the reader-writers, have all chosen intuitively to respond to the work of Peter Fitzpatrick. But our work, in turn, has been precipitated by Fitzpatrick's own writing-as-response. This writing-as-response is not only a response to previous authors but also (like the law and the literary arts of which Fitzpatrick speaks) a receptive and creative responsiveness to the possibility of future encounters with interlocutors yet to come. All of which brings to bear the extraordinary ethical force, in law and in the creative arts more generally, of the idea initially incapsulated in the phrase 'extravagant as it may seem' (Fitzpatrick 2001b: 1).

Notes

1 I discuss this in the first chapter of my forthcoming book *Drawing the Line*.
2 A careful reading of Plato's dialogue shows the relation between paired and opposed terms (such as philosophy and poetry, law and the creative arts) to be far more intricate than I suggest here. I discuss the dialogue in more detail in my essay 'Ancient antagonisms' (2008).

References

Borges, J. (1964) *Dreamtigers*, trans. M. Boyer and H. Morland, New York: E. P. Dutton.
Carroll, L. (1976) *Complete Works*, New York: Vintage.
Clarkson, C. (2008) 'Ancient antagonisms', *English Academy Review* 25(2): 101–10.
Clarkson, C. (forthcoming) *Drawing the Line: Towards an Aesthetics of Transitional Justice*, Bronx, NY: Fordham University Press.
Coetzee, J. M. (1992) *Doubling the Point*, ed. D. Attwell, Cambridge, MA: Harvard University Press.
Coetzee, J. M. (1993) 'Homage', *The Threepenny Review* 53: 5–7.
Cornell, D. (1992) *The Philosophy of the Limit*, New York: Routledge.
Davies, M. (1996) *Delimiting the Law: 'Postmodernism' and the Politics of Law*, London: Pluto Press.
Davies, M. (1998) 'The proper: Discourses of purity', *Law and Critique* 9(2): 143–73.
Derrida, J. (1989) 'Psyche: Inventions of the other', in L. Waters and W. Godzich (eds) *Reading de Man Reading*, trans. C. Porter, Minneapolis: University of Minnesota Press.
Derrida, J. (1992) *Given Time: Counterfeit Money*, trans. P. Kamuf, Chicago: University of Chicago Press.
Fitzpatrick, P. (2001a) 'Law like poetry: "Burnt Norton"', *Liverpool Law Review* 23(3): 285–8.
Fitzpatrick, P. (2001b) *Modernism and the Grounds of Law*, Cambridge: Cambridge University Press.
Fitzpatrick, P. (2004) 'Juris-fiction: Literature and the law of the law', *Ariel* 35(1–2): 215–29.
Foster, E. M. (1982) *A Passage to India*, Harmondsworth, UK: Penguin.

Heidegger, M. (1991) *Nietzsche: The Will to Power as Art*, 2 vols, trans. D. Farrell Krell, New York: HarperCollins.
Heidegger, M. (1993) 'The origin of the work of art', trans. A. Hofstadter, in *Basic Writings*, ed. D. Farrell Krell, New York: HarperCollins.
Michaels, A. (2009) *The Winter Vault*, New York: Alfred A. Knopf.
Plato (2003) *The Republic*, 2nd edn, trans. D. Lee, London: Penguin.
Santos, B. (1995) *Toward a New Common Sense: Law, Science and Politics in the Paradigmatic Transition*, New York: Routledge.
Schmitt, C. (2003) *The* Nomos *of the Earth in the International Law of the Jus Publicum Europaeum*, trans. G. L. Ulmen, New York: Telos Press.
Trier, J. (1942) 'Zaun und Mannring', *Beiträchen zur Geschichte der deutschen Sprache und Literatur* 66: 232–64.
Ulmen, G. L. (2003) 'Translator's introduction', in C. Schmitt, *The Nomos of the Earth in the International Law of the Jus Publicum Europaeum*, New York: Telos Press.
Vismann, C. (1997) 'Starting from scratch: Concepts of order in no man's land', in B. Hüppauff (ed.) *War, Violence and the Modern Condition*, New York: Walter de Gruyter.
Young, D. (1992) *Origins of the Sacred: The Ecstasies of Love and War*, London: Little, Brown.

Chapter 11

Writing by firelight

Constructing an enduring consciousness of post-coloniality

Abdul Paliwala

Prologue – on firelight

Edward Thompson and the Subaltern Studies group share the creation of candlelight histories based on centuries-old faded paper documents and focused more on the masses than on the elites.[1] Firelight is warmer than candlelight but can also be very seductive. There are two senses to my use of firelight here. First, Papua New Guinea's recent colonization meant that the transition from colonial to post-colonial was a very condensed process, which enabled a rapid forward-wind mode of observation of the history of transition.[2] We as observers participated in the construction of our own consciousness. The second sense of firelight was of direct engagement with the ordinary people really and metaphorically sitting in houses and sharing sweet potatoes baked in the fire. The engagement was a combination of ethnographic method and active identification with perspectives and issues of the people. However, both senses of firelight have a problem. Firelight is both warmly seductive and, in its flickering quality, not a great medium for readers or writers. The headiness of being involved in the rapid progress of history can be very beguiling. The warmth of the firelight can seduce too close an identification with the perspective of the subject without full consideration of the operative context.

This chapter suggests that our intimacy in sharing the fireside with Papua New Guineans, working socially, culturally, politically with them, has remained an enduring basis for intellectual and political responses to post-coloniality through various theoretical avatars. Peter Fitzpatrick and I shared with others this transition from colonial to post-colonial in Papua New Guinea (PNG). Peter went there from Belfast in 1970 and stayed until 1976, a period that included the transition to independence. He worked on a research project for the Commonwealth Law Foundation and then for the government, subsequently moving to the Faculty of Law at the university. I was in Papua New Guinea from 1973 to 1978, being mainly at the University of Papua New Guinea but undertaking significant amounts of work for the government, including work on the reform of land law and subsequently as Secretary of the Law Reform Commission.

Fitzpatrick's 'fireside' engagement commenced with a research project on forms of PNG economic organization. His methodology was ethnographic, but involving a reflexive transgressive form of participatory engagement with people who were being subordinated. Yet, in accord with Foucault's notion of transgression, a transgressive methodology requires an understanding of limitless potential for action, but also the power of the norm, to define, to constrain and limit the transgression (Foucault 1977: 35; Fitzpatrick 2008: xiii). This involved a quality of self-critical awareness of wider contexts within which any engagement operated.[3] Among his most significant engagements were observations of PNG approaches to economic work, a critique of legal and administrative restraints on economic activity that led to ten policy papers on different aspects of the 'informal sector' in collaboration with Loraine Blaxter, legislative proposals for recognition of new legal forms of economic enterprise, as well as working with community enterprises to initiate alternative forms such as the *Tuki ni Buka* community development corporation (Fitzpatrick 1980: 6–7, 178–80; 2000; Fitzpatrick and Southwood 1976).

His intellectual engagement is evidenced in *Law and State in Papua New Guinea* (herein *Law and State*) (Fitzpatrick 1980) and *The Political Economy of Dispute Settlement in Papua New Guinea* (Fitzpatrick 1982). At first glance the fireside concerns and intellectual approach of these earlier works seem far removed from his more contemporary publications including the *The Mythology of Modern Law* (herein *Mythology*) (Fitzpatrick 1992a) and *Modernism and the Grounds of Law* (herein *Modernism*) (Fitzpatrick 2001) as well as some of his essays published in *Law as Resistance: Modernism, Imperialism, Legalism* (herein *Law as Resistance*) (Fitzpatrick 2008). Therefore, the ambition of this essay is to trace the links to the PNG 'fireside' in these later publications.

Village courts in Papua New Guinea

And yet I am unavoidably a misreader. In particular, if there was ever a commonality between autopoietic theory and theories of alterity, it is that when one is describing the other, one is describing oneself…

For this reason, I feel it necessary to begin with our mutual and different engagements with village courts in Papua New Guinea.

Village courts were introduced in Papua New Guinea in 1973 in the dying embers of Australian colonial rule. These are state-organized courts that are run by elected villagers who solve disputes without recourse to any notion of state law or formalized customary law (Paliwala 1982; Fitzpatrick 1982; Goddard 2009). In 1977, while researching the courts, I was struck by two encounters: a statement by a 'bigman' traditional leader and a case before a village court involving a woman who had run away from her husband. A Kerowagi 'bigman' traditional leader said:

> We should have got village courts long ago because then there would have been no tribal fights, and development would take place. Look at our place now! It is very peaceful, with no drunkards, stealing, swearing or gambling. People are with their families making gardens, raising pigs, looking after their children and trying to start business. They are thinking of getting loans from the Development Bank and the Rural Improvement Fund. Tribal fighting has ceased completely.
>
> (Paliwala 1982: 227)

In the other case,

> A Mendi woman had run away from her husband a second time, in spite of a preventive order from the village court which enjoined both parties to stay together in peace. The husband had beaten her very badly and the wife was brought to the court, where she refused to go back to the husband, saying she would rather commit suicide. The court insisted that she give the marriage another try and ordered the husband to give one cassowary as compensation for the injury. The wife rushed to the river. She did not commit suicide but smashed the fingers of her hand with a stone, saying to the court, 'You may force me to go back, but I will be no use to him as I can't dig his garden and can't cook his food.'
>
> (ibid.: 222)

These two responses are part of the attempted colonial construction of postcolonial ordering in Papua New Guinea. The attempted transformation of the 'bigman' traditional leader into a post-colonial entrepreneurial 'economic man'[4] obviously seemed to be working, although I noted at the time that he was probably being 'over-optimistic' and to some extent was trying to *grisim* (literally, 'grease' me by presenting what he thought I wished to hear). On the other hand, the Mendi woman represents a subaltern feminist resistant voice, but a voice within the 'traditional' context.

These two 'consciousnesses' – the *economic man* and the subaltern – endure to the present, taking different forms in different contexts as post-colonial consciousness. Echoes of these consciousnesses can be found elsewhere, including the streets of Baghdad and Kabul.

Both Fitzpatrick, in 'The political economy of dispute settlement in Papua New Guinea' (1982), and I, in 'Law and order in the village' (1982), traced the introduction of the courts to the colonial need to construct systems that would maintain order in the post-colonial period, reversing previous resistance to any kind of indirect rule. The earlier approach of Governor Murray in 1925 involved an othering of Papua New Guineans through a misunderstanding of the acephalous nature of PNG society and dispute mechanisms. Murray considered that there was no scope for support or recognition of informal dispute settlement mechanisms because there were 'no chiefs worth talking about ... no one to rule through and nothing to serve as a foundation' (1925: 57). Instead, the role of dispute settlers in village societies resided in colonial district officers known as 'kiaps'. Intelligent kiaps would in fact work with indigenous disputes machinery, while retaining power and control. In the 1960s, Professor Derham of Melbourne University proposed the introduction of a modernized system of law in a report whose findings were not revealed till 1973 (Derham 1960). The modernization involved establishment of local courts staffed by trained Papua New Guinean magistrates who would have some scope for application of 'custom' which would be promulgated in statements similar to those favoured in Restatements of African law (Twining 1963). This modernization did not acknowledge existing PNG informal dispute settlement mechanisms. Yet at the death of colonial rule there was a volte-face by two senior law officers, who said of the introduction of a village court system, 'If it is established now, it could be fitted into the existing court system ... and by a process of education secure the adoption of certain basic procedures' (Curtis and Greenwell 1971).

On political economy of law and state

Fitzpatrick's *State and Law in Papua New Guinea* has a neo-Marxist political economy framework, but he selects the less fashionable, though more anthropologically charged, *articulation of modes of production* analysis of Meillasoux (1972) to explain the nature of colonial rule:

> The function of state and law ... is oriented towards the conservation and exploitation of the traditional mode whereas, in the context of the first world, the leading role of law and state was oriented more to the elimination of pre-capitalist modes.
>
> (Fitzpatrick 1980: 2)

In near-echo of his position in *Modernism*, in contrast to Banaji (1973) and others (e.g. Snyder 1981) who argued for only a singular 'capitalist' mode of production, Fitzpatrick urges that the 'two modes can co-exist and combine with one occupying the dominant, integrative position' (1980: 6).

The articulation approach eschews the simplicity of an all-encompassing capitalism in favour of complexity of relationships which result from actual observation of cultures within a contextual frame of relationships of power. If we refer back to his engagement with the fireside of community enterprises, community groups, and community dispute settlement mechanisms,

Fitzpatrick clearly established the ways in which colonial regulations disabled local enterprises in favour of metropolitan ones whether they involved the selling of food or the establishment of bars (1980: 190–2). In his early engagement he attempted to develop solutions that were located in a critique of modernity, and favoured local ways to meet 'local needs'. However, in a self-critique he suggests that they lacked comprehension of the overall relationship between metropolitan and imperial interests and the local, and could become easy prey to either benevolent developmentalism on the part of the UN's Overseas Development Group or the romantic populism of the 'Melanesian Way' (ibid.: vii).

In this context the advantage of the 'articulation' approach that he adopted is that it provides a context for a structure which would both affirm the local fireside perspective and locate it within world structures. Even more significantly, it explained the complexity of the transition from colonial to post-colonial. In the transition to independence and beyond, the colonial state is relatively weak and less legitimate, but so is the nascent post-colonial state. Thus, there is need for stronger legitimation which can be obtained through renewed 'conservation' of the traditional mode. However, the latter has to be further restructured to check the destructive effects of the capitalist mode. Thus, state support for village courts or of 'traditional' business groups becomes part of colonial construction of the post-colonial (Fitzpatrick 1980: ch. 8).

Fitzpatrick's and my intention was to emphasize that the decisions over village courts were made in the context of these colonial and post-colonial needs. It is therefore not surprising that this interaction between the local and global would re-emerge in the contemporary period of globalization of 'good governance' strategies fuelled by global strategic and economic interests. Thus, Goddard suggests:

> After a period of relative government neglect and intermittent vilification of village courts, a wider community of economic stakeholders has recognised in them a potential to contribute to the 'law and order' effort. The recognition has manifested itself in positive attempts to make the village courts' practice compatible with development policy and to draw them into the coalition of community based institutions supported by the development-aid industry.
>
> (2009: 274)

On mythologies

Fitzpatrick's *Mythology of Modern Law* constitutes a devastating deconstruction of modern law. Whereas *Law and State* involved a critique of colonial capitalist modernity in its economic impact, and a witness to the endurance, *however colonially constrained*, of local culture, *Mythology* challenges the very basis of modern law and establishes its dependency on the othering of savage and uncivilized peoples. Thus, the myth of modernity is dependent on the denial of the savage, myth-ridden other while claiming an enduring universality for itself. However, once the mythical nature of modernity is itself exposed, the 'savage' other, our culture of the firelight, can itself be given its proper place.

Intellectually, *Mythology* is (de)constructed by a heady brew of Lévi-Strauss, Derrida, Foucault, and Edward Said. Politically, Fitzpatrick is not a voice for the global South in the sense used by Twining for Deng, An-Na'im, Ghai, and Baxi (Twining 2009). Nor is his standpoint that of a western jurist 'who is concerned to make our culture of academic law less parochial and ethnocentric' (ibid.: 1), laudable as this may be. His is a transgressive voice, of a deconstructor of the culture of the West; his immersive experience of New Guinea gives him the opportunity to gaze from the South.

The idea of articulation of modes of production in *Law and State* is now continued in a new dimension. Fitzpatrick argues that the Enlightenment period involved the mythic affirmation of western modern law through the constructive othering of the colonized as 'non-persons'. What Governor Murray of Papua New Guinea had to say about the impossibility of indirect rule in 1925 ('no chiefs, nothing to rule through ... no foundation'; Murray 1925) echoes the saintly J. S. Mill's assertion a century earlier that '[d]espotism is a legitimate mode of government in dealing with barbarians' (Mill 1962: 14; Fitzpatrick 1992a: 108) and Vattel's justification, two centuries earlier, of lawfulness of colonial occupation of territories inhabited by wandering tribes (Vattel 1971: 44–5; Fitzpatrick 1992a: 82). The figure of the Native American 'Indian' forms the iconic figure of the savage in Hobbes' notion of the brutish lawless state (1651/1952: 86–8; Fitzpatrick 1992a: 76), as also in Locke's wanderer 'not sufficiently "removed" from the common state Nature placed it in"' (Fitzpatrick 1992a: 82, quoting Locke 1690/1965: 329).

Fitzpatrick effectively links Blackstone and Austin to the savage myths of Hobbes and Locke in their idealized rationalization of property rights and sovereignty as the civilizing totems of English positive law. Thus, Blackstone suggests that without the concept of property, 'men [must] have been mere animals of prey' (Blackstone 1825: 5, 7–II, quoted in Fitzpatrick 1992a: 83). Austin contrasts the 'positive state of subjection' with the 'negative ... state of nature' of savage societies. Hence, positive laws would be useless for such 'natural societ[ies] which had not ascended from the savage state' (Austin 1861–3: 122–4; Fitzpatrick 1992a: 81, 196).

However, the myth of the 'noble savage' of Dryden and Pope formed a counterpoint to that of the wretched one. For Fitzpatrick, 'even in these accounts, if sometimes as a matter of regret, the European remained the ... ordering centre of the world' (1992: 68). The myth which became much more significant in colonial Africa is that of Lugard's 'happy African' – 'a thriftless, excitable person, lacking in self-control, discipline, and foresight, naturally courageous, and naturally courteous and polite, full of personal vanity, with little sense of veracity' (Lugard 1965: 69–70, quoted in Fitzpatrick 1992a: 131).[5] In *Mythology* it takes centuries to move from the savage Indian of Hobbes and Locke to Lugard's 'happy' African. This is an African who can be trusted with some aspects of government in customary law and indirect rule, but these are there not to liberate but to ensure that his lack of organization, conspicuous deficiency in management and control, and sense of power without responsibility are effectively controlled by the civilizing colonizer. The happy African is equated to a child who would be grateful for the benefit of English law, which would 'raise the mass of the people of Africa to a higher plane of civilization' (Lugard 1965: 546–7, quoted in Fitzpatrick 1992a: 107). In the Papua New Guinea of *Law and State* the speedy history of the culture of the firelight means that the transition from the notion of the 'savage' of Murray who needed the authority of British and Australian administrators to that of 'indirect rule' in which the natives could be given some control over their own lives in village courts in the transition to independence takes a mere 50 years. Yet in this period of the active construction of the post-colonial, Lugard's notion of strongly controlled indirect rule survives, but in a new form.

Thus, we have seen that the idea underlying the establishment of village courts was that of incorporating informal dispute-settling mechanisms into systems of controlled governance in preparation for independence. Interestingly, the idea of 'informal' or 'popular' justice, as Fitzpatrick terms it, gets reimported from the periphery to the metropolitan North (Fitzpatrick 1992a: 169–80). Fitzpatrick's treatment of popular justice in *Mythology* has parallels with his treatment of village courts. He deconstructs the positive contrast between spontaneous, nature-like, more human characteristics of popular justice with 'formal', 'alienated' justice:

> But closer observation of popular justice reveals compatibilities, even similarities, between it and ... formal modes of regulation. This could be explained, as in so many accounts, by reducing popular justice to these formal modes. Popular justice is but an extension of formal regulation, its mere mask or agent. In terms of my argument, there is point to seeing popular justice and law as both opposed and integral. The conflict is accommodated by the mythic mutuality between law and popular justice.
> (ibid.: 169)

Fitzpatrick deliberately selects San Francisco's Community Boards as his exemplar. Unlike many informal dispute-settling mechanisms, these were conceived as 'profoundly alternative' to the state and state law, which were seen as undermining the self-responsibility of individuals and communities for managing conflicts (Fitzpatrick 1992a: 171, citing Shonholtz 1984). For Fitzpatrick, the myth of the informal or popular is based on the individual's voluntary participation and willingness to enter into mediated or conciliated agreements. Yet his analysis, based on DuBow's work (1987), suggests that the disputing individual is in fact 'manoeuvred into certain defining modes of engagement with the other party and with the mediator'. The very concern with 'feelings' of the parties is a device to be manipulated to the needs of the power being exercised (Fitzpatrick 1992a: 175–6; see also Fitzpatrick 1992b).

The underlying problem is that the idea of community which is adopted as the founding model for contemporary occidental informal or popular justice systems is itself a myth. Echoing the post-colonial construction of PNG village courts, Fitzpatrick suggests that

> this idea of community is a construct of colonial experience and of the degradation of community in transitions to capitalism. The end-result is a reduced and contained 'native' or 'peasant' community, the diversity and complexity of which have been denied.
>
> (1992a: 178)

On the grounding of law

The idea of articulation which is used in different epistemologies in *Law and State* and *Mythology* achieves its apotheosis in *Modernism and the Grounds of Law* (Fitzpatrick 2001). The underlying relationship between civilization and its savage other is that the savage is constructed by civilization itself, as its antithesis, yet is indeed the sustaining force of its origin. The creation of international law, with its founding principle of the comity of nations, was an intrinsic part of colonial imperialism, as it was 'initiated and sustained in the suppression of peoples marked in their very being as inimical to that enterprise' (ibid.: 125).

This contradictory presence explains the failure of colonial imperialism, which

> as an affirmation of the universal was integrally committed to the civilizing of the colonized,... [who were] seen as yearning in the depths of their being for this very consummation ... [and yet] in seemingly stark contrast were ... rendered as essentially different and irredeemably backward, marking the point of constant, unmediated exclusion and of ultimate alterity.
>
> (Fitzpatrick 2001: 64)

The great totems of liberal modern law, from Vitoria to Vattel, from Justice Marshall to Hart, are surgically disembowelled to reveal these contradictions. Vitoria may be noted for his concern for the interests of the Indian, but he others them because of their barbarism and therefore justifies their semi-permanent subjugation under the Spanish colonial power (Vitoria 1532/1934; Fitzpatrick 2001: 163). Similarly, Vattel's natural society of sovereign states excluded those peoples such as 'wandering tribes' whose small numbers and uncertain occupancy made it entirely lawful for a colonial power to occupy the country (Vattel 1971: 44–5; Fitzpatrick 2001: 157). Chief Justice Marshall in the case of *Johnson v. M'Intosh* (1823) similarly justified the colonial right of imperium through 'discovery'. While Indians had natural rights in their lands, these were negated because they were 'fierce savages ... whose subsistence was drawn chiefly from the forest.... [T]o leave them in possession of their country, was to leave the country a wilderness' (Fitzpatrick 2001: 167; *Johnson v. M'Intosh* at 590).

Hart similarly grounds his concept of law in the othering of savage society, which he claims on the basis of dubious anthropology to lack the attributes of civilized legal systems (1961: 89–94). In particular, these societies based on custom only have 'primary rules of obligation' and lack a system to determine what the rules are, or how to change them or maintain an efficient system of adjudication (ibid.: 89–94; Fitzpatrick 2001: 98). It is only modern law that has the crucial 'internal aspect' of rules and officials who accept secondary rules of behaviour.

Underlying these approaches is a manufactured contrast between modern law and custom. The former is elevated as being flexible and responsive in opposition to the fixity of custom; but is equally elevated as being enduringly stable and predictable, in contrast to custom's arbitrariness and everchanging practice (Fitzpatrick 2001: 69). This double othering sustains the ability of law to appear stable and predictable while at the same time to ensure that it is ever responsive to change: 'Otherwise law will eventually cease to rule the situation which has changed round it' (ibid.: 71). The othering also gives colonial law the privilege of controlling and constraining custom even when the latter is given some role, as we saw in the case of the village courts (ibid.: 181).

These contradictions of colonial imperialism persist in the construction of the post-colonial. Fitzpatrick suggests, following Balibar (1991: 25), that the orientalist division of humanity between a universalist and progressive civilized camp and an 'irremediably particularistic and primitive' has been merely 'reworked' in the post-colonial era through the introduction of new languages of development and underdevelopment, modernity and backwardness (Fitzpatrick 2001: 125). Thus, the era of national independence saw states such as India invent for themselves new universalist and progressive identities to join the civilized camp. In order to do so, they had to create new mythologies of historic nationhood located, for example, in ancient pre-colonial India. However, these mythologies had contradictory elements. On the one hand, the new identities served the interests of the national bourgeoisies that replaced the colonial power, but at the same time, becoming the antithesis of the rogue barbarian other was the only way in which they could participate in the world community. In this respect, national liberation, however achieved, is a constructed path to post-coloniality.

Such modern constructions then become part of the new imperialism, and specifically the new legal imperialism, which takes place in an era of the complementary universalist discourses of globalism with its legal incidents of global law, human rights, and the rule of law. And yet these universalisms define themselves through the othering of particularisms. Fitzpatrick (2001: ch. 6) critiques both the universalism of these discourses and the opposing particularisms. In particular, the universalism of globalization theory is akin to the impulses that justified colonial imperialism – globalism suggested as being the only game in town. Even those adopting nuanced globalization approaches, such as Appadurai's diversity (1990: 7) and de Sousa Santos's cultural relativity (1995: 337), still promote a quasi-universalism (Fitzpatrick 2001: 196). Even when accepting the necessity for recognition of the other or of diversity or coexistence, this has to be in terms established by the global (Hannerz 1990: 239–40; Fitzpatrick 2001: 197–8). For Fitzpatrick, there is an impasse between an orientation towards the universal and the determinedly particular. Quoting Sakai to the effect that 'universalism and particularism reinforce and supplement each other; they are never in real conflict' (Sakai 1988: 487, quoted in Fitzpatrick 2001: 198), he suggests that each assumes its identity in opposition to the other. Globalism, in particular, bases itself on the exclusion of the other – the savage particular. 'The universal [of globalism] had been almost achieved by some particular but exemplary nations at one end of the scale, but it was decidedly not achieved by those little more than savage nations at the other end' (Fitzpatrick 2001: 200).

The universalism of human rights discourse is particularly instructive here. For Rhoda Howard, human rights are a universal good, which has to fight off the claims of cultural relativism or absolutism arising from 'culture-bound, closed, exclusionary, traditional, authoritarian, status-ridden, static, pure and inviolable community' (1993: 325, quoted in Fitzpatrick 2001: 209). Human rights are located in cultural relativism's opposite: in liberalism, democracy, and individualism – the cultural attributes of the West. Thus, we return to a new era of universalization of western attributes by the othering of the savage particular. And yet, Howard manages at the same time to exclude the savage and to say that the savage also has aspirations for human rights, and is not different from the universal after all (1993: 326–9; see Fitzpatrick 2001: 211).

Underlying these new universalisms is the new imperialism, which, unlike the old imperialism of the colonial state, involves a new twist of the post-colonial in which a combination of powerful states and international financial institutions promote new contractual modes of domination such as structural adjustment conditionalities (and more recently Poverty Reduction Strategy papers; Tan 2007) in which the formally equal nation-state has 'little choice in the terms it formally agrees to, and these are more explicit, more wide-ranging and tentacular than those which characterized neo-colonialism' (Fitzpatrick 2001: 212–15). These constitute new modes of discipline that go beyond economic conditions and include governance of the social including education and health. Significantly, there is a new and enhanced emphasis on rule of law and good governance through an engagement with legal and judicial reform characterized in the past as 'law and development' (Fitzpatrick 2001: 214).

The new imperialism of globalism suggests a human universality which claims that there are no others in a universal market or in civil and bourgeois society. However, nation-state-based imperialism is contrasted with globalism in that whereas in the former, rights belonged to the citizen qua citizen of a nation-state; in the latter, human rights inhere in the quality of being human. Yet such a system of rights exists only in the context of a system of domination constituted by a new imperium of which the capitalist market forms an integral part (Fitzpatrick 2001: 217). In this respect, Fitzpatrick's argument is similar to that of Baxi's notion (2005) of trade-related, market-friendly human rights.

On resistance

And what then of resistance? Is there a space in Fitzpatrick's analysis for the resistance of the Mendi woman and her broken fingers? His Foucaultian perspective might suggest that resistance itself is an integral part of the pervasiveness of power and systems of domination. Briefly at the end of *Modernism*, and more extensively in his collection of essays *Law as Resistance* (2008), Fitzpatrick engages with the very forms of resistance that were part of the PNG firelight.

In 'Tears of the law: Colonial resistance and legal determination' (Fitzpatrick 2008) and also in 'Passions out of place: Law, incommensurability, and resistance' (Fitzpatrick 1999) he engages with resistance to colonial legality. In Sri Lanka the people skilfully adapted and subverted the colonial courts' processes to achieve ends that were quite different and contrary to colonial ones (ibid.: 54). A different form of struggle is involved in the case of harsh colonial indentured labour laws in Papua New Guinea (Fitzpatrick 2008: 104). These laws, supplemented by equally oppressive Native Regulations, provided criminal punishment for breach of contract by the labourers. Their authoritarian, yet formally legal, nature provided the widest discretion to colonial administrators and to the employers. The resulting resistance included strikes and a final mass desertion at the end of the Second World War, which led not only to the phasing out of the indentured labour system but ultimately to the granting of independence.

However, Fitzpatrick's response to forms of resistance remains complex. Resistant voices are very real but they are absorbed either by the 'determinate particularity' of law's power or by law's survival strategy of limitless responsiveness (2008: xii). In responding to struggles and in changing, law arrogates to itself the perspicacity that led to the change, with an amnesic denial of the history of the struggle. Thus, in Papua New Guinea the history of the struggle remained silent. Strikes were blamed on one or two foreign agitators as Papua New Guineans were deemed not capable of the sophistication required of struggles. More significantly, the role of the struggles was hidden in the rationalization of the phasing out of the indentured labour system and move towards independence. While in the post-colonial times, colonial history may be rewritten from the colonial civilizing mission to one of continuing resistance, the law itself continues to be insulated in its civilizing and universalizing framework (ibid.: 113).

Resistance, change, human rights, and the struggle for justice are not denied. They are problematized as bearing 'involving promise, yet also seductive oppressions' or, citing Arnold's 'The scholar gipsy' (1956), faces of 'unconquerable hope' (Fitzpatrick 2001: 218). In the introduction to *Law as Resistance*, Fitzpatrick suggests that for Foucault power and resistance are intertwined, but there are two dimensions of resistance (2008: xii). The first is as a subordinate role in which resistance gets easily incorporated by power. The second, stronger role is one in which resistance is integral to or 'inscribed' in power relationships and is an 'irreducible opposite' of power which is 'not doomed to perpetual defeat' (ibid.: xii, citing Foucault 1981: 95). In this integral role, Foucault would even suggest that we should explore the nature of power relationships by starting with forms of resistance, because it is the form of resistance, for example illegality, that will enable us to define legality (Foucault 1981: 96; Fitzpatrick 2008: xii). Fitzpatrick suggests that in this stronger role, Foucault's term 'transgression' from *Language, Counter-memory, Practice* (Foucault 1977: 35) may provide a better descriptor than *resistance* because the former is limitless and yet may always be returned to its integral relationship with the interior and sovereign power (Fitzpatrick 2008: xiii).

This version of the power–resistance embrace is closer to a yin–yang Daoist relationship. Far from taking sides on which version of Foucault's power–resistance relationship should predominate, Fitzpatrick suggests that both notions of resistance are relevant:

> It fits the weak notion where it is subjected to power, and it fits the strong notion advocated by Foucault where it is 'inscribed in' relations of power 'as an irreducible opposite'. Such irreducibility entails not only a dependence of power on resistance, on law as resistance, but also the ability of resistant law to encompass and disintegrate, even displace the power in question. It is the very pointedness and potency of the resistances through law described in these chapters that result in their being so assiduously, if uneasily, crimped and marginalized.
>
> (2008: xxiii)

This contradiction in this portrait of resistance–transgression is integral to the nature of resistance. On the one hand, it warns us of power's tendency to control resistance, but it also suggests that there is power in resistance to 'encompass and disintegrate, even displace the power in question'. In this sense, law itself becomes resistance. How these relationships develop is a matter for real politics of specific relations and struggles of power. Resistance is in this respect liberated in all its diversity, and yet the resister–trangressor must be aware of power's and law's power to 'crimp and marginalize'. In the example of the PNG indentured labour laws cited earlier, the resistance succeeds and leads to the new law which abolishes indenture, but law claims the change as the new resistant law, marginalizing the role of the real resisters.

To return to the beginning of this chapter, in which we have chased the firelight in Fitzpatrick, his epistemology can be said to be transgressive, with the spirit of transgression derived from the glow of PNG firelight. It is always engaged with the claims of the oppressed and subaltern even though his preferred terminology is that of Derrida, Foucault, and Said in speaking from the broader compass of the other.

Notes

1 The allusion is to E. P. Thomson's *Writing by Candlelight* (1980). On the ethos of the Subaltern Studies Group, see Guha (1982).

2 Papua New Guinea was colonized by the Germans and British in 1884 and subsequently by the Australians. It became independent in 1975. This 'fireside' observation is distinct from the observation of oral historians because of historians' core interest in chronology. It is also distinct from ethnographic participant observation because the process of speeded-up historical change makes history part of what is being observed.

3 In this respect, Fitzpatrick's approach is both similar to and different from the 'Transgressive Methodology' as articulated by de Sousa Santos (1981). It similarly signifies an activist research engagement which, while intellectually independent, nevertheless participates on the side of the subaltern other. Fitzpatrick's combination of ethnographic method and activist engagement is different from de Sousa Santos's methodology in being non-Utopian and its stronger emphasis on the constraints of power.

4 Robinson Crusoe was the quintessential economic man model who could be copied by the colonized (Grapard 1995).

5 For the racist undertones of Lugard, see Taiwo (1999).

References

Appadurai, A. (1990) 'Disjuncture and difference in the global cultural economy', *Public Culture* 2(2): 1–24.

Arnold, M. (1956) 'The scholar gipsy', in J. Hayward (ed.) *The Penguin Book of English Verse*, Harmondsworth, UK: Penguin.

Austin, J. (1861–3) *The Province of Jurisprudence Determined*, 2nd edn, and *Lectures on Jurisprudence*, 3 vols, London: John Murray.

Balibar, E. (1991) 'Racism and nationalism', in E. Balibar and I. Wallerstein (eds) *Race, Nation, Class: Ambiguous Identities*, trans. C. Turner, London: Verso.

Banaji, J. (1973) 'Backward capitalism, primitive accumulation and modes of production', *Journal of Contemporary Asia* 3(4): 393–413.

Banaji, J. (1977) 'Modes of production in a materialist conception of history', *Capital and Class* 3: 1–44.

Baxi, U. (2005) 'Market fundamentalisms at the altar of human rights', *Human Rights Law Review* 5(1): 1–26.

Blackstone, W. (1825) *Commentaries on the Laws of England*, 16th edn, London: T. Cadell and J. Butterworth.

Curtis, L. and Greenwell, J. (1971) *Joint Review of the Lower Court Systems*, Canberra: Department of External Territories.

Derham, D. (1960) *Report on the System of Administration of Justice in the Territory of Papua and New Guinea*, Canberra, Department of Territories, Australian Government Printing Service.

DuBow, F. (ed.) (1987) 'Conflict and community: A study of San Francisco Community Boards', unpublished manuscript, Chicago: University of Illinois, Chicago Center for Research in Law and Justice.

Fitzpatrick, P. (1980) *Law and State in Papua New Guinea*, London: Academic Press.

Fitzpatrick, P. (1982) 'The political economy of dispute settlement in Papua New Guinea', in C. Sumner (ed.) *Crime, Justice and Underdevelopment*, London: Heinemann.

Fitzpatrick, P. (1992a) *The Mythology of Modern Law*, London: Routledge.

Fitzpatrick, P. (1992b) 'The impossibility of popular justice', *Social and Legal Studies* 1(2): 199–215.

Fitzpatrick, P. (1999) 'Passions out of place: Law, incommensurability, and resistance', in E. Darian-Smith and P. Fitzpatrick (eds) *Laws of the Postcolonial*, Ann Arbor: University of Michigan Press.

Fitzpatrick, P. (2000) 'Magnified features: The underdevelopment of law and legitimation', *Journal of South Pacific Law* 4. Online, available at: www.paclii.org/journals/fJSPL/vol04/5.shtml.

Fitzpatrick, P. (2001) *Modernism and the Grounds of Law*, Cambridge: Cambridge University Press.

Fitzpatrick, P. (2008) *Law as Resistance: Modernism, Imperialism, Legalism*, Farnham, UK: Ashgate.

Fitzpatrick, P. and Southwood, J. (1976) *The Community Corporation in Papua New Guinea*, Boroko: Institute of Applied Economic and Social Research.

Foucault, M. (1977) 'A preface to transgression', in M. Foucault, *Language, Counter-memory, Practice*, trans. D. Bouchard and S. Simon, Ithaca, NY: Cornell University Press.

Foucault, M. (1981) *The History of Sexuality: An Introduction*, vol. 1, trans. R. Hurley, Harmondsworth, UK: Penguin.

Goddard, M. (2009) *Substantial Justice: An Anthropology of Village Courts in Papua New Guinea*, Oxford: Berghahn Books.

Grapard, U. (1995) 'Robinson Crusoe: The quintessential economic man?', *Feminist Economics* 1(1): 33–52.

Guha, R. (1982) 'On some aspects of the historiography of colonial India', in R. Guha (ed.) *Subaltern Studies I: Writings on South Asian History and Society*, New Delhi: Oxford University Press.

Hannerz, U. (1990) 'Cosmopolitans and locals in world culture', in M. Featherstone (ed.) *Global Culture: Nationalism, Globalization and Modernity*, London: Sage.
Hart, H. L. A (1961) *The Concept of Law*, London: Oxford University Press.
Hobbes, T. (1651/1952) *Leviathan*, Chicago: Encyclopaedia Britannica.
Howard, R. (1993) 'Cultural absolutism and the nostalgia for community', *Human Rights Quarterly* 15: 315–38.
Johnson v. M'Intosh (1823) 21 U.S. 543.
Locke, J. (1965) 'The second treatise of government', in J. Locke, *Two Treatises of Government*, New York: New American Library.
Lugard, Lord (1965) *The Dual Mandate in British Tropical Africa*, 5th edn, London: Frank Cass.
Meillasoux, C. (1972) 'From reproduction to production: A Marxist approach to economic anthropology', *Economy and Society* 1(1): 93–105.
Mill, J. S. (2003) *On Liberty and Other Essays*, Oxford: Oxford University Press.
Murray, H. (1925) *Papua of Today*, London: P. S. King.
Paliwala, A. (1982) 'Law and order in the village: Papua New Guinea's village courts', in C. Sumner (ed.) *Crime, Justice and Underdevelopment*, London: Heinemann.
Sakai, N. (1988) 'Modernity and its critique: The problem of universalism and particularism', *South Atlantic Quarterly* 87(3): 475–504.
Shonholtz, R. (1984) 'Neighbourhood justice systems: Work, structure and guiding principles', *Mediation Quarterly* 5: 3–30.
Snyder, F. (1981) *Capitalism and Legal Change: An African Transformation*, New York: Academic Press.
Sousa Santos, B. de (1981) 'Science and politics: Doing research in Rio's squatter settlements', in R. Luckham (ed.) *Law and Social Enquiry: Case Studies Research*, Uppsala: Scandinavian Institute of African Studies.
Sousa Santos, B. de (1995) *Toward a New Common Sense: Law, Science and Politics in the Paradigmatic Transition*, New York: Routledge.
Taiwo, O. (1999) 'Reading the colonizer's mind: Lord Lugard and the philosophical foundations of British colonialism', in S. Babbitt and S. Campbell (eds) *Racism and Philosophy*, Ithaca, NY: Cornell University Press.
Tan, C. (2007) 'The poverty of amnesia: PRSPs in the legacy of structural adjustment', in D. Stone and C. Wright (eds) *The World Bank and Governance: A Decade of Reform and Reaction*, London: Routledge.
Thompson, E. P. (1980) *Writing by Candlelight*, London: Merlin Press.
Twining, W. (1963) 'The restatement of African customary law: A comment', *Journal of Modern African Studies* 1: 221–8.
Twining, W. (2009) *Human Rights, Southern Voices: Francis Deng, Abdullahi An-Na'im, Yash Ghai and Upendra Baxi*, Cambridge: Cambridge University Press.
Vattel, E. de (1971) 'Emer de Vattel on the occupation of territory', in P. D. Curtin (ed.) *Imperialism*, London: Macmillan.
Vitoria, F. de (1532/1934) 'De Indis', in J. Scott, *The Spanish Origin of International Law: Francisco de Vitoria and His Law of Nations*, Oxford: Clarendon Press.

Chapter 12

Reading slowly

The law of literature and the literature of law

Peter Fitzpatrick

> To fill a Gap
> Insert the Thing that caused it –
> Block it up
> With Other – and 'twill yawn the more –
> (Emily Dickinson 1999: 290 [647])

Reversals

As for law and literature, there are doubtless differences to be observed – the bailiff does not usually come to the door armed with a poem – but here my impelling concern will be with similarity. Not, or not just, the similarity usually found in the combining of law and literature, where each at times can instance the other. And not even, or not just, the similarity that comes from an epochal sameness that the contents of law and literature may come to share (Reichman 2009). Rather, the focus will be on a constituent correspondence between law and literature. That prospectus goes against several grains where law is starkly set against the dangerously unbound creativity, fictive quality, and evanescence of literature – a contrast often instanced in Plato's uneasy aversion to poetry (1993: ch. 13 [Book X]). Instead, it is this very creativity or fictive quality, so my argument runs, that law and literature share. There could, then, in this chapter be a sustaining affinity with 'the more radical teachings of the law and literature school, towards an understanding that one can read law as literature and literature as law' (Tuitt 2004: 78; see, for example, Heinzelman 2010: 104–14).

The strain on originality is lessened further in companionable claims made by archons of my argument. Taking only a few of these claims for now, Derrida would see law as 'fictional', as 'artifice' (2002a: 240). Likewise, he finds that 'narrativity and fiction' are at 'the very core of legal thought' (1992: 190). And for Nancy the law comes to be 'modeled or sculpted (*fictum*) in terms of right', and thence '[j]urisdiction is or makes juris-fiction' (2003: 157). As the conveniently stark notion of the legal fiction would suggest, law can hardly be outdone in making similar claims for itself. To take an instance from a period of Roman law, for some claims it was the case that one had to be a Roman citizen, but eventually for this purpose foreigners were simply deemed citizens while 'the letter of the law' remained unchanged (Maine 1931: 21–2). The law in its very stability, in its posited, its 'positive' quality, is fictional.

A precarious originality may emerge when considering, by way of literature, what this fictive quality of law may be. As the legal fiction would intimate, law fuses its seeming stability, its determinate 'order', with a receptive creativity. The very rule of law fitfully characterizing modernity, while elevated in its endowment of stability and predictability, must also respond as 'newness enters the world' (Rushdie 1991: 394, for the phrase). Otherwise, the law would cease to rule a situation changing inexorably around it. And with modern law, a resolution or determination of this divide cannot be sought by reference to transcendent determination.

This allusive introduction – 'some familiar strokes and faint designations', to anticipate *Tristram Shandy* (Sterne 1967: 94) – can at best evoke the challenge of saying what the fictive quality of law is. The difficulty is compounded when that quality has in some way to be experienced or worked. Yet some grasp of it may be derived from showing it to be integral to modern politico-legal formation and in discerning what disasters would ensue if it were absent.

Literature I

> Spender told Auden he wondered whether he, Spender, ought to write prose. But Auden put his foot down. 'You must write nothing but poetry, we do not want to lose you for poetry.' 'But do you really think I am any good?' gulped Spender. 'Of course,' Auden frigidly replied. 'But why?' 'Because you are so infinitely capable of being humiliated. Art is born out of humiliation.'
>
> (Fenton 2001: 209)

And as the Eliot of 'Burnt Norton' would confirm: 'Humility is endless' (1974: 199). Or, in Nancy's terms, poetry involves 'an effacement', a withdrawal (1993: 308–9). All of which can be put more affirmatively. The poet, says Rilke, is 'he or she who is ready for everything' (see Fenton 2001: 248). And even submerged within a grim modernity, Pessoa/Caeiro would still want to be 'everyone and everywhere' (1998: 90). Or there is Muriel Spark's exuberant 'everything happens to an artist' (2007: 87). In a somewhat more muted vein, Conrad extends the imperative to fiction specifically – fiction that

> demands from the writer a spirit of scrupulous abnegation. The only legitimate basis of creative work lies in the courageous recognition of all the irreconcilable antagonisms that make our life so enigmatic, so burdensome, so fascinating, so dangerous – so full of hope.
>
> (see Miller 2009: 48)

This resonates readily with Keats's 'negative capability', a 'quality' found 'when a man is capable of being in uncertainties, mysteries, doubts, without any irritable reaching after fact and reason'; and despite naming the capability as 'negative', for Keats this was a positive 'quality' that 'went to form a Man of Achievement, especially in literature' (1947: 72). And if that is all starting to smack too much of the evanescent, there is the palpable corrective of that undoubted 'man of achievement' Tristram Shandy (Sterne 1967). If one were to rely on his title, Sterne is going to reveal the life and opinions of Tristram Shandy, Gentleman, but the novel tells us little of either explicitly. Yet devotees of the novel do feel they know Tristram Shandy, know him as a totally engaging character and narrator. The genius of Sterne gives us Tristram Shandy in person, as it were, through the narrator's receptive regard for other characters. Even with its notorious playing with possibility, its shifts in subject, in tone, time, and place, *Tristram Shandy* is a work which either as a whole or through its particulars has a felt and formed quality.

Yet for all the force of literary formation, there remains still an insistence of the negative. A much-noted concentration of the case is Auden's 'poetry makes nothing happen' (1979: 82). His meaning is rather more pointed than the one usually extracted from this line. It is not that nothing ever happens as a result of poetry. Quite the contrary. If one looks at where Auden says this, the tender yet monumental 'In memory of W. B. Yeats', we find him calling on poetry to make much happen. What Auden means with 'poetry makes nothing happen' is that it brings nothingness into happening. In the same poem he describes poetry as '[a] way of happening, a mouth' (ibid.: 82). Or as Blanchot puts it even more expansively, 'Nothingness is the creator of the world in man' (1999: 398–9). Or we have nothing as our 'flowering' in Celan's 'Psalm' (2002: 153). (The evocation of nothing can make the academic feel the need of copious reference.)

Literature II

This is yet a 'positive emptiness' (Raine 2005: 34). For Blanchot, it is an 'opening' to what is beyond, to alterity and possibility, to 'what is when there is no more world', or 'to what would be if there were no world', to the 'void' (1999: 388). But this void is of the kind encountered by Blanchot's protagonist in *The Madness of the Day* for whom it was 'disappointing', a void which inexorably becomes a presence and protean: 'one realizes the void, one creates a work' (1981: 8; 1999: 395). Between the realized and the unrealizable, between the appropriated and that which is still 'ours for being nobody's', there is a 'shifting', a 'passing', a 'movement' impelled by 'a marvellous force' which is the impossibility of the movement being otherwise (Blanchot 1988: 43; 1999: 363–5, 369, 387–9). This is an activity always situated, an emplaced 'affirmation', 'an operation' that cannot be separated 'from its results' (Blanchot 1999: 365, 397). Literature for Blanchot, then, is a work like any other – he instances building a stove – even if it is such 'to an outstanding degree' (1999: 371).

Admittedly, a work of literature can assume a stove-like solidity: witness the tenacity of literary forms and genres – a tenacity that spectacular deviations serve to confirm rather than confound. Yet, Kermode would add, 'we should expect only the most trivial work to conform to pre-existent types' (1967: 24; cf. Plato 1970: 91–2 [656–7]). And could any work thoroughly subordinated to some imperative be called literature? Such a question could be provoked by, say, 'literature' written with the overriding instrumental aim of promoting some cause. Pushing the point to an extreme, the insistently literary has found itself set against totalitarian regimes, regimes that characteristically seek to appropriate the aesthetic.

This resistance to containment emanates intrinsically from the literary work, and not just from 'its measurelessness ... hidden within the work' (Blanchot 1982: 171), but also in the very modes that would delimit it. 'We cannot, of course, be denied an end; it is one of the great charms of books', pronounces Kermode, 'that they have to end', only then to go on and charm forth this conclusion: literary '[e]nds are ends only when they ... frankly transfigure the events in which they are immanent' (1967: 23, 175). The delimiting yet generative force of ending, of completion, is poignantly evoked in Auerbach's epilogue to *Mimesis* (1968), where he apologizes at length for the deficiencies of the book brought about by his writing it in Istanbul, where he was an exile from Nazi Germany and where his access to apt scholarly sources was limited:

> [I]t is quite possible that the book owes its existence to just this lack of a rich and specialized library. If it had been possible for me to acquaint myself with all the work that has been done on so many subjects, I might never have reached the point of writing.
>
> (1968: 557)

The epigraph to this great work is Marvell's opening line 'Had we but world enough and time...'

To take for now just one further generative limit of the work, one that perhaps focuses most canonical constriction, in asking, 'What is an author?' Foucault distances himself from those who would pronounce the author dead, and he does so by advancing the author as a 'necessary and constraining figure' (1988: 209). This comes from the same Foucault who charged, in *The Archaeology of Knowledge*: 'Do not ask who I am and do not ask me to remain the same: leave it to our bureaucrats and our police to see that our papers are in order. At least spare me their morality when we write' (1974: 17). Yet in this work we find also a similar and quite explicit alternation in Foucault's regard for the author's oeuvre, an alternation between its multiple diffusions and its being a set construction (ibid.: 23–5). And both dimensions are somewhat accommodated in Foucault's once proposing a law that would break up the oeuvre and counter the 'grotesque' uniformity that consolidates in reading several of an author's books (1989: 315). This law would 'prohibit the use of the author's name more than once, with the additional right to anonymity and the use of pseudonyms, in order that each book might be read for itself' (ibid.: 315). That would, supposedly, enable the work to be read in the way of the 'first book that one writes', a book that is read 'because one is not known, because people don't know who we are, and it is read in disorder and confusion' (ibid.: 315). Yet familiarity does not necessarily breed uniformity, grotesque or otherwise. A spectacular instance of ambivalent effect is offered with the 'books' of the Abrahamic religions managing to generate both mass uniformity and conflicted diversity, and both at the same time. The formative force of the reader starts to come into contention.

Reading

> ...you read me, and I write you. *Somewhere*, this takes place.
>
> (Nancy 2008: 51, emphasis in original)

The fragile author has been conspicuously beleaguered by varieties of reader response theory, a theory that would consign the work to effective existence only as read – as a 'performance' by the reader (Blanchot 1999: 364; and see Kivy 2006). The work comes to existence only as it goes forth 'to find the reader' (Auerbach 1968: 557). Yet there is still something that has to be brought to an end and assume some determinate existence, something which is then impelled searchingly into the world. The work, it may readily be granted, cannot exist apart from the practical infinity of its readership, yet the work does not simply dissipate in relation to its readers but remains a focus for the diversity of responses to it. Your reading and my reading will be different, but in some sense we read the same thing. Still, the work now in the world cannot exist apart from the relation to its readers. That relation, in turn, will generate an endless variety of determinate existences of the work, concentrations of professional regard for example. Yet the work is not, or not just, enclosed in any particular reading, but remains a continually formative opening onto what lies beyond its realizations (Blanchot 1981: 16; 1999: 365–6). In always extending receptively beyond any determinate realization in its reading, the work does not become simply evanescent but continues also to assert an existence that stills the importunate world and makes for some contained determinacy, transient as that will be in turn.

Reading, then, comes to have the same constituent dimensions as the 'original' author. 'What does it matter that there was one to write and another to read?', asks Le Clézio: 'In the last resort, in the very last resort, they are one and the same' (2008: 3). In reading, with Alberto Manguel, 'we are transformed: reader into writer into reader' (2010: 181). And for Blanchot, the work 'reveals itself within' some such 'shared existence' (1999: 365). Or in terms of Shandean 'just boundaries of decorum and good breeding':

> The truest respect which you can pay to the reader's understanding, is to halve this matter amicably, and leave him something to imagine, in his terms, as well as yourself.
>
> For my own part, I am eternally paying him compliments of this kind, and do all that lies in my power to keep his imagination as busy as my own.
>
> (Sterne 1967: 127)

Indeed, the work may go into the world carrying a large expectation of the reader's creativity. So, it could be spare, 'minimal', in its content. Or the work could leave it to the reader to make connections between its different parts or perspectives.[1] And the imperative of interpretation can be heightened by incompleteness. Apparently the earliest written version of both the Koran and the Hebrew scriptures 'lacked vowels; the words aided recitation but weren't definitive. No doubt later clerics, in choosing which vowel to put in the blank, occasionally found themselves with real semantic leeway' (Wright 2009: 373). All of which slants matters towards the reader's rendering the work determinate. Such decisiveness is gently confronted by Nietzsche's injunction to read slowly, and indeed to write slowly – an injunction to counter 'an age of "work", that is to say, of hurry, of indecent and perspiring haste, which wants to "get everything done" at once', an injunction 'to read slowly, deeply, looking cautiously before and aft, with reservations, with doors left open, with delicate eyes and fingers' (Nietzsche 1982: 5; see Goodrich 2005: 189–97). The slower the reading, the greater the receptiveness to the work. Not that this receptiveness can encompass the work. By itself it would generate nothing but dissipation, and necessary as such 'indecisiveness' is (see Nietzsche 1968: 169–70 [52]), the receptive alone cannot encompass anything. 'In any case', the reader's absorptive ability is limited, even as the possible readings of the work are limitless.[2] A reading, as Nietzsche would also have it, can only ever be 'approximate', and we must thence 'invent' it – 'people are much more artistic than they think' (2002: 81–2 [192]). Like the author, and recalling Auerbach's exilic genius, in the limiting the reader creates. A summary statement of the case: in his panegyric *On Reading*, Proust demotes his hero Ruskin to the extent of rejecting his advocacy of subservience to the author, along with Ruskin's assuming the 'continually open' in reading (1984: 23, 25). While embracing a profound responsiveness in reading, Proust would affirm that we 'remain ... on our own', that we make the reading – 'create it for ourselves' (ibid.: 26, 30). The panegyric thence becomes one to reading as self-forming. No less than the author (see Clarkson 2009: ch. 5), the reader's going to the work is to a finding of self. The reader does not bring to the work only an already shaped layering of self, some template of truth.

In sum, and in writing/reading, we are left with 'this strange institution called literature' (Derrida 1992: 36), an institution whose work must be delimited and illimitable, determinate and indeterminate, and both at the same time. Perhaps, then, an affinity with the resolving law may help us engage with these seeming contraries.

The law of literature

> ...sense the solving emptiness
> That lies just under all we do,
> And for a second get it whole...
>
> (Larkin 1964: 33)

Summarizing with distressing brevity much of the argument so far, Derrida finds that this same strange institution 'allows one to *say everything*, in *every way*. The space of literature is not only that of an instituted *fiction* but also a *fictive institution* which in principle allows one to say everything' (1992: 36 – his emphasis). He then somewhat abruptly introduces the law, the law as delimiting, and does so by way of a contrast with '[t]he law of literature [which] tends, in principle, to defy or to lift the law', only to add immediately that the law of literature 'allows one to think the essence of the law in the experience of this "everything to say"' (ibid.: 36).

Affinities loom, and these are soon amplified. In the same volume, Derrida comes to consider 'the law of genre' (1992: 221). The genre-marker of a literary work will identify with the work yet also be set apart in identifying it:

> [T]his singular *topos* places within and without the work, along its boundary, an inclusion and exclusion with regard to genre in general, as to an identifiable class in general. It gathers together the corpus and, at the same time, in the same blinking of an eye, keeps it from

> closing, from identifying itself with itself. This axiom of non-closure or non-fulfillment enfolds within itself the condition for the possibility and the impossibility of taxonomy. This inclusion and this exclusion do not remain exterior to one another; they do not exclude each other. But neither are they immanent or identical to each other. They are neither one nor two. They form what I shall call the *genre-clause*, a clause stating at once the juridical utterance, the designation that makes precedent and law-text, but also the closure, the closing that excludes itself from what it includes (one could also speak, without winking, of a floodgate [*écluse*] of genre).
>
> (1992: 230–1, emphasis in original)

The wink could be taken as mischievous. In English, but not French, legal argumentation, the image of the floodgate is often invoked as a caution against change – change that could, by opening the floodgates, be overwhelming. Yet it is in both a containing and an uncontained opening, as well as in the generative 'contamination' between the two, that the floodgate becomes a figure not only of genre but also of the law. There is both a dimension of containing division and one of uncontained combining, and inseparably, which means there may be too much fixity and division in the floodgate metaphor since these two dimensions combine repeatedly in both literary and legal invention. A better, if less enjoyable, translation could have been a canal lock. When considering legal invention in the next section of this chapter, I will return to Derrida's compressed elegance here. As a prelude to that return, the law of literature will first be somewhat refined.

There is an initial difficulty. Given the seeming irresolution of the conundrum just outlined – the 'genre clause', in sum, being 'neither one nor two' – how can there be a cohering literature that can be given or give law? We have seen already that literature rejects instrumental containment, and likewise Derrida would want it to be free from coherence in terms of 'thematism, sociologism, historicism, psychologism' (1981: 70). Literature, we have seen also, rejects any ultimate containment. Hence, to counter a common instance, the novel as genre cannot simply be a product of the emergence of 'bourgeois society', strong as its connections to that emergence may have been (cf. Said 1993: 84, 92–3). Indeed, the novel has provided the paradigm of a literary modernism. Whence, as Kundera has it, 'the author was no longer content with a mere "story" but opened windows onto the world that stretched all around' (2008: 153). Or, more engagingly, if still too simply in its contrast with the pre-modern: 'A magic curtain, woven of legends, hung before the world. Cervantes sent Don Quixote journeying and tore through the curtain. The world opened before the knight errant in all the comical nakedness of its prose' (ibid.: 2008: 92). The related and standard point is that Cervantes introduces a modernist individualism, a questioning of everything, including the genre doing the questioning. Yet this is an individualism of connectedness, of relation – something attested in the disasters of Quixote's blinkered adherence to outmoded codes and perceptions. It is in modernity, as Nancy has it, that literature would 'seem devoted to communicate the common and to offer itself thus as its own space, as the *in* and the *between* of the common' (1992: 386, emphasis in original).

Still, the unencompassed world, the uncontainable, without more, lacks the concentrated efficacy to give law, and law in its commonality. Yet further, there were and are 'laws and conventions which fixed what we call literature in modernity' (Derrida 1992: 40). What happens, then, is that literature 'plays the law', and in so doing takes on a 'power to produce performatively the statements of the law' (ibid.: 216). So, what is 'proper' to, say, literary form is a matter of 'law' – 'the legislative, form-grounding aspect' of literature, even as the law of literature is 'inexhaustible' (Heidegger 1991: 130–1, 212).[3] The literary–legal determination will straddle, in Derrida's terms, 'both sides of the line', the line that will separate the form from 'its' alterity, holding both all the while in a generative relation (1992: 216; 2002a: 269–70). Such separation and such holding require of literature, then, that it be an 'institution', one 'with authorization to say everything' (Derrida 1992: 36–7).

With this authorization, literature 'finds itself' far from being confined to giving formed law to itself. The inevitable next sentence has to be Shelley's: 'poets are the unacknowledged legislators of the world' (1911: 58). In a like exaltation, literature is directed by Heidegger 'to prepare and ground standards and laws for historical, intellectual existence' (1991: 92). An instance may prove more pointed. Each of the tragic plays surviving from ancient Athens 'was originally written for a single performance in a competition at the Great Dionysia, a festival to the god Dionysus' (Goldhill 2007: 120). The festival was 'truly a civic event' in which the tragedies were to promote normative imperatives of political and social order (ibid.: 123). Yet this was decidedly not narrowly didactic 'political theatre'. Rather, conformity was mocked and debate was generated with a 'political seriousness' that would, in Goldhill's estimation, challenge a modern 'sense of political order' (ibid.: 123–4).

Law

> But neither arrest nor movement. And do not call it fixity...
>
> (Eliot 1974: 191)

At the outset, archons of my argument summarily inverted the story so far when they invoked law as literature, as with Nancy's 'juris-fiction' (2003: 157) and Derrida's finding that 'narrativity and fiction' occupied 'the very core of legal thought' (1992: 190). Coming to the crux, the engagement so far with literature as law now informs the concern with law as literature, and the object of the exercise at last emerges – finding what literature, or the literary, tells us about law. In the previous section, Derrida encapsulated the comparison in an elegant topos of 'the genre-clause', an ordering category of literature which he endowed with 'juridical' content (1992: 231). Aptly enough, there is a mirroring passage in Derrida's 'Force of law' (2002a: 257). That passage comes as a culmination of Derrida's account of justice and law and of the distinction, and 'lack' of distinction, between them. Before we come to this passage and its pivotal part in my argument, something needs to be said about this distinction.

In 'Force of law', Derrida would want to 'make explicit or perhaps produce a difficult and unstable distinction between justice and *droit*, between justice (infinite, incalculable, rebellious to rule and foreign to its symmetry)' on the one side and, on the other, 'the exercise of justice as law or right, legitimacy or legality, a ... calculable apparatus..., a system of regulated and coded prescriptions' (2002a: 250). This justice for Derrida imports an unlimited responsiveness to the other, an 'other' that extends to an illimitable, an uncontained alterity or otherness. This unlimited responsiveness of justice, its being ready for anything, is impossible 'in itself', always beyond attainment. To be made possible, become existent and take on operative force, justice must be 'cut' into, limited, and thence in a sense denied (ibid.: 252). For Derrida, the decision creating law cuts into and enacts justice, even while denying justice as illimitably responsive. In this, 'law is the element of calculation' (ibid.: 244). Law, in the legal decision, can never be 'presently and fully just' (ibid.: 252).

Yet if law is necessary for justice, justice for Derrida is also necessary for law. Law 'itself' must ever inchoately respond to an unattainable justice, to a justice that 'exceeds law but at the same time motivates movement, history, and becoming of juridical rationality' (2002a: 252; 2005: 150). In rendering justice, making it possible, law must somehow extend beyond justice and bring it to bear. In all, although 'justice exceeds law and calculation', calculable law has also to be conceived as 'exceeding' justice, and 'one *must* [*il faut*] negotiate the relation between the calculable and the incalculable' (ibid.: 257, emphasis in original). Snatching a segue, I must now focus on the imperative quality of this process and then on the negotiated quality of its outcome.

Derrida's enigmatic genre-clause provided an instance of the 'marking' of the literary by way of combining its constituent dimensions – combining the determinate gathering 'together [of] the corpus' with a holding of it open, responsive, to alterity, a keeping of 'it from closing, from identifying itself with itself' (1992: 231). And there is a simultaneity to this combining. It happens 'at the same time, in the same blinking of an eye' (ibid.: 231). Likewise with law: it is a calculable determinacy, yet this determinacy must be held in a 'suspense' allowing law to empty itself of existing content, respond to alterity, and do so utterly (Derrida 2002a: 269). This constituent combining becomes a 'moment of law', a moment instanced in the legal decision, a moment which '*takes place and never takes place in presence*' (ibid.: 269–70, emphasis in original). Reversing this perspective through the lens of responsiveness to what is ever beyond, we may, with Blanchot, 'grant that law is obsessed with exteriority, by that which beleaguers it and from which it separates via the very separation that institutes it as form, in the very movement by which it formulates this exteriority as law' (1993: 434).

The combinatory force of these dimensions and of the 'presence' and 'form' that this force generates can all be sensed by posing its absence. This is a sense in which the existence of each dimension becomes a condition of the existence of the other. If the holding open to alterity were simply receptive beyond any determinacy, it could not be realized. And for the determinate dimension to stand alone, it would have to be a fixed and total comprehension. The truth of such a comprehension would for Nancy be 'the truth of death', death as terminal (1991: 12). The like inexorability would attend the putative containing of some determinate part immune to the formative force of 'exteriority' since a totalized comprehension would be needed both to hold the part in an ungiving stasis and to predetermine its relation or possible relation to everything else (cf. Derrida 1979: 125). The inability of either dimension to subsist without the other is underscored by the simultaneity touched on a short while ago – the simultaneity of constituent dimensions of both the genre-clause and 'the moment of law'. There is 'no time' in which either can exist apart from the other.

Matters obviously are becoming too resolved for a Derridean reading. There has to be some failure in the imperative that combines dimensions, preferably a failure in which that imperative is reversed, a failure producing a counter-imperative in which the dimensions 'must' not be combined. And such there is. With the genre-clause, for instance, the dimensions can be neither 'immanent to' nor 'identical to each other' (Derrida 1992: 231).[4] Nor can their mutual involvement be simply in part – a compromise or trade-off of some kind. The separation must be complete. Still, 'one *must* ... negotiate the relation between', in effect, law and justice (Derrida 2002a: 257, emphasis in original). The composition of that negotiation begins to look crucial. It does raise a further and telling dissonance.

Derrida often directed us to negotiate, *négocier*, comparable divides. On one such occasion in an interview with Nancy, and to the latter's evident surprise, after emphasizing his use of *négocier* Derrida proceeds to render it in terms of '*une transaction*', to render it as something that operates as a compromise, as a mutual accommodation and transformation (Derrida and Nancy 2004: 179–80).[5] Some reassurance to the contrary could have been got from Derrida's having said elsewhere that '[t]here is negotiation when there are two incompatible imperatives that appear to be incompatible but are equally imperative. One does not negotiate between exchangeable and negotiable things' (2002b: 13). The imperatives in contention here have already been visited. The determinate cannot simply compromise with the openness and hold something of itself back 'in part' – still 'identifying itself with itself' (Derrida 1992: 231) – since that holding would have to be, as we have just seen, a totalized stasis. Neither can the openness compromise with the determinate since it cannot be delimited or contained either in part or at all. As with Auden's 'poetry makes nothing happen' (1979: 82), in the sense of bringing nothing into happening, making law happen involves its responsive reaching to 'nonlaw' (Derrida 2002a: 269), to the 'exteriority' with which, Blanchot again, law is necessarily 'obsessed' as 'it formulates this exteriority as law' (1993: 434).[6]

For Blanchot, then, the exteriority becomes law – it is becoming to law and law is what it becomes. This may seem at odds with Derrida's distinguishing law as calculable from an incalculable justice, yet as he is a professed follower of Blanchot, we may also expect him to see matters otherwise. And Derrida does also see law as inclusive of justice even as it 'cuts' into and denies justice. Two varieties of law can be involved here. One is a 'law of originary sociability', a law of the law in which there is an indwelling of alterity and which is generative of and 'prior to all *determined* law,... but not prior to law *in general*' (1997: 231, emphasis in original). This paves the way for a corresponding distinction between 'law' and 'laws' – 'law above the laws' (Derrida 2000: 79). And that brings matters full circle, since such 'law' is unconditional, ever beyond and impelling of the conditioned 'laws'. Indeed, Derrida (1987) also wrote in a sustained way of 'law' as combining what became in 'Force of law' a differential law and justice. In sum, and returning to the terms of 'Force of law', law and justice, now as constituent dimensions of law in its amplitude, have to combine yet remain distinct and uncompromised by each other. They are 'undissociable ... in their very heterogeneity' (Derrida 2002a: 257).

Law thence is doubly aporetic. There is, in terms of a Greek derivation of aporia, no road, no already assured passage, between law's separate dimensions, as well as no such passage between the separation of the dimensions and their inseparate combining. As Derrida has it, no enduring resolution can 'come to pass' (1993: 23). And even as there must, 'this *il faut*' again, be a combining, that is not 'reducible to the application and deployment of a program' (Derrida 2002a: 257; 2005: 145). Law is held 'in suspense' (Derrida 2002a: 269). It can have no set content of its own. As Cixous would confirm, it 'has no material inside' (1991: 18). It can, says Derrida, have no history of its own, nor any self-encompassed origin (1992: 191). This imperative, this particular 'must', ensues if law is '[t]o be invested with its categorical authority' (ibid.: 191), an authority which, adds Blanchot, is 'an empty authority', but an authority nonetheless (1992: 24).

Like the crowded 'void' encountered in Blanchot's *Madness of the Day* (1981: 8), this is a 'positive emptiness' akin to that involved in literary creation (Raine 2005: 34, for the phrase). More to the point, for Derrida the aporia is not classically confined to an irreducible opposition. It is generative. Reverting again to the terms of his 'Force of law', the 'order' generated as law 'does not *properly* belong either to justice or to law. It only belongs to either realm by exceeding each one in the direction of the other' (2002a: 257, emphasis in original). The exceeding leaves the 'calculable' law and 'incalculable' justice autonomous, yet 'at the same time' integrally related through an 'order' orienting each in the direction of and beyond the other (see also Derrida 2000: 79, 81).

Yet 'order' would indicate something resolved, even a ranking between them. The inevitable problem becomes how anything that must be constituently and illimitably open could ever be resolved or ranked. The aporetic linking to the determinate will not suffice because the openness must not only be related to the determinate but also remain uncompromisingly apart from it. Nor can resolution or ranking be sought elsewhere. The openness and illimitability 'in' and as law frees law from any possibility of anterior or exterior determination – from 'any possible derivation', as Derrida put it (1992: 191). And, the companionate Blanchot would add, law 'affirms itself as law and without reference to anything higher: to it alone pure transcendence' (1992: 25).

Yet if law is '[t]o be invested' with the autonomous 'categorical authority' endowed by its openness (Derrida 1992: 191), it must have a posited efficacy. It must be able to give itself the law, 'affirm ... itself as law and without reference to anything higher' and, Blanchot would continue, '[t]his is why it does not authorize any question about it or beyond it' (1992: 25). Law, then, must share literature's constituent aversion to instrumentalism, to an end that would precede any beginning. The type of political trial where the outcome is predetermined provides a pointed instance. Characteristically, it is seen as 'political' and not 'legal' exactly because the result is fixed, in two senses of the word, beforehand. And as with literature, the instrumentalism to be resisted would extend to any attempt to render law in terms of 'thematism, sociologism, historicism, psychologism' (Derrida 1981: 70).

So, like that law we encountered when literature 'plays the law', the law takes on a 'power to produce performatively the statements of the law' (Derrida 1992: 216). Law's self-affirmation in this could also be seen as akin to Derrida's 'law' of the archive (1995), a law which inheres in the political 'privilege' endowed on the archons, on the keepers of the archive, giving them 'the right to make or to represent the law' (ibid.:

2–3). The keepers of the law gather 'the corpus' together in a creative and in-forming responsiveness to 'its' exteriority (cf. Derrida 1992: 231). For Nancy, then, this '*corpus*' is the 'space of the law', and as such it is

> neither chaos nor organism: it doesn't fall in between the two, but lies somewhere else. It's prose from a different space, not abyssal, systematic, grounded or ungrounded.... The *corpus* obeys a law that passes from case to case, a discrete continuity of rules and exceptions, of demands and derogations. *Jurisdiction* consists less in enunciating the absolute of the Law, or in unfolding its reasons, than in saying *what* the law can be *here*, there, now, in this case, in this place.
>
> (2008: 53, emphasis in original)

And, again, '[j]urisdiction is or makes juris-fiction' (Nancy 2003: 157). The creative and formative reading of the law, like that writer–reader fusion we delved into earlier, is not confined to some authority apart from us, to those archons more prosaically known as officials, for example. The 'juridical', as Derrida notes, is 'grounded on the sovereignty of the subject, that is, the intentional auto-determination of the conscious self' (2002c: xix).

Further reading

Reading being an ever self-subverting activity, my reading of works to do with reading compounds the subversion. And so we come to another variation on the end, the engaging 'weariness' in the chapter that ends Ecclesiastes: 'of making many books there is no end' (12:12). Returning to Kermode's 'sense of an ending' (1967), with his guiding instance of Apocalypse or the Revelation of St John the Divine, the end is a beginning: all things are made new (21:5). This sense of an ending accompanies rather than counters the imperative which has it that 'one cannot, of course, be denied an end' (Kermode 1967: 23). The end, in and as the act of literary and legal creation, is terminal, but only and ever 'for the time being'. Yet matters, inevitably, are more mixed. Apocalypse concludes with a malediction against adding to it (22:18).

The 'one' who cannot be denied an end, the 'one' who '*must* ... calculate, negotiate the relation between the calculable and the incalculable' (Derrida 2002a: 257, emphasis in original), this one is a finite, singular, political being subsisting in the history implied by this chapter, a history inseparable from the coming to law through literature which it attempted. This history has its own complicit relation to the type of scriptural completeness, the last word, claimed for Apocalypse, but it also imports a rejection of transcendent resolution and advances an ultimate reliance of the political on 'the sovereignty of the subject, that is, the intentional auto-determination of the conscious self' (Derrida 2002c: xix). The archons of my argument do not engage in extensive histories but resort rather to telling evocations. Derrida, for instance, would take 'the French Declaration of the Rights of Man' as obliging 'one ... to reinterpret the very foundations of law such as they had previously been calculated or delimited' (2002a: 257). This obligation he would extend to various 'emancipatory battles' once won or still envisaged (ibid.: 257–8). And while the outcome of these battles will provide some sense of an ending necessary for 'one ... to reinterpret the very foundations of law', Derrida would find, aptly enough, that the generative force of emancipation lies in the movement ever beyond the determinacy of the 'calculated or delimited' (2002b: 35–6). With studied irony, he also finds this force to be 'a weakness', weak in its being uncontainable and evanescent (ibid.: 35). That weakness, brought to the ever-present incipience of being otherwise, is a transformative strength capable of being the 'strongest' (ibid.: 35). Something of the sense and efficacy of that force was found in Nietzsche's 'slow reading' with the attuned responsiveness it called for (1982: 5). In conversation with his 'stillest hour', Nietzsche's Zarathustra protests that he lacks 'the lion's voice for all commanding', only to be countered by the response, a response 'like a whispering': 'thoughts that come on the feet of doves steer the world' (Nietzsche 2006: 116–17).[7]

Acknowledgements

This chapter draws on a talk given at the University of Alberta on 11 March 2008 in a series entitled The Future of the Arts and the Humanities. The present variation comes, then, with thanks to George Pavlich, Lois Harder, Debra Cairns, and Dennis Sweeney for the invitation and for the unsurpassed hospitality. It comes as well with thanks to Maria Carolina Olarte Olarte for the conversation, along with apologies for there not being more Nietzsche.

Notes

1 The mosaic quality sometimes attributed to 'Indigenous' literature would be an instance (see, for example, Arguedas 1978).

2 Authorial challenges to comprehension can sharply inhibit the reach of the reader. Few could have the linguistic range to accommodate Amitav Ghosh's *Sea of Poppies* (2008), for instance.

3 Here and in later references Heidegger is reflecting Nietzsche. The concern is with 'art', but in a sense that includes literature.

4 The divide here is taken from Derrida's engagement with the 'genre clause' in the midst of the last section. In this present setting the divide is brought forward, as it were, to fit the further elaboration of it that has just been offered in relation to the law 'in' literature as well as to the constituent connection between law and justice.

5 I am grateful to Pablo Ghetti for the reference. See also the use of 'compromises' in Derrida (1988: 266–7).
6 Notes being an apt repository for temptations too big for the text, there is some resonance here with the sensed distinction Wallace Stevens offers in 'The snow man' between '[n]othing that is not there and the nothing that is' (2006: 9).
7 Second part 'The stillest hour'. My thanks to Johan van der Walt for placing it in this context.

References

Arguedas, J. M. (1978) *Deep Rivers*, trans. F. H. Barraclough, Austin: University of Texas Press.

Auden, W. H. (1979) 'In memory of W. B. Yeats', in W. H. Auden, *Selected Poems*, London: Faber & Faber.

Auerbach, E. (1968) *Mimesis: The Representations of Reality in Western Literature*, trans. W. R. Trask, Princeton, NJ: Princeton University Press.

Blanchot, M. (1981) *The Madness of the Day*, trans. L. Davis, Barrytown, NY: Station Hill Press.

Blanchot, M. (1982) 'Orpheus's gaze', in M. Blanchot, *The Space of Literature*, trans. A. Smock, Lincoln: University of Nebraska Press.

Blanchot, M. (1988) *The Unavowable Community*, trans. P. Joris, Barrytown, NY: Station Hill Press.

Blanchot, M. (1992) *The Step Not Beyond*, trans. L. Nelson, Albany: State University of New York Press.

Blanchot, M. (1993) *The Infinite Conversation*, trans. S. Hanson, Minneapolis: University of Minnesota Press.

Blanchot, M. (1999) 'Literature and the right to death', trans. L. Davis, in M. Blanchot, *The Station Hill Blanchot Reader: Fiction and Literary Essays*, Barrytown, NY: Station Hill Press.

Celan, P. (2002) *Poems of Paul Celan*, trans. M. Hamburger, New York: Persea Books.

Cixous, H. (1991) *Readings: The Poetics of Blanchot, Joyce, Kafka, Kleist, Lispector, and Tsvetayeva*, trans. C. V. Andermatt, Minneapolis: University of Minnesota Press.

Clarkson, C. (2009) *J. M. Coetzee: Countervoices*, Basingstoke, UK: Palgrave Macmillan.

Derrida, J. (1979) *Spurs: Nietzsche's Styles*, trans. B. Harlow, Chicago: University of Chicago Press.

Derrida, J. (1981) *Positions*, trans. A. Bass, Chicago: University of Chicago Press.

Derrida, J. (1987) 'The laws of reflection: Nelson Mandela, in admiration', trans. M. A. Caws and I. Lorenz, in J. Derrida and M. Tlili (eds) *For Nelson Mandela*, New York: Henry Holt.

Derrida, J. (1988) 'The deaths of Roland Barthes', trans. P.-A. Brault and M. Naas, in H. J. Silverman (ed.) *Philosophy and Non-philosophy since Merleau-Ponty*, London: Routledge.

Derrida, J. (1992) with D. Attridge '"This strange institution called literature": An interview with Jacques Derrida', trans. G. Bennington and R. Bowlby (33–75); 'Before the law', trans. A. Ronell and C. Roulston (181–220); 'The law of genre', trans. A. Ronell 221–52), in J. Derrida, *Acts of Literature*, New York: Routledge.

Derrida, J. (1993) *Aporias: Dying – Awaiting (One Another at) the 'Limits of Truth'*, trans. T. Dutoit, Stanford, CA: Stanford University Press.

Derrida, J. (1995) *Archive Fever: A Freudian Impression*, trans. E. Prenowitz, Chicago: University of Chicago Press.

Derrida, J. (1997) *Politics of Friendship*, trans. G. Collins, London: Verso.

Derrida, J. (2000) *Of Hospitality*, trans. R. Bowlby, Stanford, CA: Stanford University Press.

Derrida, J. (2002a) 'Force of law: The "mystical foundation of authority"', trans. M. Quaintance, in J. Derrida, *Acts of Religion*, New York: Routledge.

Derrida, J. (2002b) '"Negotiations": An interview with E. Rottenberg', in J. Derrida, *Negotiations: Interventions and Interviews, 1971–2001*, trans. E. Rottenberg, Stanford, CA: Stanford University Press.

Derrida, J. (2002c) *Without Alibi*, trans. P. Kamuf, Stanford, CA: Stanford University Press.

Derrida, J. (2005) *Rogues*, trans. P.-A. Brault and M. Naas, Stanford, CA: Stanford University Press.

Derrida, J. and Nancy, J.-L. (2004) 'Responsabilité du sens à venir', in F. Guibal and J.-C. Martin (eds), *Sens en tous sens: Autour des travaux de Jean-Luc Nancy*, Paris: Galilée.

Dickinson, E. (1999) *The Poems of Emily Dickinson*, Cambridge, MA: The Belknap Press of Harvard University Press.

Eliot, T. S. (1974) 'Four quartets', in T. S. Eliot, *Collected Poems 1909–1962*, London: Faber & Faber.

Fenton, J. (2001) *The Strength of Poetry*, Oxford: Oxford University Press.

Foucault, M. (1974) *The Archaeology of Knowledge*, trans. A. M. Sheridan-Smith, London: Tavistock.

Foucault, M. (1988) 'What is an author?', trans. J. V. Harari, in D. Lodge (ed.) *Modern Criticism and Theory: A Reader*, London: Longman.

Foucault, M. (1989) 'An aesthetics of existence', in M. Foucault, *Foucault Live* (Interviews, 1966–84), trans. J. Johnston, New York: Semiotext(e).

Ghosh, A. (2008) *Sea of Poppies*, London: John Murray.

Goldhill, S. (2007) *How to Stage Greek Tragedy Today*, Chicago: University of Chicago Press.

Goodrich, P. (2005) 'Slow reading', in P. Goodrich and M. Valverde (eds) *Nietzsche and Legal Theory: Half-Written Laws*, New York: Routledge.

Heidegger, M. (1991) *Nietzsche*, vol. 1: *The Will to Power as Art*, trans. D. F. Krell, New York: HarperCollins.

Heinzelman, S. S. (2010) *Riding the Black Ram: Law, Literature, and Gender*, Stanford, CA: Stanford University Press.

Keats, J. (1947) *The Letters of John Keats*, 3rd edn, London: Oxford University Press.

Kermode, F. (1967) *The Sense of an Ending: Studies in the Theory of Fiction*, London: Oxford University Press.

Kivy, P. (2006) *The Performance of Reading: An Essay in the Philosophy of Literature*, Oxford: Blackwell.

Kundera, M. (2008) *The Curtain: An Essay in Seven Parts*, trans. L. Asher, New York: HarperCollins.

Larkin, P. (1964) *The Whitsun Weddings*, London: Faber & Faber.

Le Clézio, J. M. G. (2008) *Terra Amata*, trans. B. Bray, London: Penguin.

Maine, H. (1931) *Ancient Law*, London: Oxford University Press.
Manguel, A. (2010) *A Reader on Reading*, New Haven, CT: Yale University Press.
Miller, D. (2009) 'Biographies and memoirs', in A. H. Simmons (ed.) *Joseph Conrad in Context*, Cambridge: Cambridge University Press.
Nancy, J.-L. (1991) 'The inoperative community', trans. P. Connor, in J.-L. Nancy, *The Inoperative Community*, Minneapolis: University of Minnesota Press.
Nancy, J.-L. (1992) '*La Comparution*/The Comperarance: From the existence of "communism" to the community of "existence"', *Political Theory* 20(3): 371–98.
Nancy, J.-L. (1993) 'We need...', trans. E. McVarish, in J.-L. Nancy, *The Birth to Presence*, Stanford, CA: Stanford University Press.
Nancy, J.-L. (2003) '*Lapsus judicii*', trans. S. Sparks, in J.-L. Nancy, *Finite Thinking*, Stanford, CA: Stanford University Press.
Nancy, J.-L. (2008) *Corpus*, trans. R. A. Rand, Bronx, NY: Fordham University Press.
Nietzsche, F. (1968) *The Anti-Christ*, in F. Nietzsche, *Twilight of the Idols/The Anti-Christ*, trans. R. J. Hollingdale, Hardmondsworth, UK: Penguin.
Nietzsche, F. (1982) *Daybreak: Thoughts on the Prejudices of Morality*, trans. R. J. Hollingdale, Cambridge: Cambridge University Press.
Nietzsche, F. (2002) *Beyond Good and Evil*, trans. J. Norman, Cambridge: Cambridge University Press.
Nietzsche, F. (2006) *Thus Spoke Zarathustra: A Book for All and None*, trans. A. Del Caro, Cambridge: Cambridge University Press.
Pessoa, F. (1998) *Poems of Fernando Pessoa*, trans. E. Honig and S. M. Brown, San Francisco: City Light Books.
Plato (1970) *The Laws*, trans. T. J. Saunders, Harmondsworth, UK: Penguin.
Plato (1993) *Republic*, trans. R. Waterfield, Oxford: Oxford University Press.
Proust, M. (1994) *On Reading*, trans. J. Sturrock, London: Penguin.
Raine, C. (2005) 'Word power', *Guardian Review*, 5 February: 34.
Reichman, R. (2009) *The Affective Life of Law: Legal Modernism and the Literary Imagination*, Stanford, CA: Stanford University Press.
Rushdie, S. (1991) *Imaginary Homelands: Essays and Criticism 1981–1991*, London: Granta.
Said, E. W. (1993) *Culture and Imperialism*, London: Chatto & Windus.
Shelley, P. B. (1911) *The Art of Poetry*, Boston: D. C. Heath.
Spark, M. (2007) *Loitering with Intent*, London: Virago.
Sterne, L. (1967) *The Life and Opinions of Tristram Shandy, Gentleman*, London: Penguin.
Stevens, W. (2006) 'The snow man', in W. Stevens, *Collected Poems*, London: Faber & Faber.
Tuitt, P. (2004) *Race, Law, Resistance*, London: Glasshouse Press.
Wright, R. (2009) *The Evolution of God*, London: Little, Brown.

Index

For Product Safety Concerns and Information please contact our EU representative GPSR@taylorandfrancis.com
Taylor & Francis Verlag GmbH, Kaufingerstraße 24, 80331 München, Germany

www.ingramcontent.com/pod-product-compliance
Ingram Content Group UK Ltd.
Pitfield, Milton Keynes, MK11 3LW, UK
UKHW011004180926
475701UK00004B/561
* 9 7 8 0 4 1 5 5 2 6 4 1 8 *